Lacan to the Letter

To my brilliant and beautiful sister, Jody.

Merry Christmas 2011 ☺

I love you!

Julie

Lacan to the Letter

Reading *Écrits* Closely

Bruce Fink

University of Minnesota Press   Minneapolis ⋅ London

An earlier version of chapter 6 was published as "Knowledge and Jouissance," in *Reading Seminar XX: Lacan's Major Work on Love, Knowledge, and Feminine Sexuality,* ed. Suzanne Barnard and Bruce Fink (Albany: State University of New York Press, 2002). Copyright 2002 State University of New York. All rights reserved. Reprinted with permission.

Published by the University of Minnesota Press
111 Third Avenue South, Suite 290
Minneapolis, MN 55401-2520
http://www.upress.umn.edu

Library of Congress Cataloging-in-Publication Data

Fink, Bruce, 1956–
    Lacan to the letter : reading "Écrits" closely / Bruce Fink.
        p. ; cm.
    Includes bibliographical references and index.
    ISBN 978-0-8166-4320-2 (hc : alk. paper)
    ISBN 978-0-8166-4321-9(pb : alk. paper)
    1. Psychoanalysis.
    [DNLM: 1. Lacan, Jacques, 1901– Écrits.   2. Lacan, Jacques, 1901–
Ecrits.   3. Psychoanalytic Theory. WM 460 L129f 2004]   I. Title.
    BF173.L1434 2004
    150.19'5—dc22

                                                        2003024806

Printed in the United States of America on acid-free paper

The University of Minnesota is an equal-opportunity educator and employer.

16 15 14 13 12 11 10   10 9 8 7 6 5 4

Contents

Preface

> The more the analytic community lets Freud's inspiration dissipate, what, if not the letter of his doctrine, will allow it to continue to constitute a body?
>
> —Lacan, "The Situation of Psychoanalysis in 1956"

Afriend and former teacher of mine, Richard Klein at Cornell University, once remarked that hardly anyone working on Lacan took the trouble to explicate his texts at length, preferring, apparently, to comment on his theoretical apparatus rather than on his actual writing. The remark immediately struck me as true, and I realized that it applied to my own publications as well. The present volume is a first attempt to take up the implicit challenge: to take Lacan at his word, to read his texts *à la lettre*—that is, both literally and to the letter.

The readings I am offering here are *à la lettre* in at least two senses:

1. I take Lacan literally, in the belief—or gambling—that he comes right out and says what he means in many cases (that is, we need not always look elsewhere to grasp what he is talking about), though much of his argument must be reconstructed or pieced together from the various claims he makes on the basis of a line-by-line reading. What may at first seem nonsensical or absurd often, in my view, becomes quite comprehensible and even sensible when understood in context. I provide numerous references and quotations so that the reader can verify that Lacan in fact says what I claim he says and that he does so where and when I claim he says it.

2. I assume that the specific words and expressions he uses are not irrelevant to understanding what he means. This leads me to emphasize what we might call the "literality" of his texts: both their literal and literary qualities. The evocative aspects of his writing are central both to language in general ("For the function of language in speech is not to inform but to evoke," E 299)[1] and to the training of the future analyst-critic that he aims to effect with his unusual kind of writing. This leads him at times to deliberately use formulations that can be understood in several different ways. The emphasis on evocation should not, however, be confused with a lack of

precision. Lacan can be an extremely precise writer, even though this is not always clear in certain translations of his work, above all, the early ones.

The kinds of imprecisions found in translations of his *Écrits,* in particular, are extremely varied and can only sometimes be blamed on the difficulty of the texts themselves. These imprecisions run the gamut from the failure to recognize typical French word order in compound words like *souvenir-écran* (noun followed by adjective, E 518), which we find translated as "memory-screen" instead of the more familiar and accurate "screen-memory"; to the confusion of similarly spelled words, such as *rosière* and *rosée* (E 502), the former being translated as "dew," which is what the latter means, instead of "virgin" or "virtuous maiden"; to the misrecognition of false cognates such as the English "physician" and the French *physicien,* for we find "les méfaits [. . .] du [. . .] physicien" (E 217) translated as "errors [. . .] of the physician" instead of as "the physicist's crimes"— presumably his crimes against humanity in the form of the atom bomb; and to the amusing oversight of juxtapositions, such as that between *ici* and *là-bas,* leading *là-bas* in the text "Le plaisir donc, de la volonté là-bas rival qui stimule, n'est plus ici que . . ." (E 773) to be rendered as "down there," as if in reference to the genital region, instead of as referring back to Kant's system in juxtaposition to the Marquis de Sade's *(ici)*—a better translation might be "Pleasure, a rival of the will in Kant's system that provides a stimulus, is thus in the Marquis de Sade's work no more than . . ."

As entertaining as some of these imprecisions may be—and I have not even tried to present here the way in which Lacan's more complex grammatical constructions have been handled—they have contributed to Lacan's reputation as an extremely abstruse writer whose murky formulations are impenetrable to even highly motivated readers. I can only hope that readers will glean from my new translation of *Écrits: A Selection* (2002) and my translation of the complete *Écrits* (forthcoming) that his early translators may well have been more obscure and impenetrable than the man himself.

Some of the readings I include here are directly clinical in orientation, focusing on clinical issues raised in "The Direction of the Treatment and the Principles of Its Power" and other texts in *Écrits.* The letter of the text is never far from view in examining such clinical matters, because we must correct the earlier translation that would have Lacan, employing a bridge metaphor for analysis, recommending that the analyst "try to expose" the analysand's hand instead of recommending that "the analyst strive to get the analysand to guess *[lui faire deviner]*" his own hand (E 589)—that is, the cards/contents of his unconscious. There is a whole world between these two projects, and that world is the world of mastery. It may be a

small error, but it effaces the giant step Lacan takes away from those analysts who see themselves as masters of knowledge, ready and able, owing to
their prodigious "powers of insight," to pinpoint the subject's mainspring
and reveal it to him. If the analyst is to get the analysand to guess his own
hand, the analyst must be operating as object *a,* not as the all-knowing
subject.

Chapter 1 lays out some of the most basic features of Lacan's approach
to psychoanalytic treatment and examines in detail the longest account
Lacan ever gives in print of one of his own cases (the obsessive man discussed in "The Direction of the Treatment"). It also presents Lacan's critique of Freud's position in the transference with a young woman whom
Freud discusses in "The Psychogenesis of a Case of Homosexuality in a
Woman."

Chapter 2 elaborates on Lacan's claim that "commenting on a text
is like doing an analysis" and outlines how and why Lacan's reading of
Freud's texts is so different from those of many other post-Freudians. It
also lays out Lacan's argument that many analysts' difficulties in clinical
practice grow directly out of their rejection of certain facets of Freud's
theory. Special attention is given to the question of affect (which Lacan
is sometimes accused of neglecting), to acting out as seen in specific case
studies, and to Lacan's attempt to psychoanalyze psychoanalysis.

Chapter 3 is more theoretical in scope and provides a sustained reading of "The Instance of the Letter in the Unconscious, or Reason since
Freud," in which I attempt to delineate what Lacan means by "the letter,"
as contrasted with "the signifier." I examine the rather unique rhetorical
opacity of the first few pages of the text in light of Lacan's broader rhetorical strategy, suggesting that much of his writing from around this point
onward can be understood (at least at one level) as an analysand's discourse
designed to train its readers. My sense is that Lacan was striving to create a new audience with much of his work, a new breed of analyst-critics
adept at reading both the analysand's discourse and literary texts (which
have a tendency to become intertwined to a greater or lesser extent in
many cases). By elucidating his claim that figures of speech and tropes are
related to defense mechanisms, I try to show that even the most seemingly
theoretical of discussions is directly clinical; indeed, the attempt to divide
Lacan's work into theory (linguistics, rhetoric, topology, logic) and practice (clinical psychoanalysis, technique) is seen to founder here.

Chapter 4 offers a detailed reading of "The Subversion of the Subject
and the Dialectic of Desire in the Freudian Unconscious," with particular
attention to the workings of the Graph of Desire. The graph is shown to
grow out of Lacan's "subversion" of Ferdinand de Saussure's schemas, and

knowledge, truth, castration, and jouissance are all explored in considerable detail here. The chapter explores tasks imposed on the analyst by the theorization of psychoanalytic treatment that is built into the graph.

The meaning of the term "phallus" in Lacanian theory is addressed in chapter 4, given detailed attention in chapter 5, and then elaborated on in relation to the so-called phallic function in chapter 6. I try, in chapter 5, to make sense of Lacan's equation of the phallus with the square root of negative one (it makes a lot more sense than Alan Sokal and Jean Bricmont would allow) and to clarify the distinctions between the symbolic, imaginary, and real phalluses.

In chapter 6, I turn to the definition of the phallus as the bar between the signifier and the signified. I emphasize the fallibility inherent in the phallus, as Lacan conceives of it: the fallibility of phallic jouissance and the infallibility of the Other jouissance. In a detailed commentary on Seminar XX, *Encore, On Feminine Sexuality,* I examine the relation between knowledge and jouissance, the way speaking "of love is in itself a jouissance," and the kind of love Lacan terms "soulove."

My concern here has not been to indicate where Lacan went in later years with each of the concepts discussed in these texts—that is, to show how he revised his views as time went on—but rather to let each period of his theoretical and clinical formulation stand alone. I have devoted considerable space to the unpacking of phrases that have, in my view, been especially prone to misunderstanding, such as the "sliding of the signified under the signifier" (E 502), or that have gone seemingly unnoticed, such as "the ego is the metonymy of desire" (E 640).

These essays were mostly written while I was in the midst of retranslating Lacan's *Écrits* (1997–2000). Chapter 1 was prepared for a workshop with the Toronto Psychoanalytic Association in April 2000, at the invitation of Richard Simpson and Larry Lyons. Chapter 2 was given as a keynote address at the Catholic University of Nijmegen in Holland in the context of the conference "Lacan and the Anglo-Saxon Tradition" held in February 2000. Chapter 3 was prepared for a workshop with the LOGOS psychoanalytic group in Miami at the invitation of Alicia Arenas, and given as a keynote address at the second annual conference of the Affiliated Psychoanalytic Workgroups, sponsored by the Program in Psychoanalytic Studies at Emory University in May 2000. Early versions of chapter 4 were delivered at SUNY Buffalo in March 1998 at the invitation of the Program in Psychoanalysis and Culture and at the University of California at San Francisco Medical School in August 1998 at the invitation of the San Francisco

Lacanian Society. Chapter 5 was written for a planned but subsequently canceled special issue of a journal in response to Sokal and Bricmont's *Fashionable Nonsense*. Chapter 6 was delivered at the University of Massachusetts at Amherst in 1998 to the Department of Communications at the invitation of Briankle Chang.

1

Lacanian Technique in "The Direction of the Treatment"

> People generally ask for advice only in order not to
> follow it; or, if they do follow it, to have someone to
> reproach for having given it.
> —Alexandre Dumas, *The Three Musketeers*

Like all of Lacan's major papers, "The Direction of the Treatment and
the Principles of Its Power" is an intervention in a debate, a debate
among the different psychoanalytic societies of the time and the different practitioners and theoreticians over the correct way to train analysts
and over the relevance of Freud's work. The most immediate backdrop to
"The Direction of the Treatment" is a collection, published in 1956 by
one of the most prestigious publishers in France, Presses Universitaires de
France, entitled *La psychanalyse d'aujourd'hui*. Lacan takes this collection as a sort of slap in the face, as is witnessed by his comments on it in
the opening chapters of Seminar IV. The collection opens with a preface
by Ernest Jones, who lends it the stamp of International Psychoanalytical
Association (IPA) approval, and is edited by Sacha Nacht, a colleague of
Lacan's at the Société Psychanalytique de Paris. The contributions are by
Nacht, Maurice Bouvet, and other of Lacan's colleagues, and here is what
Lacan has to say about the book:

> I refer [to this book in this paper] only because of the naive simplicity
> with which the tendency to degrade the direction of the treatment and the
> principles of its power in psychoanalysis is presented in it. Designed, no
> doubt, to circulate outside the psychoanalytic community, it serves as an

1

obstacle inside it. Thus I don't mention its authors, who make no properly scientific contribution in it. (E 643)

This is pretty typical of Lacan: He only mentions by name worthy adversaries, enemies with whom he is at least willing to be compared in the reader's mind. As for those who are not at the same level, he ruthlessly criticizes them without even mentioning their names; this all the more effectively erases them from the reader's memory.

I will discuss the views of these unnamable authors in a moment, but first let us note that the broader backdrop for the paper is the whole psychoanalytic movement of the time and that the references at the back of the paper include a great many of the prominent figures: Anna Freud, Ernst Kris, Rudolf Loewenstein, Heinz Hartmann, Ella Sharpe, Melitta Schmideberg, and D. W. Winnicott.

This article is thus a major "position paper" for Lacan, a paper in which he defines his position on many issues of treatment, takes a stand against the majority of his fellow analysts, and even opposes a number of his own earlier positions (for example, whereas in 1950 he had endorsed medical training for analysts, here he never mentions medicine at all, suggesting instead that the analyst must be a *lettré*, a man of letters). It seems to be the only one of his published papers that follows the relatively standard *International Journal of Psycho-Analysis* format of referencing texts by numbers in brackets or parentheses, making this the article perhaps most specifically designed for the wider IPA public. It is certainly one of Lacan's most straightforwardly written texts. Many of Lacan's other papers, even those from the same period, seem to be written for a yet-to-be-determined public; perhaps they are written for posterity, or perhaps they are designed to (or at least written in such a way as to) create a new audience, an audience of analyst/philosopher/literary critics. This one seems most clearly addressed to practitioners and, for the most part, eschews long, detailed theoretical discussions.

Some of the salient perspectives embraced by Lacan's colleagues in *La psychanalyse d'aujourd'hui* are as follows: First of all, there is little fundamental distinction between psychosis, perversion, and neurosis; instead, they are located on a continuum based on the solidity of one's early object relations. Neurotics had pretty good object relations, perverts had mediocre ones, psychotics had terrible ones, and normal people had perfect ones. Note that contemporary trends, running from the political correctness movement to the fourth edition of the *Diagnostic and Statistical Manual of Mental Disorders* (DSM IV),[1] prefer the perspective that there are no fundamental or structural distinctions between psychosis, perversion, and neurosis. According to the DSM IV, one can have a psychotic episode but be normal before and afterward. There are no structures, strictly speaking (except perhaps for Axis II "personality disorders").

If there is any kind of a distinction to be made, according to the authors of *La psychanalyse d'aujourd'hui*, it is between "pregenital types" (psychotic and perverse) and "genital types" (neurotic). The goal in therapy is, predictably enough, to turn pregenital types into genital types. And those who are fortunate enough to be genital types before analysis will, through analysis, "realize the enormous difference between what they used to believe sexual joy to be and what they now experience" (55). The pregenital types have weak egos, and the genital types have strong egos.[2] Thus, the goal is to strengthen egos.

The Ego Is Already Strong Enough

> Here one is liable to make errors of judgment in the conduct
> of the treatment—such as trying to strengthen the ego in
> many neuroses that are caused by its overly strong structure,
> which is a dead end.
> —*Lacan, "Function and Field of Speech and Language"*

The position Lacan adopted in the 1950s was, I think, that *in the vast majority of cases, the ego is already more than strong enough;* as he says in "Psychoanalysis and Its Teaching," this ego is far from weak (E 453). The ego is so strong and rigid that repression occurs whenever one of the neurotic's own sexual or aggressive impulses does not fit in with his view of himself, leading to the return of the repressed in symptoms. There would be no symptoms were the neurotic's ego too weak to push such impulses outside of itself.

Thus the neurotic's ego is not necessarily any weaker than the analyst's, and the goal is not to model the analysand's ego on the analyst's stronger ego (E 425). Indeed, we might say that the goal of analysis is to loosen up the fixity and rigidity of the ego, for it is this rigidity that requires so many things to be put out of mind (E 826); it is this "overly strong structure" that results in so much repression (E 250, note 1). We aim to loosen up the ego-ideal so that the neurotic need not, in the future, bring about so many repressions. Things that would have been forced to become or remain unconscious before analysis become conscious instead, no longer needing to be rejected as unsuitable or unsavory. The unconscious is not exhausted or totally emptied out in the course of analysis, but a new relationship between the drives (id) and the ego and superego develops such that future repressions need not occur.

I am perhaps going a bit far here, but I want to bring out two points:

- Lacan clearly prefers many aspects of Freud's early work to his later work and is not overly fond of the second topography. And it is from the latter—id, ego, superego—that ego psychology as a movement took its lead. Certain parts of Freud's posthumously published *Outline of Psychoanalysis* (1940) read just like the texts from *La psychanalyse d'aujourd'hui* that Lacan criticizes in "The Direction of the Treatment." Freud talks there about the patient's weak ego and how we work to strengthen it in psychoanalysis. He never suggests, however, that the patient's ego should model itself on the analyst's; indeed, he warns us against any such temptation to serve as a model for the patient (SE XXIII, 175).[3]

- Whereas Freud sometimes suggests that the ego must be brought to face id impulses and decide to either accept them or reject them once and for all (SE XXIII, 199, for example), Lacan never uses a term like "instinctual renunciation" and never (to the best of my knowledge) proposes that the ego must either sublimate the drives or give them up altogether. He focuses instead on a loss of jouissance that the subject has to come to terms with. Lacan never characterizes the drives as "crude," as Freud so high-mindedly does, as needing to be overcome; rather, the subject is the drives at some important level and must forge a new relation to the drives at the end of his analysis (Seminar XI, 245–46/273), must learn to reckon with them differently.[4]

Indeed, Lacan's whole conception of the ego is quite different from what we find in certain texts by Freud, especially the later Freud, though it fits very nicely with certain formulations in *The Ego and the Id* (1923) regarding the ego as a projection of the surface of the body, for example.[5] Lacan never talks about the ego as struggling between three masters—the id, the superego, and external reality—attempting to reconcile their differences and satisfy their exigencies, except when commenting on others' work. Instead, we find, in "The Direction of the Treatment," a formulation that is apparently very far removed from Freud's position: "[T]he ego is the metonymy of desire" (E 640). However cryptic this definition may seem on the face of it (and I try to unpack it in the section entitled "The Topography of the Unconscious" in chapter 3), Lacan's view of the role the ego should play in analytic work is obviously quite different from that of the majority of his contemporaries, whose work is generally based on a certain interpretation—a largely Anna Freudian interpretation—of Freud's last formulations (see chapter 2).

Analysis Is Not a Dyadic Relationship

Let us turn here to the way in which this particular interpretation of Freud's later work was taken up by Lacan's colleagues in France. Nacht suggests, in the aforementioned collected volume, *La psychanalyse d'aujourd'hui*, that psychoanalysis can be understood as a two-person relationship—that is, as a relationship involving only two people. Lacan, on the contrary, makes it very clear early on in this paper (and I will assume hereafter that the reader is following along with me in reading sections of "The Direction of the Treatment" page by page) that he believes that there are always at least four parties involved in analysis: the analyst as ego and as dummy (or dead man, that is, essentially as the Other with a capital O) and the analysand as ego and as subject of the unconscious (E 589; see Figure 1.1).

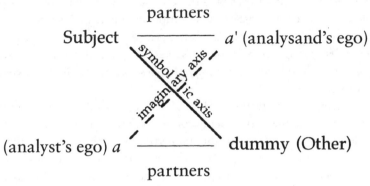

Figure 1.1. Simplified L schema I

There are thus always four different players in the analytic game, which Lacan likens here to a game of bridge that can be illustrated with the L schema.[6] The analyst as ego has a partner, the dummy (or Other as language), and the analysand as ego has a partner too, his unconscious, whose hand is an unknown. The analyst's goal is to get the analysand as ego to guess his own partner's hand—that is, to divine what is unconscious in himself.[7] (It is clear that Lacan is situating this game of analytic bridge on the L schema from his use of terms like "quadripartition" on E 590 and "the distribution of responses" on E 591.)

Lacan claims here that whenever the analyst interprets in analysis, she interprets from one and the same position: that of the Other, or dummy. Even if she interprets transference, that is, even if she interprets a projection onto her of something by the analysand, her interpretation is heard as if it were coming not from her as a living, breathing, flesh-and-blood human being with her own specific personality or ego (unless this is the only way she has situated herself in the analysis, an eventuality I will discuss a little further on) but rather from her as the person she is *imputed* to be by the analysand in his transferential relation to her (E 591). Interpreting transference does not allow her to leave behind the position in which she has been situated by the analysand in the transference and to somehow become more herself, more genuine, in the relationship.

Lacan recommends that we avoid interpreting transference for a variety of reasons, but first and foremost he wants it to be clear that we do not achieve some sort of metaposition *outside of* the transference by interpreting it. We remain in it up to our ears. As he puts it in Seminar XV (November 29, 1967), there is "no transference of the transference": Just as there is no Other of the Other—that is, no position outside of language that allows us to discuss language as a whole without having to rely on language itself in our discussion—there is no way in which we can step completely outside the transference situation and invite the analysand to do so with us in order to discuss what is happening in the transference itself.[8] For we never manage to extricate ourselves from it in this way; instead of disappearing, the transference simply changes its object. How can we describe this change?

The attempt to invite the analysand to step outside the transference with us (which is at the crux of many contemporary approaches to "psychodynamic" treatment) fosters in the analysand "self-observation," that is, the development of an observing ego that remarks upon and criticizes the patient's behavior and affect, an observing ego that is modeled on an analyst who observes the patient in such a way within the treatment. Not only does this approach to treatment lead to the oft-repeated complaint that at the end of therapy "I know myself much better, but I still act the same" ("knowledge" being acquired at the expense of subjective transformation), but it also further alienates the analysand by encouraging him to become like (identify with) someone else: his analyst. His analyst observes him from a particular point of view, involving her own personal set of ideals, values, and criticisms—in short, her own personality. Far from being dissipated, the transference simply becomes steered toward an other like the analysand (an alter ego, or "semblable"),[9] with the proviso that this other is even more objectifying in her way of seeing the analysand than he himself was before he started the treatment.

This amounts, thus, to a form of transference located on the imaginary axis as opposed to a form of transference located on the symbolic axis (as we shall see shortly), the latter being transference to an Other where the analysand presumes there to be knowledge of what makes him tick, knowledge that is inaccessible to him. The imaginary transference is based on the analyst as someone who *sees* or *views* the analysand in a certain way. The analyst, like a parent, views the analysand approvingly or critically based on her own values, beliefs, feelings, and regrets. The imaginary transference is thus to the analyst as an individual with her own personality, however balanced or unbalanced, her own foibles and idiosyncrasies, insights and blindnesses.

The symbolic transference is something else altogether. It is based on what the analyst hears—that is, on what can be heard in the analysand's discourse. In this symbolic position, the analyst strives not to analyze on the basis of her own personality (values, beliefs, feelings, regrets, foibles and idiosyncrasies, insights and blindnesses) but rather on the basis of the Other, as we shall see in considerable detail below.

The fact that there is "no transference of the transference" means that even the most "balanced" and even-handed of analysts who practice in this way (attempting to foster the development of and enlist the aid of the analysand's observing ego) cannot completely avoid unintended projections by the analysand: The analyst who believes she is adopting the most dispassionate tone of voice in speaking to the analysand is taxed with being hypercritical, like the analysand's father it may turn out, and thus another dimension of the transference, the symbolic dimension, persists despite every attempt to eliminate it. The analyst's remarks are still heard by the analysand as coming from the person he *imputes* her to be, even if that is not who she feels herself to be, even if that is not where she is trying to situate herself. The person he *imputes* her to be is not the analyst as ego but the Other (the representative of his parents' or culture's ideals and values, an authority figure, or a judge, for example).

Thus even when the analyst deliberately strives to assume the role of a "neutral" ego in making an interpretation to the analysand, what she says is heard by the analysand as coming from some Other place and, moreover, *as addressing something in him that is beyond his observing ego,* something in him that is beyond the "cooperative" ego he tries to play the role of in the therapy relationship (see Figure 1.2).

Subject

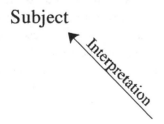

Other (who the analyst is imputed
to be by the analysand)

Figure 1.2. Interpretation on the L schema

Lacan's perspective, then, is that the analyst should not attempt to interpret on the basis of her own ego or personality in the first place (why hers, after all, and not someone else's?), since (1) it prolongs the subject's alienation by encouraging him to identify with the analyst as observing ego instead of helping reveal his own unconscious to him, and (2) it is doomed to at least partial failure in its bid to eliminate the unwieldy, uncontrollable aspects of the symbolic transference.

Lacan claims that analysts have not known what it meant to interpret from the position of the Other, to situate themselves as the Other, and this is perhaps why they have instead fallen back on situating themselves as egos, as people with their own personalities, people who supposedly have good reality contact. This leaves them, as he says, "at the level of 'I' and 'me' " with the analysand (E 591)—that is, at the level of saying, "It seems to me that you are deliberately trying to hurt me" or "*I* sense that you are angry at *me* for what I said earlier"—which is the level of imaginary relations (see Figure 1.3).

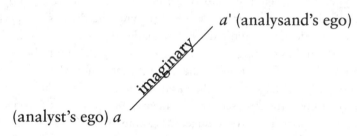

a' (analysand's ego)

imaginary

(analyst's ego) a

Figure 1.3. The ego-to-ego (two-person relation) schema

While the neurotic analysand keeps trying—wittingly or unwittingly—to situate the analyst in the position of the Other, certain analysts keep bringing everything back to themselves, collapsing the symbolic transference into the imaginary. Such analysts appeal to the "healthy part of the ego" (no doubt, the observing ego), which Lacan sarcastically refers to as "the part that thinks like us" (E 591). They try to get part of the patient's ego to model itself on their own egos, a notion Lacan critiques extensively. Analysts engage here in a narcissistic project of self-duplication, attempting to clone themselves by making new analysts in their own image. Lacan claims that the only answer such analysts have to the question "Who or what is the analyst when he or she interprets?" (this is, I think, what Lacan refers to as the "changed question," the one that corresponds to the question to the analysand "Who is speaking?") is "me" *(moi),* thus the ego— in other words, they interpret with their own personalities (E 592).

Lacan goes so far as to suggest that interpretation drops out of the picture in the way such analysts work; instead, they simply try to get the analysand to see reality as they do. Instead of interpreting, they give insight, confront the analysand with the reality he supposedly refuses to see, and make suggestions. According to Lacan, the kind of interpretations Freud made went well beyond what contemporary analysts offer up. In the case of the Rat Man, for example, Freud went out on a limb and divined events in the Rat Man's past that *must* have occurred, this divination having little to do originally with the *hic et nunc* (the here and now) of the transferential situation, but being based, rather, on the larger symbolic frame of the Rat Man's life. Freud, Lacan argues, knew how to situate himself as Other and interpret from that place, foreshadowing Lacan's own notion about how that place can be occupied by *un mort,* that is, a dead man, or a dummy.

What does it mean to occupy the place of the Other? Let us consider the bridge metaphor again here (E 598). Note that, in bridge, after the bidding has occurred and the dummy has been declared, the dummy (or Other) plays with all of his cards turned face up for all the players to see. There is nothing to guess at there in the Other: Like the cards turned faceup, the language spoken by the analysand and the analyst is *public knowledge,* in a sense. The double meaning of what the analysand says or the meaning of certain of his slips is already there in the Other. People who are not in the room with them could hear the very same double meanings and perhaps occasionally divine some of the meanings of the slips simply by listening to a recording or reading a transcript. There is nothing *hidden* in the Other.

This Other may include something as abstract as the Koranic law, as we see in an example Lacan provides in Seminar I (221–22/196–98) in which a patient with a number of symptoms related to one of his hands came to Lacan after an unsuccessful analysis with someone else. The Koran, of prime importance in the northern African land of the patient's birth, stipulates that a thief must have his hand cut off, and part of the analysand's family backdrop included the fact that his father was at one point accused of stealing and even lost his job because of the accusation. Although the Koranic law was not sovereign in France where the analysand lived as an adult, it continued to operate as part of his social, cultural, and religious background; it played a role in the patient's life unbeknown to him, written ("inscribed") in his unconscious. This portion of his unconscious coincided with something that was publicly available, in some sense: namely, the Other as the locus of those laws known to virtually everyone from a certain culture. The Other, in this sense, has to do with the existing symbolic codes and the interrelationships among words and phrases in a language.

Analysts may be ignorant of many aspects of their analysands' backgrounds, and that will skew their understanding of the situation. Analysts must always strive to learn more about their analysands' cultures and tongues. If they do not, they allow their "inadequate information"—that is, one aspect of their countertransference, which Lacan defines as "the sum total of the analyst's biases, passions, and difficulties, or even of his inadequate information, at any given moment in the dialectical process" (E 225)—to interfere in the analytic work. For example, the analyst who had worked with Lacan's northern African patient before Lacan had simply attempted to apply preformed analytic knowledge to the patient's hand-related symptoms, chalking them up to masturbation and the supposed prohibition thereof. Time and again, neglecting the Other has led analysts in the wrong direction (the Other is not psychoanalytic theory per se).

The Other is the level at which analysts must situate themselves: listening for slips, telling idiomatic expressions, and double entendres, all of which can be heard and understood by anyone with the proper linguistic and analytic training. Hearing a slip of the tongue has little if anything to do with one's personality! It has to do with adopting a symbolic position and listening from that position, instead of always considering how, as a person, one is being taken up and treated by the analysand: as a good object or a bad object, as a punitive parental figure or as a loving one, and so on. In other words, it has to do with listening, not from the position of one's ego or personality but from the vantage point of the Other.

That is the analyst's overarching *strategy,* as Lacan describes it. He suggests that analysts can situate themselves in the game of analytic bridge in such a way as to play before or after the fourth player (the analysand's unconscious), which allows them a degree of freedom in their *tactics,* leaving them freer in their tactics than in their overall strategy (E 589). These two possibilities are represented in Figures 1.4 and 1.5, where the straight lines connect the two sets of partners and the arrows indicate the order of play.

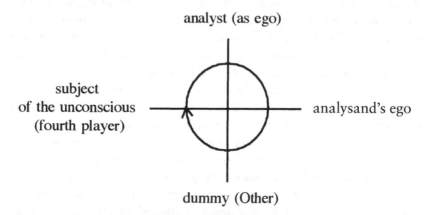

Figure 1.4. The tactics of analytic bridge I: Dummy plays before the subject

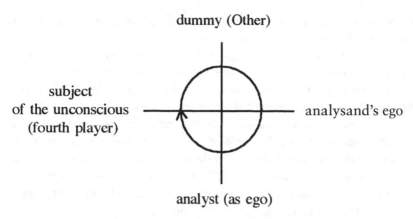

Figure 1.5. The tactics of analytic bridge II: Dummy plays after the subject

What might this difference in tactics look like concretely? Perhaps in one case (Figure 1.4), the analyst says something relying on the Other—that is, she says something evocative or oracular that has two or more possible meanings graspable by virtually anyone who speaks the same language— and waits to see the effect it has on the analysand's unconscious, whether in the form of a spontaneous association or a thought or dream produced afterward. In the other case (Figure 1.5), the analyst might wait until the analysand says something unintentionally polyvalent and then have the Other play its hand by, for example, repeating back one or more of the analysand's words, allowing the double or triple meanings to resonate. In both cases, the analyst's overarching strategy remains the same: to situate herself in the analysis not as an ego but as the Other. And since this is a never completely realizable ideal, the analyst must try to keep her ego from interfering with her ability to occupy the position of the Other as much as possible.

Why We Should Not Analyze with Our Own Being:
On an Interpretation Discussed by Margaret Little

> If we train analysts, it is so that there will be subjects in whom the ego will be absent. This is the ideal of analysis, which, of course, remains virtual. There is never a subject without an ego—a fully realized subject—but this is what we must always try to obtain from a subject in analysis.[10]
> —*Lacan, Seminar II*

Having mentioned "personality"—more specifically, the difference between interpreting from the position of the Other and on the basis of one's own personality—let us consider how it is related to what Lacan refers to as "being" in this paper.

In section I.3 (E 587), Lacan quotes Freud's expression from *The Interpretation of Dreams,* "Kern unseres Wesens" (SE V, 603), translated by James Strachey as "the core of our being."[11] In that text, Freud tells us that the core of our being consists "of unconscious wishful impulses." It is the primary processes that characterize us first and foremost, compared to the secondary processes, which only come to characterize us over the course of many years and merely direct and divert the primary processes instead of overwriting or eradicating them. The "core of our being" is thus our wishful impulses (governed by the primary processes) dating back to early childhood and our enduring "primitive" impulses.

"Being" next appears in Lacan's text a few lines further down, when he quotes Nacht's view that "the analyst cures not so much by what he says and does as by what he is" (E 587). In Nacht's work, the analyst's being ("what he is") is the analyst's personality. Nacht emphasizes "the importance of the analyst's personality" (*La psychanalyse d'aujourd'hui,* 134), which should be "as harmoniously and profoundly balanced as possible" (135). He even goes so far as to say that one's personality does not necessarily become suitable for being an analyst by undergoing training analysis; "certain innate gifts are necessary" (136). In other words, either one is born with the right stuff or one is not; and if one is not, no amount of analysis will ever enable one to occupy the proper analytic position. Nacht thus proposes that only certain kinds of people, people with certain kinds of personalities, can be analysts. He seems, however, to be circumspect enough not to try to define which ones they are! Clearly there is "no transcendence in this context" (E 587), that is, no way to go beyond one's own personality traits, no way to work from something more objective, such as that which is provided by the Other.

Let us compare Nacht's approach with what Lacan says in section I.4: "[T]he more his being is involved, the less sure he is of his action" (E 587). In other words, the more the analyst lets his personality be his guide, the less sure he is of what he is doing.

In section I.6, Lacan adds that the analyst "would do better to take his bearings from his want-to-be (or lack of being) than from his being" (E 589). He would do better to take his bearings from his *lack of personality,* we might say, from what he is or stands in for when his personality has slipped into the background: the Other. Hearing a slip or a slur has nothing to do with his being but rather has to do with his lack of being. As I mentioned earlier, the analyst is able to hear a slip precisely because he has managed to put himself aside, so to speak, precisely because he has managed to take the analysand's speech not as a personal attack but rather as directed elsewhere, directed at something or someone else.

Let me turn to an example of what it means to analyze with one's being, or personality. In this example (Seminar I, 40–43/30–33), which is taken from a case presented by Margaret Little in "Counter-Transference and the Patient's Response to It," a patient comes to see his analyst a few days after giving a brilliant talk during a radio broadcast.[12] The patient seems particularly anxious and confused during his session, and his analyst "interpreted the patient's distress as being due to a fear lest he, the analyst, should be jealous of what had clearly been a success and be wanting to deprive him of it and of its results" ("Counter-Transference," 32).[13] The analyst thereby asserts that the patient's affect—his anxious and confused state—is related to his analyst: He must be anxious either because he thinks his analyst is jealous of him and might take revenge, or because he is trying to ward off or dissipate the analyst's jealousy and vengeance (if he acts anxious, perhaps the analyst will not be able to hold his success against him).

Lacan comments that it took the patient a full year to get over this interpretation, that is, to realize that he was in fact depressed at that time because his mother had died three days before his radio show and that he was quite ambivalent about having performed so well so soon after her death and at a point in time when she could no longer hear him![14]

The mother's death is what Lacan points to as the *symbolic backdrop* of the patient's affect here. He does not ignore the analysand's feelings and does not try to claim that the analysand was unaware of the analyst's jealousy; indeed, he asserts here that "feelings are always mutual" (Seminar I, 43/32), suggesting thereby *not* that we always have the same feelings about each other, but that we can at least elicit feelings in another person by asserting or demonstrating that we have them ourselves (if, for example, I get very angry at someone and manifest my anger to him, he is likely to get angry at me in turn). Lacan's point is that there is more going on here than meets the eye and that we must take into account not only the here and now of the imaginary relationship but also the symbolic axis. We must consider the symbolic relationship rather than proffer an interpretation at the imaginary level, that is, an interpretation of the transference that essentially proceeds from our own personality.[15] Lacan is not trying to deny the existence of the analyst's feelings; he indicates that he is quite sure the analyst had them. He simply suggests that the analyst needs to learn to put them aside and not allow them to intervene in the therapy.

In the case at hand, it is as if the analyst had reasoned as follows: "I feel that he feels that I begrudge him his success in an area where I would like to be that successful myself, and therefore he must be angry with me;

that is why he is in the state he is in." He assesses the situation on the basis of his conscious feelings and makes an interpretation based on his own personality. To interpret from the position of the Other, instead, is to take into account the larger symbolic picture: the recent death of the patient's mother and the patient's ambivalence about his success in relation to her.

The forcing of one's own feelings and personality onto the analysand is an abuse of power that Lacan decries in "The Direction of the Treatment." Freud, by the 1910s, did not try (in theory) to influence his patients with his own personality—which he never seems to have believed to be particularly wonderful or special (see, for example, SE XII, 160–61)—and instead gave us the metaphor of the analyst as a mirror that reflects back the analysand's projections (SE XII, 118; cf. Seminar VIII, 435). Contemporary analysis, Lacan argues, in its cult of personality and the importance it gives to the body-to-body, ego-to-ego, person-to-person relationship, leads to a kind of forcing of one person's view of reality and of what is healthy onto another, something Lacan considers to be quite foreign to the analytic enterprise.[16]

He announces this point of view right in the very first subsection of the paper when he says, "I intend to show how the inability to authentically sustain a praxis results, as is common in the history of mankind, in the exercise of power" (E 586). Later in the paper he says, "What I want to convey is that the more impasses researchers and groups encounter in conceptualizing their action in its authenticity, the more they end up forcing their action into the direction of the exercise of power" (E 612). According to Lacan, post-Freudians have been unable to grasp the essential thrust of Freud's work, its essential content or substance, and have thus latched onto the form alone while completely modifying the substance: "They half-suspect as much, and that is why they are so punctilious about preserving its forms" (E 590).

Lacan's comment about their latching onto its forms here comes, of course, in the context of the controversy over Lacan's experimentation with psychoanalytic technique, in particular, his introduction of the variable-length session, which he claims follows the spirit of Freud's work. Note that it was the post-Freudian institutes and the IPA that codified session length, not Freud, for Freud did not run his sessions strictly by the clock. Freud explicitly tells us in his *Papers on Technique* that there are occasionally patients "to whom one must give more than the average time of one hour a day, because the best part of an hour is gone before they begin to open up and to become communicative at all" (SE XII, 127–28).

Why We Should Not Interpret the Transference:
Freud's Case of Homosexuality in a Woman

We saw above that Lacan criticizes analysts for interpreting on the basis of their own being, personality, or feelings, but *not* because those feelings are not indicative of the analysand's transferential feelings; indeed, they are indicative of them, since "feelings are always mutual" (or can easily be elicited in the other). Their very mutuality is indicative, however, of their imaginary status: They reflect the reciprocal relations characteristic of the relationship between egos, between the analyst as ego and the analysand as an ego like the analyst's ego. Lacan argues that "[t]here is, in fact, an imaginary element and a symbolic element in the transference, and there is thus a choice to be made" (Seminar IV, 135). If, as Lacan claims, "the symbolic dimension is the only dimension that cures,"[17] we must confine our interventions to the symbolic component of the transference, setting the imaginary component aside. Where then is the symbolic component of the transference, and what would it mean to interpret it?

To answer these questions, let us turn to Lacan's commentary in Seminar IV on Freud's case of a young homosexual woman (SE XVIII, 147–72). I will not summarize the case here, assuming that the reader is familiar with it. I will begin with Freud's remarks on "a series of dreams" the analysand had. He says that these dreams, which were

> distorted according to rule and couched in the usual dream-language, could nevertheless be easily translated with certainty. Their content, when interpreted, was, however, remarkable. They anticipated the cure of the inversion through the treatment, expressed her joy over the prospects in life that would then be opened before her, confessed her longing for a man's love and for children, and so might have been welcomed as a gratifying preparation for the desired change. The contradiction between them and the girl's utterances in waking life at the time was very great. She did not conceal from me that she meant to marry, but only in order to escape from her father's tyranny and to follow her true inclinations undisturbed. As for the husband, she remarked rather contemptuously, she would easily deal with him, and besides, one could have sexual relations with a man and woman at one and the same time, as the example of the adored lady showed. Warned through some slight impression or other, I told her one day that I did not believe these dreams, that I regarded them as false or hypocritical, and that she intended to deceive me just as she habitually deceived her father. I was right; after I had made this clear, this kind of dream ceased. But I still believe that, beside the intention to mislead me,

the dreams partly expressed the wish to win my favour; they were also an attempt to gain my interest and my good opinion—perhaps in order to disappoint me all the more thoroughly later on. (SE XVIII, 164–65)

Lacan begins his commentary by providing his own paraphrase of Freud's last sentence here: "They were an attempt to wrap me around her little finger, captivate me, and make me find her very pretty." Lacan then continues,

> This extra sentence suffices to tip us off. This young girl must have been truly ravishing for Freud, as with Dora, not to feel completely free in the matter. In affirming that he had to expect the worst, what he wanted to avoid was to feel disillusioned. Which means that he was quite ready to create all kinds of illusions for himself. In guarding himself against these illusions, he had already entered into the game. He was already bringing the imaginary game into being. He made it become real [by telling her she intended to deceive him] because he was already inside the game. (Seminar IV, 108)

Lacan's point is not that this series of dreams was completely devoid of wishes to deceive Freud, the person they were dreamt for. But, as he puts it, the woman had not yet formed an *intention* to trick him; "it was only a desire." Freud makes it into something more than a desire, something real, by naming it, by symbolizing it, by "interpreting it too soon" (Seminar IV, 108).

What exactly does Freud do? He makes a classic transference interpretation: "You're trying to fool me just like you're trying to fool your father." Let us recall that she submits to the treatment to get her father off her back but has no intention of changing, and that she considers getting married just to appease her father while fully intending to pursue her homosexual activities behind her father's and her future husband's backs.

This might seem to be a perfect reading of the situation at the symbolic level, a reading that brings out a structural similarity between the analysand's relationship to her father and to her analyst: She wants to dupe Freud just like she wants to dupe her father. Lacan implies, however, that this only means she has put Freud in the same imaginary position as her father: in the position of an other like herself with whom she rivals for mastery of the situation. She will simply turn the tables on the masters and become the master herself. This does not reach the level of her symbolic relations per se. Why not?

Lacan indicates right away that the analysand's wish to pull the wool over men's eyes is a preconscious wish: She is well aware of the fact that she wants to dupe her father and her future husband. She is perhaps not immediately aware that she wants to do the same thing to Freud, but the very fact that she admits she is going through the motions of the analysis for her father's sake suggests that she is, at least at some level, aware that to fool Freud into believing she has changed is to fool her father into believing the same.

Freud, with his transference interpretation, situates himself as one in her series of dupes even as he shows her that he, for one, is not duped —that is, he situates himself as a slightly smarter master for her to master. In so doing, he does not situate himself elsewhere than on the imaginary axis; he does not point to his role as placeholder of the Law and the unconscious. Does he already play a symbolic role for her and inadvertently reduce his twofold role to the one-dimensional imaginary role by his intervention, or would it be by intervening in a different way that he would first come to play a symbolic role for her? That is an open question.

By focusing on the imaginary dimension of the transference, Lacan suggests that Freud misses the larger symbolic picture. Lacan often congratulates Freud for seeing the larger symbolic picture, which many contemporary analysts still do not do (though Lacan feels that when Freud misses it, it is usually with his more attractive female analysands, for example, Dora and the young homosexual woman). Lacan no doubt believes that this is partly where his own categories, the symbolic and the imaginary, are useful to analysts: His categories allow analysts to consider at what level they are situating their action at any particular moment.

What is the larger symbolic picture in the case of the young homosexual woman? Since the unconscious is the Other's discourse, the discourse constituted by her dreams is her father's discourse. And since the analysand desires what the Other desires, the unconscious desire in her dreams—which must be rigorously distinguished from her preconscious wish to fool her analyst—is her father's desire, with the caveats that her father's desire as presented in the dreams is the daughter's interpretation thereof and that she interprets his desire as the inverted form of her own message. Her message or wish is "You are my daddy/husband and you'll give me a baby." The message or wish in the dreams inverts her message so that it sounds like it comes from the Other: "You are my daughter/wife and you are going to have my baby." (Even though Freud does not present the dreams themselves, he tells us that they expressed a longing for a husband and children.)

Lacan refers to this message as "the promise on which a girl's entry into the Oedipus complex is based" and says that the dream articulates "a situation that satisfies this promise" (Seminar IV, 135). According to Lacan, a girl enters into the Oedipus complex—leaving behind her mother as her primary love object—on the basis of a promise she considers to be made by the father that "[y]ou will have my child" (144). In Lacan's view, this implies that Freud's patient had moved from the castration complex to the Oedipus complex but had not gone beyond the latter. Indeed, on Lacan's reading, it is precisely because her father gave her mother a real child when the girl was sixteen that she was unable to go beyond the Oedipus complex.

To go beyond the Oedipus complex would, according to Freud, require that she replace her father with another man; in other words, the promise would have to remain intact long enough to put a different agent in the place of the promise-maker. Yet her dreams seem to suggest that the promise *did* remain intact in her unconscious.

Lacan articulates the change that occurs when the mother's new baby is born differently than does Freud. The father refuses to give his sixteen-year-old daughter his love, preferring the mother to her. In this sense, the mother becomes a rival who *has* more than the daughter, and *having* is always phallic in Freudian and Lacanian theory. The mother is thus perceived as someone who has the phallus. According to Lacan, "What the daughter demonstrates to her father here [by getting involved with a "society lady"] is how one can love someone [. . .] for what that person does not have" (145); and who better to select for this than an unmarried, childless woman—a person who has neither a penis nor a child of her own, a person who clearly does not wield the phallus?

This interpretation is based on Lacan's many discussions of the notions that we love in our partner something that is beyond our partner and that love involves giving what we do not have, notions that I will not elaborate on here (see E 618 and especially Seminar VIII). But note that Lacan finds corroboration of his view in the fact that the girl clearly used her relationship with the "society lady" *to send a message to her father:* She regularly strolled with her "near her father's place of business" (SE XVIII, 160) as if to be sure to be seen with her by him. And her platonic or courtly style of love for the lady, which involved considerable idealization, suggests a repudiation of the father's rather more material (real) form of love for the girl's mother. Indeed, a regular figure in women's homosexual fantasies is a man who must be shown how it is done—that is, how a woman should be loved and desired for what she does not have, for her lack of a phallus.

Thus, the symbolic situation is, according to Lacan, one in which the phallus has been situated. The young homosexual woman still wants to be loved for what *she herself* does not have, as her series of dreams suggests, and Freud overlooks this. He seems convinced that she has, quite simply, adopted a masculine position in relation to the lady and thus that she has the phallus and is not looking to receive it from a man. Freud's belief in her masculine position would be characterized by Lacan as a prejudice or bias and thus as part and parcel of Freud's countertransference. Freud seems to assume that in a relationship between a man and a woman, even if the one is an analyst and the other is an analysand, either he has the phallus or she has it and there is likely to be a struggle over who is going to end up with it. (After all, a female analysand must, in Freud's view, be led to give up her claim on the phallus and agree to wait to gratefully receive it from a man.) It is this countertransferential belief that stops Freud from seeing that the phallus is still elsewhere: *It is not situated in the imaginary space of exclusive having,* where if one has it, the other cannot have it (for example, in the imaginary space of sibling rivalry, where if my sister has the new toy, I cannot have it). To get ahead of ourselves here, the phallus must be situated in a different register: in the symbolic register, which Lacan associates with the realm of being—"to be or not to be the phallus."

In order for Freud to take up his symbolic role in the transference here, he would have to keep the space of this elsewhere open for the analysand, not collapse it into the imaginary space of a struggle between the two of them over who is going to end up having it. (I will discuss what it means to keep open the space of that elsewhere in the example of a dream dreamt by the mistress of one of Lacan's analysands a bit further on.) Lacan does not tell us exactly what he would have recommended Freud do, but his view here seems to involve an additional dialectical move beyond Freud's perception of the situation: In the game of analytic chess or bridge, Lacan is thinking a move ahead of Freud—with twenty-twenty hindsight, of course.

Lacan's view at this point in his work seems to be that analysts must not identify in the transference with the position of having or not having the phallus but must somehow situate themselves in the position of the symbolic Other, where the phallic signifier is found. This, it would seem, is the symbolic element of the transference. There may be a degree to which analysts are automatically situated in that position by a neurotic analysand, but they have to actively work to stay in that position and are easily ousted from it by the level at which they situate themselves in their own interpretations.

Interpretation of the symbolic element of the transference is then, it seems to me, nothing but interpretation of the symbolic situation as a whole. Hence, Lacan's overall recommendation not to interpret transference is a cautionary statement: *Whenever analysts are inclined to interpret "the transference," they are likely to be interpreting the imaginary component alone and not the overall symbolic framework.* [18]

Unconscious Desire Must Not Be Confused with Conscious Desire: The Butcher's Witty Wife

Lacan's discussion of another of Freud's cases, that of the "butcher's witty wife" from *The Interpretation of Dreams* (SE IV, 146–51), also relies on the distinction between (pre)conscious and unconscious desires and similarly introduces the dialectic of having and being the phallus. Here is the dream she tells Freud:

> I wanted to give a supper-party, but I had nothing in the house but a little smoked salmon. I thought I would go out and buy something, but remembered then that it was Sunday afternoon and all the shops would be shut. Next I tried to ring up some caterers, but the telephone was out of order. So I had to abandon my wish to give a supper-party. (SE IV, 147)

Part of the backdrop to the dream is that the patient has noticed that her husband the butcher, while very much enamored of her and seemingly very satisfied with their relationship in every respect, speaks highly of a female friend of hers who is not at all his type (she is very skinny, and he generally only likes plumper women like his wife). The patient begins to wonder how it is that he could desire something more, how it is that he might not be entirely satisfied with his wife. How could he desire a woman who is not even his type, a woman who would seem to be unfit to satisfy him? Lacan puts the following question in her mouth: "Couldn't it be that he [the husband] too has a desire that remains awry when all in him is satisfied?" (E 626).

The day before the dream, the patient's friend had told the patient that she would like to gain some weight and inquired of her, "When are you going to ask us to another meal? You always feed one so well." One wish in the dream would then seem to be to thwart the friend's wish to eat at their house; as Lacan puts it, "a fine thing it would be, indeed, for [her friend] to fatten up so that her husband could feast on her!" The manifest dream wish to throw a dinner party ("I wanted to give a supper-party") would thus seem to be undone by the latent wish to thwart her friend's request to put on a few pounds under the butcher's appreciative gaze. This is Freud's first interpretation of the dream, which brings out the contradiction between the conscious wish (to prove Freud wrong) and unconscious wishes.

His second interpretation and Lacan's commentary on it take us quite a bit further, examining as they do the unconscious meaning of one of the patient's wishes that appears in the dream—not in the story or plot itself, but in one of the signifiers that constitutes *the text of the dream:* "smoked salmon." If we consider the dream as a simple story, we are likely to view the smoked salmon as an incidental detail or pretext. But, as Freud insists, we have to examine every dream element, and as Lacan stresses, "Desire must be taken literally *[à la lettre]*," in other words, we have to look at the *letter* of the dream in which desire is expressed.

This second interpretation is somewhat roundabout. We know from Freud's discussion of the case that this woman adores caviar and would love to eat a caviar sandwich every morning, yet she tells her husband not to buy caviar for her, "teasing" him about it. In other words, by depriving herself of it, she takes pleasure in simply wanting it (and in bringing out a "want-to-give" in her husband, keeping him on his toes, so to speak, or in suspense). She is well aware that she has a wish—that is, it is not an unconscious wish—to keep her wish for caviar unsatisfied; as Freud puts it, she has a wish for "an unfulfilled wish."[19] Lacan terms that a (preconscious) "desire to have an unsatisfied desire" (E 621). So despite her admitted love for her husband, she wants something more: She wants to go on wanting.

We also know that she has detected an interest on her husband's part in her skinny female friend. This leads her to wonder what her friend has that she does not have. She attempts to look at her friend from her husband's perspective, wondering what makes her interesting to him. One thing she seems to note is that her friend loves *smoked salmon* and yet deprives herself of it, an intriguing configuration: Why would anyone do such a thing? Freud does not argue that she puzzles the question out consciously, but it would seem that she finds motives for depriving oneself of something that resonate with her own motives. Indeed, Freud seems to suggest that his patient modeled her wish to be deprived of caviar on her friend's wish to be deprived of salmon. In other words, Freud suggests that his patient has detected or imagined a reason for this kind of desire in her friend and has made this kind of desire her own, thinking that she herself has a similar reason for having such a desire. What is that reason? It would seem that it is the pleasure one can take in desiring itself, in simply going on desiring without ever having one's desire go away due to the satisfaction of that desire. The butcher's wife identifies with her friend on this particular point, a process Freud refers to as "hysterical identification."

Let us recall the example Freud gives of hysterical identification in the context of his discussion of the dream: A number of female patients on a hospital ward all develop the same symptom, a symptom originally developed by one woman upon receiving a letter from home reminding her of an unhappy love affair (SE IV, 149–51). The other women do not simply imitate the first but identify with a particular trait of hers; in essence, they too have reasons for feeling jilted or wronged or for feeling depressed and panicky. In other words, they all put themselves in her place, unconsciously substituting themselves for her.[20]

When another woman begins to attract the butcher's attention, begins to function as the object of his desire for something else, the patient plumbs his desire to try to fathom its object and become it—that is, she wants to be what causes him to desire and thus strives to become what Lacan at this point in his work refers to as the phallus, the phallus as "the signifier of the Other's desire" (E 694). This is a general truth for Lacan: Since what every person desires is for the Other to desire him or her, everyone wants to be the signifier of the Other's desire (at other times he formulates this by saying every person wants to be the cause of the Other's desire; see, for example, E 691).

What, then, is the unconscious meaning of the patient's desire for an unsatisfied desire? *To become the phallus for her husband by identifying with a woman who has begun to captivate him.* (Freud points out the identification, whereas Lacan points out the desire to be the phallus for her husband that motivates the identification.)

Note that in the dream, the patient does not directly frustrate her friend. She frustrates herself directly, frustrating her friend indirectly (because she will not be able to invite her friend over for dinner). Freud comments on this (SE IV, 149) but does not go any further than saying that she also wanted to "to bring about a renounced wish in real life." It is Lacan who emphasizes the incompatibility between desire and satisfaction in so many ways, notably in the expression "Don't give me what I ask for because that's not it." This, according to Lacan, is not some pathological feature of this particular patient but rather a general, structural feature of human desire.

Desire is the result of a fundamental want-to-be or lack of (or in) being, a wanting or lacking that is represented and relayed in each new desire that inhabits us. This lack is what makes us neurotic rather than psychotic, and it is important for all of us to ensure that it is not saturated or smothered in some way. As Lacan says here, "desire is the metonymy of the want-to-be": Desire is the continual displacement of the ever-same structural lack or split. This split is essentially the same as that between the signifier and the signified (discussed at length in chapter 3). For whatever I say, whatever signifiers I pronounce, the meaning or signified is never absolutely clear. If I say "Lacan is an idiot," you may be thinking idiot savant or thinking of the word's Greek root, which means "particular" or "peculiar." Indeed, you may have in mind the fact that in Seminar XX Lacan refers to masturbation as the jouissance of the idiot and think I am calling him a masturbator! Or you may be thinking of *The Idiot* by Fyodor Dostoyevsky and assuming that I am associating Lacan with Dostoyevsky's protagonist. Every attested usage of the word is a valid signification, and I can say virtually nothing that is not ambiguous.

This means that there is a structural disjunction between everything I say or think I want, desire being formulated in words, and the "content" or "signified" of my desire. The referent—as some specific object that could satisfy my desire—is never isolated or discerned as such by my speech. Rather, my speech evokes numerous meanings, none of which entails a specific object or external referent (for example, an attention or caress that, if supplied exactly as requested, will really be what was desired). If I say I want a woman who will treat me like a king, you can be sure that once I have found a woman who seems to do so, I will find something to quibble about in the definition of "king" and what it means to be treated like one. (Is a king mothered? waited on hand and foot? betrayed? badly served? sucked up to?)

This suggests that desire is structurally unsatisfiable. Whereas need can be satisfied, desire cannot: There is always something left to be desired. I will not go into this point any further here, having discussed it at great length in my *Clinical Introduction to Lacanian Psychoanalysis,* but I want to mention that, at the end of "The Direction of the Treatment," Lacan points to the inherently unfulfillable nature of desire by saying that whereas hysteria is characterized by unsatisfied desire, obsession is characterized by impossible desire: They are both strategies for keeping desire in the picture, on the map, or on the menu (as we shall see in the case of Kris's patient, discussed in chapter 2). To try to continually be what incites the Other's desire is obviously a never-ending quest—a quest to be something that is subject to displacement or metonymic slippage—as opposed to the quest for caviar, which one can have and then be done with.[21] Having is static; being is a pursuit.

There are many other aspects of the patient's dream and case that could be discussed here: for example, the facts that the husband also expressed an interest in losing weight (to be more like or more attractive to his wife's friend?), that the wife also identified with her husband in trying to figure out what the other woman had that she did not have, and that Lacan suggests that there is some relationship between the slice of smoked salmon ("which comes to occupy the place of the Other's desire"), the slice of a pretty girl's rump (could we say that the husband's desire for that slice "does not suffice for anything," that is, that she wants him to desire something else?), and the phallus ("To be the phallus, even a somewhat skinny one—isn't that the final identification with the signifier of desire?"). But I would like to continue my discussion of the phallus by taking up Lacan's discussion in "The Direction of the Treatment" of one of his own cases. Lacan very rarely wrote of his own cases, and this is, I believe, his longest discussion of one in print.

Evoking Absence: Lacan's Case of an Obsessive Man

Regarding case discussions, Lacan says something quite paradoxical toward the beginning of "The Direction of the Treatment": He asks us to excuse him for always referring to the same Freudian cases and seems to want to explain to us why he almost never "make[s] use of [his] own analyses to demonstrate the level interpretation reaches." He mentions the problem of anonymity that can arise "in the communicating milieu in which many of [his] analyses take place" but nevertheless indicates that he has "succeeded at times in saying enough about a case without saying too much, that is, in conveying [his] example without anyone, except the person in question, recognizing it" (E 598).

We might expect Lacan to discuss one of his own analyses immediately after such a preamble, but he does not; instead, he provides a somewhat cryptic thumbnail sketch of Freudian technique. Indeed, we have to wait thirty-two pages—and they are rather dense pages—before we come across an example taken from Lacan's own consulting room.[22]

It will be helpful to briefly discuss the road map of Freudian technique Lacan provides before turning to the case itself. Lacan claims that Freud's approach differs from that adopted by Lacan's contemporaries in the order in which Freud proceeded; in particular, Freud did not reserve interpretation until the last stage of the treatment, when it would apply only to the transference. Lacan says,

> [I]t is in a direction of the treatment, ordered, as I have just shown, in accordance with a process that begins with rectification of the subject's relations with reality, and proceeds to development of the transference and then to interpretation, that is situated the horizon at which the fundamental discoveries, which we are still living off, surrendered themselves to Freud concerning the dynamics and structure of obsessive neurosis. Nothing more, but nothing less either. (E 598)

"Rectification of the subject's relations with reality" seems to be a reference to Freud's remarks to the Rat Man during their very first sessions (SE X, 169, 173) regarding the "errors of memory" and "displacements" involved in the pince-nez matter. Freud has to get the Rat Man to tell the story three times before being able to begin to piece it together, and Freud eventually points out to the Rat Man that he must have *known* that the woman at the post office paid the C.O.D. charges for his pince-nez before the cruel captain incorrectly told him that Captain A. had paid them. It should be noted that this "rectification" has to do with something the Rat Man must have known and thus concerns his psychical reality; it is not a reference to the concept of "external" or "objective" reality.[23]

Freud also does something similar with Dora: He says that it seems she has participated in her father's dalliance with Frau K.; indeed, although complaining about it—as the beautiful soul blames the "disorder" found in her world on others—she seems to have played the part of its linchpin, the sine qua non of the relationship (SE VII, 35–36). Freud's comment can be understood as concerning her subjective involvement in the situation, not as some sort of "objective" judgment by Freud about the "real situation." Lacan refers to this maneuver on Freud's part with Dora as "subjective rectification" (E 601), suggesting that such rectification is always necessary with the "beautiful soul" who criticizes the havoc of her own world rather than seeing her own contribution to the havoc (E 219, 596; see also SE VII, 67).

We shall see how this discussion of the order in which Freud proceeded— rectification, development of the transference, and then interpretation— echoes in Lacan's discussion of his own case.

Lacan does not give us a detailed overview of the case (E 630–33). Instead, he tells us about "an incident that occurred at the end of the analysis of an obsessive, that is, after a great deal of work" in which Lacan did not limit himself, he says, to "analyzing the subject's aggressiveness"; in other words, Lacan did not spend his time analyzing the resistances and defenses that arise in the dyadic relationship between two egos, as so many of his contemporaries recommended doing.

Let us note in passing that Lacan severely criticizes the constant use of the verb "to analyze" by certain analysts, who show thereby that they no longer know what it means *to interpret*. According to Lacan, when an analyst says he "analyzes" something, it almost always means that he situates his work at the imaginary level instead of interpreting at the symbolic level. To "analyze" is to work on the basis of oneself, one's own personality, one's own way of seeing the world, one's own notion of reality, one's own biases—in short, one's own countertransference. To say that one "analyzes" implies that one was lucky enough to have been born an analyst, to have received at birth the special, ineffable gifts necessary to be an analyst—gifts that usually turn out to be terribly difficult to impart or communicate to other people. In Lacan's view, it is the analysand who analyzes, not the analyst; the latter is "up against the wall of the task of interpreting" (E 591).

Now the analysand cannot help but fall back into the imaginary realm of defenses and resistance when the real that she is trying to put into words (trauma and other experiences that have never before been articulated by the subject) resists symbolization. Imaginary phenomena arise when the analysand cannot manage to say what she has to say due to "desire's incompatibility with speech" (E 641). The analysand takes her frustration out on the analyst (Seminar I, 59–60/48–49) and how could it be otherwise given that there is no one else physically present with the analysand in the office? The analyst is experienced by the analysand as refusing to help and even as impeding the analysand's progress. But the analyst must not situate himself at that level and must not feel attacked personally by the analysand in such situations. The analysand is not suddenly resisting the analyst deliberately out of some ill will or perfidy, as some analysts seem to think (see the comments by Dr. Z* in Seminar I). The real that the analysand is up against always resists symbolization.[24] Indeed, the analysand *and* the analyst are both situated on the same side of what we might call the "wall of the real," the analyst needing to try to help the analysand symbolize the real that resists their combined efforts (cf. Lacan's "wall of language," E 282, 291, 308, 316). As Lacan puts it in 1968, "What resists in analysis is obviously not the subject. What resists is discourse" (Seminar XV, January 24, 1968).

Regarding the case at hand, Lacan asserts that instead of analyzing his obsessive patient's aggressiveness, he brought him to recognize "the part he had played in the destructive game foisted by one of his parents on the other parent's desire" (E 630). He tells us later that the patient's mother was critical of his father's "overly ardent desire" (E 633), and thus it was the mother who was directing a game that involved destroying the father's desire. Lacan therefore brought his patient to recognize the part he himself had played in this game, which seems quite similar to the "subjective rectification" Lacan points to in Freud's work with Dora. He thus proceeds with this patient exactly as in the summary he provides of Freud's technique (E 598): He begins by rectifying "the subject's relations with reality, and proceeds to development of the transference and then to interpretation."

He goes on to tell us that the patient "surmised his powerlessness to desire without destroying the Other, thus destroying his own desire insofar as it was the Other's desire *[devine l'impuissance où il est de désirer sans détruire l'Autre, et par là son désir lui-même en tant qu'il est désir de l'Autre]*" (E 630). The French here is, as is often the case with Lacan, quite ambiguous: Does the patient *surmise* both his powerlessness and his desire insofar as it is the Other's desire, or does he *destroy* both the Other and his desire insofar as it is the Other's desire? Furthermore, should we understand *désir de l'Autre* in the sense in which the patient's desire is the same as the Other's desire (Lacan does not tell us whether it is his mother's or his father's) or in the sense in which the patient's desire is the desire he has for the Other?

In following the oft-repeated indications Lacan provides, I will put forward the prudent hypothesis that the Other with a capital O is the father here and the other with a lowercase o is the mother. Having made this hypothesis, we see that if the patient desires he becomes like his father, who desired ardently. Since the patient agrees to play his mother's game, he is supposed to destroy his father's excessive desire and thereby destroy his own desire (since the patient's desire is identical to his father's desire). This is what leads him to put his real desire aside or on hold, or, as Lacan says further on, to tuck his being away (E 633); in this way, he keeps his own desire out of the line of fire. While the patient is ostensibly engaged in the project of destroying the Other for his mother's sake, at the same time he is striving to protect the Other (E 630).

Indeed, Lacan tells us that he revealed to his patient "how at every moment [the patient] manipulated the situation so as to protect the Other" and that this manipulation consisted in arranging "the circus games between the two others (little *a* and the ego, its shadow)"—the two others being, at this point in Lacan's work, his mother as ego (or alter ego, *a'*) and the patient's ego *(a)*. The patient thus arranged circus games between himself and his mother (presumably pretending to ally with her in destroying the father's excessive desire) "from the spectator's box reserved for the Other's [. . .] boredom" (E 630). The Other here is placed on the sidelines, in the position of a spectator in his box, a spectator who is bored precisely because he does not participate in the games but who remains intact thanks to his isolation.

We can situate this on the L schema as in Figure 1.6.

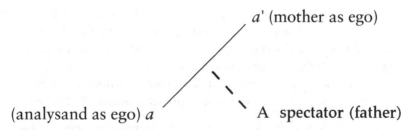

a' (mother as ego)

(analysand as ego) *a*   A spectator (father)

Figure 1.6. L schema for Lacan's obsessive analysand

We might say that Lacan's obsessive—and, by extension, the obsessive in general—presents the entire L schema minus the place of the subject. The symbolic axis is truncated here, deprived of its continuation toward the position of the subject (for the subject of the unconscious is hidden or tucked away here); or we might say that the subject position is collapsed into the Other position. The subject's unconscious desire is removed from the game and retracted into the position of the spectator.

This is related to what Lacan says in "The Function and Field of Speech and Language in Psychoanalysis" about the place of the Other in obsession:

> The obsessive [. . .] addresses his ambiguous homage toward the box in which he himself has his seat, that of the master who cannot be seen *[se voir]*.
>
> [The obsessive] puts on a show *[donne à voir]*.
>
> [. . .] In the case of the obsessive, you have to get yourself recognized in the spectator, who is invisible from the stage, to whom he is united by the mediation of death. (E 304)

What may not seem terribly clear in this citation is stated far more clearly in Seminar IV. It is even quite possible that what Lacan says in Seminar IV in November 1956 is inspired by the same patient he tells us about a year and a half later when he writes "The Direction of the Treatment":

> What is an obsessive? In short, an obsessive is an actor who plays his role and assures a certain number of acts as if he were dead. The game he gives himself over to is a way of sheltering himself from death. It is a lively game that consists in showing that he is invulnerable. [. . .] It is important for him to show [. . .] how far the other—the small other, who is merely his alter ego, the double of himself—can go. The game is played out in front of an Other who watches the spectacle. The obsessive himself is merely a spectator here; the very possibility of the game and the pleasure he takes in it lies therein. However, he does not know what place he occupies, and that is what is unconscious in him. [. . .]
>
> He participates in an illusory game [. . .] that consists in getting as close as possible to death while remaining out of the range of all the blows, because the subject has, in some sense, killed in advance the desire in himself; he has, so to speak, mortified it. [. . .]
>
> The point is to demonstrate what the subject has articulated for this Other spectator that he is unbeknown to himself. (Seminar IV, 27–28)

The obsessive thus situates himself (through identification with the father, the master, and even death itself) as the Other who is the spectator of the scene. While his ego participates in the games—that is, in the spectacle staged for the Other—his desire, his unconscious desire, remains on the sidelines as if it did not exist. Whereas the hysteric identifies with the spectacle itself, the game played out before the Other's very eyes (E 304), the obsessive, according to Lacan, puts on a show for the spectator that he himself is and that the analyst becomes for him in the course of analysis.

The Incident

Such are the basic, albeit highly theoretical, coordinates of the analysis according to Lacan. This brings us to the incident mentioned by Lacan at the very beginning of his commentary: "Here my subject was at the end of his rope, having reached the point of playing a game of three-card monte with me that was of a rather peculiar kind, in that it revealed a structure of desire" (E 631).

Three-card monte, often played on the streets of New York City and other cities, is a game in which a player (often an out-of-towner who does not yet know the ruses of the big city streets) must find a certain card, after having seen it faceup, among three cards lying facedown on a flat surface, after the other player, the rip-off artist, has moved them around with rapid sleight of hand. The rip-off artist usually allows the tourist to win once or twice to raise the ante, but once he begins to bet seriously, the sleight of hand accelerates and he never manages to find the right card even when he is sure he knows which it is (often it has simply been taken off the table by prestidigitation).

The rapid movement of the cards evokes Lacan's remark here that obsessive neurosis is an "architecture of contrasts" and presents us with a wide variety of facades; the analyst must thus possess "the general combinatory that no doubt governs their variety, but which also, even more usefully, accounts for the illusions or, better, shifts in the labyrinth that take place right before one's very eyes" (E 630). It also evokes the games between the two egos that are orchestrated for the spectator.

Note that Lacan does not say that his patient deliberately tries to dupe him; the obsessive does not even realize that he is directing the game. According to Lacan, this is part of the very nature of obsessive neurosis, which is a structure whose "great mass [. . .] nevertheless remains" after an analysis (E 631). This formulation seems to me to mean that the obsessive does not become something else after an analysis; he does not become "normal," for example. But that does not stop him from changing in the course of his analysis.

The Hidden Card

What, then, is the card the patient hides from Lacan? The card would seem to be the phallus. Lacan continues his account of the incident as follows:

> Let's say that being of mature years, as the comical expression goes, and of a disillusioned turn of mind, he would have willingly misled me into thinking his menopause was the cause of the impotence that struck him, and accused me of the same. (E 631)

In other words, the patient was trying to blame his sudden impotence with his mistress either on his age and so-called male menopause (or climacteric) or quite simply on Lacan. The analysand insinuated either that Lacan, too, was going through menopause and was thus similarly impotent or else that it was because of Lacan's impotence as an analyst that the analysand was having this particular problem.

The patient comes up with the idea of asking his mistress to "sleep with another man to see" (E 631)—a formulation that might seem, at first glance, to indicate a belief on his part that jealousy would have an effect on his libido. After all, it was not yet the age of Viagra, and the patient thus could not resort to such stimulants. But it turns out that this "to see" has to do with the fact that the patient is convinced he must harbor within himself some repressed homosexual desires (latching onto certain psychoanalytic "truths" he had heard), a belief Lacan refuses to either confirm or refute ("I remained, as you may well have expected, rather off-putting on that point," E 631). In effect, the patient plans to be present during the scene between his mistress and another man.[25] Now he does not simply come up with the idea: He explicitly asks his mistress to sleep with another man.

The Dream

That very night, his mistress has a dream that she immediately tells her lover.[26] This dream, according to Lacan (E 632), constitutes a response to the patient's request (*demande,* in French, also meaning "demand"), but the response does not take the form of a simple yes or no. The mistress responds from a certain place, the place assigned to her by the patient's neurosis—in other words, she responds not from the place he consciously wants her to occupy but from the place where he cannot help but situate her. This recalls what Lacan had said earlier about interpreting transference: One cannot find a point outside of the transference on the basis of which one makes one's interpretation, since interpretation is always heard by the analysand as coming from the place where the analysand has already situated the analyst. To interpret the transference thus does not mean that one leaves the transference behind or somehow steps outside of it, were it only for an instant; the impact of an interpretation depends on where it comes from. One is always already situated.

Let us return to the mistress's dream. In this dream, "she had a phallus—she sensed its shape under her clothing—which did not prevent her from having a vagina as well, nor, especially, from wanting this phallus to enter it." Lacan adds that "[o]n hearing this, our patient's powers were immediately restored and he demonstrated this brilliantly to his shrewd paramour" (E 631).

Now what allows Lacan to interpret this dream, which is not one of his patient's own dreams? Desire being the Other's desire, the desire in the dream dreamt by the mistress is the same as the patient's desire. The dream, says Lacan, "was designed to satisfy the patient's desire beyond his request," in other words, beyond the patient's request that his mistress sleep with another man. The patient requests that she do something, but the mistress, unlike the kinds of analysts Lacan often criticizes, hears something else in his request *(demande)*: a desire, a desire that is elsewhere. And it is this desire—the patient's desire which lies beyond his request—that is fulfilled in the dream.[27]

An obsessive, Lacan tells us, maintains "his desire in an impossibility that preserves its metonymic conditions" (E 632), and the patient's desire here was sustained in a fantasy in which his mistress was formerly able to occupy the position of the erotic object. But the analysis had disturbed the metonymic conditions necessary to the patient, and his mistress could no longer occupy the right place for him, the place of the cause of his desire. Instead, it would seem that she had come to occupy the place of the object of his adoration (that of the mother in the obsessive's madonna/whore dialectic).

Are we to think that it is the fact that she presents herself in the dream "as having a phallus" that restores "her erotic value"—in other words, that reinstates her in the place of cause of desire in the patient's fantasy? If that were true, it would seem to confirm the hypothesis about male homosexuality proposed by Lacan in Seminar VIII, which affirms that, for the male homosexual, "the sign of desire"—namely the erect penis—is "the object of desire, the object that attracts desire" (307). According to this hypothesis, it would seem that it is the sign (of desire) that the male homosexual seeks rather than the signifier (of desire). His cause of desire would thus be a presence (the presence of the erect penis as a sign of the partner's desire) instead of an absence (a lack that points to the partner's desire for something).

Lacan proposes this notion in the context of his discussion of the *Symposium*. In Plato's dialogue, Alcibiades, unlike the butcher's wife, does not seem concerned with the signifier of the Other's desire, that Other being Socrates for him. Instead, he demands a sign of Socrates' desire for him; he wants Socrates to have an erection; that alone can serve for him as a sign of the Other's desire. This is why Lacan speaks of the "degrading" of capital Phi (Φ, the phallus) into lowercase phi (-φ, imaginary castration), which is not exactly the reduction of the symbolic to the imaginary (Seminar VIII, 296) but, more precisely, it seems to me, the reduction of the signifier to the sign. Alcibiades wants a sign of Socrates' desire because "the Other's desire is essentially separated from us by the mark of the signifier" (274–75). The Other's desire—that is, what the Other wants, and more specifically, what the Other wants from us—is hidden from us or presented to us by a signifier, an intangible signifier: the phallus. It is not immediately obvious, like a demand that we do *x, y,* or *z*. A desire is never directly spoken as such, for all speech is demand, as Lacan tells us: All speech constitutes a demand of some sort (for a response, for example, or for recognition or acknowledgment).[28] A desire is something that has to be deciphered, since desire proper is unconscious desire; it is beyond what one consciously intends to say one wants. To content ourselves with a sign of the Other's desire is, in Lacan's scheme of things, a shortcut: a way of relieving the anxiety aroused by the obscurity of the Other's desire and the uncertainty of our interpretation thereof.

Like a good analyst, Socrates does not give Alcibiades the sign he is seeking. According to Lacan, Socrates wants to set Alcibiades on the path of his own desire, a desire linked not to a sign but rather to the signifier of an absence. Socrates tries to "dialectize" Alcibiades' desire. The modern psychoanalyst must do the same: He must not, Lacan says, represent *something* to the analysand, "[f]or the sign that must be given [is the sign of the] lack of a signifier" (Seminar VIII, 275). This is obviously related to S(Ⱥ), the signifier of the lack in the Other (the signifier of the lack in the signifying order itself): the lack in the Other that the analysand must be brought to grapple with for analysis to have a chance of reaching its proper end.

This formulation is not the only nor necessarily the most complete one Lacan ever gave of male homosexuality. Note, in particular, that in his discussion of it in Seminar VIII, Lacan introduces Psyche and Eros, Dora, and other references as well. Moreover, he tells us that in obsessive neurosis in general, "capital Phi emerges in forms that I call degraded" (Seminar VIII, 298). In other words, this "degrading" seems to be a general feature of obsession. Furthermore, since capital Phi is "the signifier that is excluded from the signifier," that is, from the signifying system as a whole, "it can only return there by artifice, contraband, and degradation.... [T]his is why we never see it except as the function of imaginary phi" (306). Capital Phi thus never appears as such, but it seems that it can be evoked nevertheless by its very absence.[29]

Note that when Lacan proposes this formulation in chapter 16 of Seminar VIII, he refers to Rabelais's statement that "science without conscience is the ruin of the soul." In his discussion of the mistress's dream in "The Direction of the Treatment," he refers to the same expression by Rabelais, inverting it into "conscience without science" (E 632), evoking it again when he mentions "the science included in the unconscious" (E 632). Note, too, that "The Direction of the Treatment" was published for the first time in 1961 and that the several classes of Seminar VIII devoted to the phallus were held in April 1961. This perhaps justifies us in elucidating the one text in relation to the other.

In any case, we might say that the mistress's dream shows us "the science included in the unconscious" in the sense that this dream brings forward both the present sign of desire—the erect penis—and absence, namely, the vagina associated with the desire that the penis enter it. We have thus the two at once: the "real presence" of the erect penis and the simultaneous absence of the penis that evokes the dreamer's desire.[30]

It is thus not simply by presenting herself in the dream as having a phallus that the mistress restores her value as an erotic object for the patient. Certain analysts might believe that her possession of a penis serves him as a guarantee that she will "not have to take [his penis] from him," but according to Lacan, "such a guarantee is too strong not to be fragile" (E 633). The "maternal phallus" that she presents—why not call it that?— can relieve the subject's castration anxiety momentarily, but this presence does not in any way help him overcome it. I refer to the phallus she presents as the "maternal phallus" because it seems that if she had previously been able to occupy the position of cause of desire in his fantasy but was no longer able to do so because of the work he was doing in his analysis, it was because he had begun to see her as too much like his own mother.

What restores her value as an erotic object for the patient would thus seem to be the fact that the absence of the phallus is *also* presented in the dream. The place of lack is preserved, despite all possible presences, and thus the place of desire remains intact: the place of the dreamer's desire but also of the patient's desire. The lack in the dreamer is the patient's desire; stated differently, the lack in the dreamer gives rise to the patient's desire. And this lack must remain intact.

Winding His Way between a Desire and Contempt for That Desire

Why must this lack remain intact? The mother of Lacan's patient showed contempt for her husband's desire. The patient thus "wound his way between a desire and contempt for that desire" (E 633), in other words, between his father's desire, which had become his own desire, and contempt for that desire coming from the mother and thus from any woman situated in the place of the mother by the subject. If I contemn someone's desire, I signify to him that his desire does not correspond to any lack in me. If I stop him from seeing any sort of lack in me, his desire vanishes and his being evaporates.[31]

If the mistress had a penis but no vagina (and no desire that some other penis enter it) in the dream, she would have no need of anything from the patient and would have nothing but contempt for his desire. Indeed, it would seem that the patient viewed her in precisely that way prior to her dream: as lacking in nothing and having no use for his desire—hence his impotence with her. But in the dream, she presents herself as nevertheless lacking in something, and it is in this respect that the patient can be of some use to her, that he can lend his being to something: to holding the place of the phallus for her. It is in this way that his own "want-to-be was touched" (E 633).

If the reference to Rabelais does not suffice to indicate a certain relationship between "The Direction of the Treatment" and the section of Seminar VIII I have been quoting, note that the word *contrebande* (contraband) is used to qualify the obsessive's object in both texts and that it takes on a rather particular meaning in the case of Lacan's obsessive here, where the question is *bander ou ne pas bander* (to get an erection or not to get an erection).

Indeed, I would propose as a working hypothesis that what is contraband here is the maternal phallus itself, the fake or counterfeit phallus that is fraudulently introduced. One might say that it is the imaginary phallus, the phallus that is there but that might not be there, the phallus that is capable of falling off. As Lacan says in "The Subversion of the Subject," it is the phallus's "position as a 'pointy extremity' in the [human] form [that] predisposes it to the fantasy of it falling off—in which its exclusion from the specular image is completed as is the prototype it constitutes for the world of objects" (E 822).

The imaginary phallus is never sure; its possession is not assured to us. This is perhaps why it is not a very strong guarantee to Lacan's obsessive to attribute one to his mistress (E 633). But the presence of a fake phallus can evoke the phallus that is not presented; in fact, that is exactly what Lacan says several pages later in "The Subversion of the Subject":

> Such is woman concealed behind her veil: it is the absence of the penis that makes her the phallus, the object of desire. Evoke this absence in a more precise way by having her wear a cute fake one under a fancy dress, and you, or rather she, will have plenty to tell us about: the effect is 100 percent guaranteed, for men who don't beat around the bush, that is. (E 825)

I doubt if, in the age of Viagra, people still resort to such games, where it is the obviously fake nature of the phallus worn under one's clothing that allows the equation "woman = symbolic phallus" to be made, "symbolic phallus" to be understood here in the sense of the signifier of the Other's desire and even as the cause of the partner's desire. The presence of the obvious fake forcibly evokes the absence of a real, biological penis; it evokes, in other words, a not-having that calls for symbolization. It calls for a signifier of the lack in the Other, that signifier being essentially equated with the symbolic phallus at this stage in Lacan's work, the symbolic phallus being what elicits the subject's desire. The analyst must lead the analysand to an encounter with the symbolic phallus as signifier of the lack in the Other—not by orchestrating this sort of sexual encounter, but through the work of analysis—if the analysand is to arrive at the proper end of analysis.

Prior to this encounter, it is the imaginary phallus that determines the fate of all the obsessive's objects, that makes them into a series, renders them equivalent to each other, and keeps them metonymically slipping from one to the next. The exact formulation of the obsessive's fundamental fantasy that Lacan gives us in Seminar VIII is

$$\mathcal{A} \lozenge \varphi\, (a, a', a'', a''', \ldots)$$

On the left of the lozenge we have the fact that the obsessive situates himself in relation to the Other in such a way as to "never be where he seems to designate himself at any particular moment in time" (Seminar VIII, 297); his being is, in other words, tucked away, somewhere else. On the right of the lozenge we have the fact that

> objects are for him, as objects of desire, situated as a function [mis en function] of certain erotic equivalences—something we are used to indicating by speaking of the eroticization of his world, and especially of his intellectual world. This "situating as a function of" [mise en function] can be noted by φ. [. . .] φ is precisely that which underlies the equivalence established between objects at the erotic level. φ is, in some sense, the unit of measure by which the subject accommodates the function of little a—namely, the function of the objects of his desire. (297)

If, as I am proposing, this φ can be understood as the maternal phallus, at least in one sense, it is by the light of that phallus that all the obsessive's objects shine. The characteristic of contraband that they all share comes from the contraband object par excellence: the maternal phallus. (We will return to the importance of the contraband object in the case discussed by Kris in chapter 2.) The obsessive's objects are able to cause his desire as long as their association with the mother is not unveiled. Once this association is unveiled, the contraband object (mistress, "whore") can no longer be desired but only idealized (madonna) or abandoned.

Taking my interpretation here one step further, we might say that the obsessive's objects remain determined by his obstinate unconscious attribution to a woman of a phallus (the so-called maternal phallus) until he comes to grips with castration, which as Lacan repeatedly states is "first and foremost [. . .] the Other's castration (the mother's, first of all)" (E 632; see also E 686). The obsessive refuses to accept that his mother is castrated, which simply means that she does not have everything she wants and is thus lacking in something. He refuses to accept this because he feels that it means something about him: It means that she wants something unthinkable from him, his very being perhaps. Better to deny the existence of her lack ("the lack in the Other") than face the horrible anxiety her desire ("the Other's desire") elicits in him. Nevertheless, his jouissance remains tied to her, and it is only by veiling the connection between her and the contraband that excites him that he can find any satisfaction. It is only through the analytically orchestrated encounter with the lack in the Other as symbolized, that is, with the signifier of the lack in the Other (which, as I said earlier, is equated by Lacan with the symbolic phallus, Φ, at this stage in his work), that the obsessive can come to terms with castration and put a stop to the endless serialization of objects all destined to eventually reveal their connection to the mother. It is only then that the imaginary phallus, φ, can stop serving as the condition of the subject's desire.

Perhaps Lacan is suggesting, then, that the mistress's dream helped bring about the analysand's encounter with the lack in the Other and helped symbolize this lack for him as something beyond the penis in the dream (the imaginary, maternal phallus), as a desire for something else—not for his being per se, not for an organ he has, but for something he can give from time to time, even though he does not have it. Or perhaps Lacan is suggesting it was just a temporary fix, one that temporarily moved him in the same direction as the analysis was moving him.

Such are, in any case, some of the interpretations we can draw from Lacan's account of this incident in his obsessive analysand's analysis. What did Lacan himself do with this patient? In the end, we know more about what he did not do than about what he did. We know that he did not speak to him of his "castrating mother": Lacan indicates that "it's of no value [to do so] in interpretation, where to invoke [her] would not have taken us very far, except to bring the patient back to the very point where" he already was, to the point where "he wound his way between a desire and contempt for that desire" (E 633). The mistress's dream "addressed the analysand just as well as the analyst could have" (E 632). Perhaps better?

Lacan nevertheless devoted his attention "to get[ting] the patient to grasp the function the phallus as a signifier serves in his desire" (E 632), but it seems we will never know *how* Lacan did so. It would appear, in any case, that he oriented all of his interventions around the symbolic axis and that he strove, like the patient's mistress, to preserve "the place of desire in the direction of the treatment" (E 633). This is what Freud seemingly failed to do in his work with the young homosexual woman, as we saw above, grasping the phallus, as he did there, only as something tangible one could either have or not have, not as something she could give in love without having and something for which she could be loved precisely for not having.

Why We Should Not Encourage Our Analysands to Identify with Us

By way of concluding this commentary on "The Direction of the Treatment," I would like to point to one more fundamental difference between Lacan's technique and that of other analysts. A number of Lacan's contemporaries formulated the explicit goal of trying to bring about identification between the analysand and the analyst, which, according to Lacan, involves "reduc[ing] their patients' desires to demands, which simplifies the task of converting them into the analysts' own demands" (E 626). This identification satisfies the analysand's demand for being, the analysand's "passions for being" (E 627); I know who and what I am because the analyst (as Other) tells me who and what I am. This corresponds to the position $s(A)$ on the Graph of Desire (E 817; see chapter 4 below).

Lacan, rather than seeking to satisfy the patient's passion for being—which *can* be satisfied through identification—tries to get the analysand to encounter her *manque-à-être* (lack of being, failure to be, want-to-be). The analyst should strive to bring the analysand to encounter the absence of a signifier in the Other, a signifier given by the Other that can take her under its wing and justify her existence, say why she is here and what her purpose is—this corresponds to the position $S(\cancel{A})$ on the Graph of Desire.

The Graph of Desire spatially differentiates these two approaches. Identification is a way of avoiding the question of my lack-of-being. If I identify with the analyst or a leader (see SE XVIII, chapter 8), I do not have to ask myself the difficult questions—my being is never at issue, the question of my being is already answered. Lacan, as Colette Soler argues in "The Relation to Being: The Analyst's Place of Action," refers to such identification with another's ego as the *malheur de l'être* (misfortune of being, unhappiness of being) (E 615, 636).[32] It is a misfortune to identify with someone, for it keeps me from grappling with and going beyond my lack of being. It leaves me with the same inadequacies or failings as my analyst. Now that is unfortunate!

2

Lacan's Critique of the Ego Psychology Troika: Hartmann, Kris, and Loewenstein

> To wipe desire off the map when it is already covered
> over in the patient's landscape is not the best way of
> following Freud's teaching.
>
> —Lacan, "The Direction of the Treatment"

Psychoanalyzing Psychoanalysis

Lacan rarely gives us a full summary of a position he criticizes, laying out the various theses and arguments attributable to it and then going on to refute them one by one. Lacan is probably never demonstrative in that sense: He never demonstrates that his opponents are wrong by carefully explaining his opponents' positions and then critiquing them step by step. He tends, rather, to make a snide, ironic, or offhanded remark here or there, dismissing the entire edifice of a theory with a half a sentence.

His seemingly casual attitude toward such offensive tendencies within psychoanalysis is, however, offset by a rather different attitude we find in his work, one that shows Lacan psychoanalyzing psychoanalysis itself, or more specifically, psychoanalyzing the historical evolution of new trends in psychoanalysis since Freud's time. Lacan seems to want to read the history of analytic theory the way Hegel reads history (in his *Lectures on the Philosophy of History*). Lacan does not do so because he believes analytic history is somehow inexorably tending toward Truth, the way Hegel believes history is pursuing its most perfect course; rather, he wants to "get out of this true impasse, which is both mental and practical, to which analysis has now come" (Seminar I, 32/24).[1]

He hopes that, by analyzing the various changes in direction within the analytic movement, he will be able to overcome the impasse to which these changes have led. Lacan seems to suggest that since analysis "is a detour for acceding to the unconscious" (Seminar I, 32/24)—that is, analysis is a roundabout path that avoids and circles around without going to the heart of things (namely, truth)—there must be a logic to its detours and avoidances, a logic to its tangents and new directions. He says, "[W]e must posit that the evolution and transformations of analytic experience teach us about the very nature of this experience insofar as it is also a human experience that is hidden from itself" (32/24).

The attempt to understand the internal logic of the series of twists and turns within psychoanalysis—the major ones Lacan takes up being ego psychology and object relations[2]—is a theme Lacan returns to again and again: We find it in Seminar I, "Function and Field of Speech and Language," "Variations on the Standard Treatment," and "The Direction of the Treatment," to mention just a few of the places where this project is discussed. I will attempt to elucidate Lacan's analysis of the place of ego psychology in the logic of the evolution of psychoanalysis—and of how it can help us go beyond a certain impasse—after I have first presented some of the particular features of ego psychology itself.

Ego Psychology's Theoretical Base

Ego psychology, as defined by its self-proclaimed founders, Ernst Kris, Heinz Hartmann, and Rudolf Loewenstein, traces its very name to Freud's work in the 1930s.[3] Its founders find their inspiration above all in *Inhibitions, Symptoms, and Anxiety* (SE XX), which is, incidentally, the text most often cited by Anna Freud in her 1936 book *The Ego and the Mechanisms of Defense*.[4]

Anna Freud's book must certainly be considered to be the primary source of the ego psychology movement, legitimating, as it did, a wholesale endorsement of the ego as an object of independent study, with its own arena of activities worthy of investigation. Written by Freud's daughter and published during Freud's own lifetime, it was taken to be approved of in its entirety by the master himself. Lacan tells us in 1954 (Seminar I, 76/63) that Anna Freud's book has the value of a "legacy": It is the "faithfully transmitted" legacy of Freud's last conceptualization of the ego. Note, however, that in his 1955 paper "The Freudian Thing," Lacan says something rather more ironic: The ego's stormy liaison with the second topography has been "legitimized by the ministry of Miss Anna Freud in a marriage whose social credit has done nothing but grow ever since, so much so that people assure me it will soon request the Church's blessing" (E 420–21)

It is as if a number of analysts in the international psychoanalytic movement had been waiting for just such a legitimation of what they had wanted to do all along: Hartmann wasted little time in bringing out his book *Ego Psychology and the Problem of Adaptation,*[5] manifesting his sense that analysts could finally, in good conscience, study all the things psychologists had been studying for years—how children learn, how they develop from year to year, and how they respond to different forms of early education—all under the auspices of the ego. The ego no longer had to be understood as simply a mediator between the id's drives and the superego's judgments, or between id impulses and the demands of external reality. Suddenly, it was possible to imagine the existence of a "nonconflictual zone" or "conflict-free sphere" in which the ego could develop and extend its "mastery of reality"[6] free from the distracting or nefarious influence of the other psychical agencies. A number of ego functions were now claimed to develop in a zone "largely outside of the reach of psychic conflict," in a sphere "free from conflict."[7]

There was a sense at that time that psychoanalysis could now be brought back into the fold of general psychology and that analysts could now study the minute details of child development and the positive achievements of the ego as it masters languages, mathematics, science, everyday tasks, and so on. The ego's defenses no longer needed to be seen as negative attributes or deficits: They could now be seen as highly productive, as necessary for *the laudable task of adaptation.* Indeed, we might say that the ego's adaptive faculties could suddenly be celebrated by psychoanalysts, whereas before that adaptation always seemed to place excessive restrictions on the id, to be fraught with difficulties and uncertainties, and to remain ever precarious.

In their writings, Hartmann and Kris credit Freud with tracing in fine detail the development of the libido (the id) and the superego, but they claim that he did little to elucidate the development of the ego. They set out to make good that "gap in our knowledge." Part of Freud's failing, according to them, is that he did not sufficiently take into account the "influences of the environment," and they refer to those influences as "development" ("The Genetic Approach," 24).

Curiously enough, in their next major paper, "Comments on the Formation of Psychic Structure," a paper written jointly with Rudolf Loewenstein, Lacan's former analyst, Freud is taken to task for attributing *too much* importance to development when it comes to the ego. For Freud tells us that the ego does not exist at all at birth: It is a precipitate or sedimentation of a child's abandoned object-cathexes, a crystallization of the child's successive identifications with objects that have been given up (*The Ego and the Id,* SE XIX). This strikes our troika as going too far, for it is inconsistent with things that Freud says about the ego elsewhere (*New Introductory Lectures on Psychoanalysis,* SE XXII), where he claims, on their reading, that the ego is in charge of "motility, cognition and perception."[8] Rather than reading Freud as Lacan attempts to, placing each text and each formulation in the context of the theoretical and clinical problems Freud was grappling with at the time he wrote it, the troika simply discards the parts of the theory that contradict the aspect of the theory of the ego that they like.

Freud said a great many things about the ego that are virtually impossible to accord in a single coherent account of the ego. In *The Ego and the Id* alone, there are at least four different theses about the ego, two of which portray the ego as object-like in character and two of which portray the ego as agent-like in character. Freud tells us there that the ego is (1) a projection of the surface of the body and (2) a precipitate of former object-cathexes, both of which suggest that the ego is characterized by fixity and stasis (that of an image or a sediment). He also tells us that the ego is (3) the representative of reality in the psyche and (4) a part of the id that has been specially modified (desexualized), both of which could at least be construed as active functions, the ego actively "representing" the demands of reality before the pressing impulses of the id, and the "desexualized" id energies being actively harnessed and put to work by the ego (SE XIX, chapter 2). Clearly, it would not be easy to reconcile or harmonize the four distinct theses contained in this one text alone. And the problem is only further complicated by notions Freud adds in *Inhibitions, Symptoms, and Anxiety, New Introductory Lectures,* and *An Outline of Psychoanalysis.*

How do Kris, Hartmann, and Loewenstein deal with such a conundrum? They conclude that *Freud must simply be wrong* when he says the ego does not exist at first and only gradually evolves out of the id because, if that were true, the id would be in charge of action, perception, and thought at the outset. This strikes them as altogether unacceptable, and they "suggest a different assumption, namely that of an undifferentiated phase during which both the id and the ego gradually are formed" ("Comments on the Formation of Psychic Structure," 19). The notion that the ego does not exist to begin with is, of course, perfectly compatible with Freud's formulations that the id is in charge of virtually everything at the beginning of life, but this is an affront to the dignity of the ego as the triumvirate understands it: In their view, the ego must somehow be there at the outset if it is ever to acquire the autonomy from the id that they believe it has.

The reasoning process here seems to be as follows: If in 1933 Freud asserts, according to their reading, that the ego is "the psychic system that controls perception and motility, achieves solutions, and directs actions" ("The Genetic Approach," 24), then, according to the triumvirate, the ego is always and has always been in charge of those things, and it cannot ever have left these precious tasks to the id. If that means the ego is not entirely a product of development, so be it. And if Freud's 1933 assertion means that the ego is a highly active agent and hardly characterized by the kind of stasis that is implied by the first two theses about the ego in *The Ego and the Id,* then those two theses should simply be discarded. There is no need to ponder the paradox of active and static sides or aspects of the ego, no need to keep both of them in mind in a fruitful dialectical tension, as a challenge for thought.

Kris, Hartmann, and Loewenstein refer to their approach as the "synchronization" of Freud's concepts: the attempt to make a synchronic whole, a self-consistent system, out of Freud's work ("Notes on the Theory of Aggression," 14). Indeed, at the beginning of their 1946 paper "Comments on the Formation of Psychic Structure," they lament that there is as yet no "handbook" or textbook of psychoanalysis that would spare us the trouble of studying the entire history of psychoanalysis.[9] What they would obviously like is a manual or user's guide to psychoanalysis that would allow us, like students in the hard sciences such as physics and chemistry, to learn all the essential concepts and features of psychoanalysis in the most consistent, concise, and up-to-date manner. This, they feel, would spare us a lot of wasted effort, a lot of time spent reexamining old theories that have since been rejected for good reason. In a word, it would spare us from having to learn the messy, unruly *history* of psychoanalysis.

Freud's work does not easily lend itself to such a synchronization, but textbooks and handbooks were nevertheless published soon thereafter.[10] According to Lacan, the relationship between history and psychoanalysis is a very intimate one indeed, psychoanalysis having taken as its first task to fill in the gaps in the subject's history and to probe the unusual temporality of the subject's history—the past being what is repressed, as he says (Seminar I, 45/34). To Lacan's way of thinking, there is no such thing as a psychoanalysis in which history does not play an important part (E 254–65). Lacan in fact criticizes the troika precisely for this attempt to create a system out of Freud's work where there is, in fact, only a series of attempts to grapple in theoretical terms with ever-evolving clinical problems.

Psychoanalysis, according to Lacan, is a *method of reading texts,* whether those texts be oral—the analysand's discourse—or written. And every text, whether doctrinal or therapeutic, is riddled with tensions and contradictions that must be read, reread, and pondered. Not necessarily *resolved,* but explored and worked on. Lacan even says that "[c]ommenting on a text is like doing an analysis" (Seminar I, 87/73).

It is noteworthy here that, while Lacan often explores in great detail the tensions and contradictions in Freud's definitions and theses, his approach in the case of the ego is somewhat different. We might formulate his approach as follows: Because psychoanalysts since Freud's death have dwelt exclusively on the active face of the ego, a corrective is needed, and I will dwell exclusively on its static face. I will stress its object-like character to the exclusion of all else. His paper "The Freudian Thing" is one of the clearest testimonies to this strategy, and Lacan justifies it by saying that Freud

> in fact wrote *Das Ich und das Es [The Ego and the Id]* in order to maintain the fundamental distinction between the true subject of the unconscious and the ego as constituted in its nucleus by a series of alienating identifications. (E 417; see also E 433)

This is obviously an interpretation by Lacan of Freud's intent in *The Ego and the Id,* situating Freud's reasons for introducing the second topography in a way that runs counter to the way Freud's reasons were interpreted by virtually everyone else at Lacan's time. Anna Freud and the troika interpret *The Ego and the Id* as introducing a topography that *supersedes* the old conscious-preconscious-unconscious topography so completely that they frequently remind us that what was called the unconscious in the old topography is now called the id in the new. They seem to see no reason to even distinguish between the id as the seat of the drives and the unconscious as the site of the repressed (a point that is repeated as if it were Gospel in many contemporary psychology textbooks).

It seems to me that Lacan's juxtaposition of the unconscious to the ego is an attempt to revitalize the debate and that his claim that this was in fact Freud's intent is a moot one, convincing as it may be in certain respects. We could, for example, do a detailed analysis of Freud's text here and examine it in light of what analysts were doing with Freud's work at the time, attempting to extrapolate his intention from his letters and from the internal logic of this and other texts. Or we could simply say that Lacan perceived that this new obsession with the ego was so great that, although Anna Freud and the troika continued to pay lip service to other parts of Freud's theory—that is, although they occasionally say that their emphasis on the ego is *not* designed to invalidate interest in the id and the superego—in fact, they neglected the unconscious altogether. It is virtually absent in their writings and, as we shall see, plays little or no role in their approach to practice. Seeing this *forgetting of the unconscious,* Lacan introduces a new and paradoxical polarity: the ego versus the unconscious. In the sense that this polarity opposes agencies or instances from two different Freudian topographies, we might even refer to it as a mixed metaphor or chiasmus, in the etymological sense of the term.

First Topography	Second Topography
Conscious	Ego
Preconscious	Superego
Unconscious	Id

It seems to be an attempt to compare or juxtapose apples and oranges. Alternatively, we might say that it constitutes a fundamentally new topography: the ego and the Other, or the other[11] and the Other.

Other   other

But since Lacan seeks to bring out the subject in the unconscious, or what he calls "the subject of the unconscious," this can also be expressed as

subject   ego

The term "subject" obviously comes from a different tradition: either from the philosophical tradition, where it is juxtaposed to object (here the ego is an object), or from the medical tradition, where the subject is simply the patient in the broadest sense of the term. In Lacan's case, this particular topography might be understood as corresponding to the distinction he finds in Freud's work between the use of *Ich* by itself and of *das Ich.*[12] The former has to do with oneself, broadly speaking, the latter with the agency known as the ego.

In a word, we might say that faced with the ever more dominant role of ego psychology in the psychoanalysis of his time, Lacan introduces a new cut, a new opposition, a new or renewed polarity: in essence, a new topography.[13] He does not simply ignore the theoretical apparatus of ego psychology or sidestep it to introduce his own concepts. We might say, on the contrary, that it is through his debate with ego psychology that he comes to formulate his own position.

This debate is two-pronged: It is theoretical and clinical. I will only briefly discuss a few aspects of his critique of ego psychology as a theory, focusing primarily here on his critique of ego psychology as a clinical practice.

Lacan claims that ego psychology radically misunderstands the central thrust of Freud's work at both theoretical and clinical levels, which are obviously intertwined. His claim is outlined in the first chapters of Seminar II, where he puts forward the notion that Freud follows in the footsteps of a moralist like François de la Rochefoucauld, who sees a fundamental discrepancy or disjunction between what we believe our motives to be and what they really are, a disjunction or split in man that is ineradicable. Nietzsche picked up this theme of the fundamentally deluded or deceptive nature of our self-understandings, and Freud did too, according to Lacan. To try to eliminate this disjunction through the introduction of a "conflict-free sphere" of ego functioning is to miss a crucial axis of Freud's work from the beginning to the end. Freud's Copernican revolution involves the decentering of the human subject, a decentering Lacan sees as central, associating it with Arthur Rimbaud's *Je est un autre* ("I is an other").[14] The center is not the ego or self (two terms that I use interchangeably here), for the ego or self is always fundamentally deluded.

Lacan also points out that the second topography was provided by Freud in response to what he calls a crisis in analytic technique wherein the formerly striking results achieved in a relatively short space of time gave way to less and less striking results that took longer and longer to achieve. He claims that *The Ego and the Id* must be read alongside *Beyond the Pleasure Principle* and *Group Psychology and the Analysis of the Ego,* both of which preceded it, and that it becomes clear that Freud was not in any way rejecting the category of the unconscious, as the ego psychologists claim. Lacan also points to one of Freud's very last works, *An Outline of Psychoanalysis* (SE XXIII), where we see the first and the second topographies subsisting side by side, the latter *not* replacing the former as Anna Freud suggests.[15]

I find Lacan's reading of Freud's intention and central thrusts quite convincing, but I learned to read Freud with Lacan. I find Lacan's reading far more interesting, far more dialectical, and far more illuminating in most ways. Nevertheless, there is textual evidence for the ego psychologists' position in numerous texts, and it is, as always, a question of the meaning of those texts. This is why I stated earlier that in a certain sense we can say that whether Lacan has a truer reading of Freud than Hartmann does is something of a moot point. What we can say is that, historically speaking, Hartmann's reading was sterile and unproductive. It led to very little in the way of a renewal of research and theorization, whereas Lacan's led to a huge increase in both (like a good interpretation in the analytic setting, it generated a lot of new material). We can also say that Lacan's approach gave a considerable impetus to practice, whereas Hartmann's contributed to the effective death of psychoanalysis in America: Virtually all of the classical analytic institutes in the United States are dying, training very few new analysts per year.[16]

As for the emphasis on development that analysts like Hartmann spearheaded, all of that accrued to general psychology. It led to the popularization of psychoanalysis only in the guise of a three-stage developmental theory—of oral, anal, and genital stages—that is taught to first-year psychology students and then promptly forgotten. Lacan argues that the focus on development leads to nothing but a "rut" (Seminar XX, 52/55), neglecting, as it almost always does, the role of symbolic structure: the role of the phallus when it comes to the discussion throughout the 1920s and 1930s of early female development (see Jones's articles on "The Early Development of Female Sexuality," "The Phallic Phase," and "Early Female Sexuality"),[17] and the Name-of-the-Father when it comes to the etiology of psychosis. Here is what Lacan, already in Seminar II, says about the developmental approach:

> The idea of a unilinear, preestablished individual development, made up of stages each of which appears in its turn in a specific typical manner, amounts purely and simply to the giving up, conjuring away, camouflaging—or, strictly speaking, to the negation or even repression—of the essential contribution made by psychoanalysis. (24/13–14)

Ego Psychology's Clinical Approach

> [T]he handling of transference and one's notion of it are one and the same. [. . .] However deficient the theory with which an author systematizes his technique, the fact remains that he really does analyze people, and that the coherence revealed in the error is the guarantor here of the wrong turn practice has taken.
>
> —*Lacan, "The Direction of the Treatment"*

Lacan's critique of the kind of analytic *practice* that grew out of ego psychology is found in an especially detailed form in Seminar I, and in some detail in "The Direction of the Treatment." I will begin with his discussion of Anna Freud's approach in chapter 6 of Seminar I.

Anna Freud's Contemptuous Analysand
Lacan begins by complimenting Anna Freud's book, *The Ego and the Mechanisms of Defense*, claiming that "if we consider her book as a description given by a moralist, then she indisputably speaks of the ego as the seat of

a certain number of passions, in a style not unworthy of the manner in which La Rochefoucauld points out the unflagging ruses of pride *[amour-propre]*" (Seminar I, 76/63). Since Lacan sees La Rochefoucauld's work as a precursor of Freud's, this is seemingly high praise.

However, since "what determines what each author means is his technique" (E 609), Lacan soon waxes critical in turning his attention to a short sketch of a clinical situation that Anna Freud provides in her book. I will quote it at some length:

> A young girl came to me to be analyzed on account of states of acute anxiety, which were interfering with her daily life and preventing her regular attendance at school. Although she came because her mother urged her to do so, she showed no unwillingness to tell me about her life both in the past and in the present. Her attitude toward me was friendly and frank, but I noticed that in all her communications she carefully avoided making any allusion to her symptom. She never mentioned anxiety attacks which took place between the analytic sessions. If I myself insisted on bringing her symptom into the analysis or gave interpretations of her anxiety which were based on unmistakable indications in her associations, her friendly attitude changed. On every such occasion the result was a volley of contemptuous and mocking remarks. *The attempt to find a connection between the patient's attitude and her relation to her mother was completely unsuccessful.* Both in consciousness and the unconscious that relation was entirely different. In these repeated outbursts of contempt and ridicule the analyst found herself at a loss and the patient was, for the time being, inaccessible to further analysis. *(The Ego and the Mechanisms of Defense,* 35–37 [emphasis added])

In this passage, we see that the analysis got off to a bad start, and we also see how Anna Freud conceived of the initial situation. The analysis made no progress because the patient was unwilling to say anything about the anxiety that was interfering in her life and schoolwork. And when Anna Freud brought up the girl's anxiety and tried to interpret it, the girl made ironic and derisive remarks about Anna Freud herself. This led Anna Freud to immediately assume that her patient was identifying her analyst with her mother, that is, effecting a mother transference.

As Lacan says, "Anna Freud immediately approached the material from the perspective of the dyadic[18] relationship between the patient and herself," that is, from the perspective of the imaginary relationship *a-a'* on the L schema. Lacan goes on, "She mistook the patient's defense for what it [seemingly] manifested itself as, namely, as an aggressive act toward herself, Anna Freud." The patient's ironic reaction was interpreted by Anna

Freud as an ego defense only because of the way Anna Freud situated herself in the transference right from the outset. According to Lacan,

> [S]he wanted to see in [the patient's reaction] a manifestation of transference, according to the formulation that transference is the reproduction of a situation. . . . [T]his formulation is incomplete since it does not specify how that situation is structured. (Seminar I, 78/65)

In other words, this formulation of the transference leaves out both the unconscious subject (S, for subject of the unconscious) and the Other (A, for *Autre,* meaning Other in French): the whole of the symbolic axis.

Lacan asserts,

> She should have distinguished between dyadic interpretation, in which the analyst enters into an ego-to-ego rivalry with the analysand, and the kind of interpretation which moves forward in the direction of the subject's symbolic structuration, which is located beyond the ego's present structure. (Seminar I, 78/65)

It is, according to Lacan, because Anna Freud situates herself incorrectly in the transference right from the outset that she finds herself "at a loss" (as she herself says) as to how to proceed.

Let us turn now to the kind of solution Anna Freud tells us she found to the initial stagnation in the treatment.

> As the analysis went deeper, however, we found that these affects [ridicule and contempt] did not represent a transference reaction in the true sense of the term and were not connected with the analytic situation at all.[19] They indicated the patient's customary attitude toward herself whenever emotions of tenderness, longing, or anxiety were about to emerge in her affective life. The more powerfully the affect forced itself upon her, the more vehemently and scathingly did she ridicule herself. The analyst became the recipient of these defensive reactions only secondarily, because she was encouraging the demands of the patient's anxiety to be worked over in consciousness. The interpretation of the content of the anxiety [. . .] could have no result so long as every approach to the affect only intensified her defensive reaction. It was impossible to make that content conscious until we had brought into consciousness and so rendered inoperative the patient's method of defending herself against her affects by contemptuous disparagement—a process which had become automatic in every department of her life. Historically this mode of defense by means of ridicule and scorn was explained by her identification of herself with her dead father, who used to try to train the little girl in self-control by making mock-

ing remarks when she gave way to some emotional outburst. [. . .] The technique necessary in order to understand this case was to begin with the analysis of the patient's defense against her affects and to go on to the elucidation of her resistance in the transference. Then, and only then, was it possible to proceed to the analysis of her anxiety itself and of its antecedents. (*The Ego and the Mechanisms of Defense*, 36–37)

Thus, we can say that Anna Freud, having excluded any third term or Other from the situation at the outset by reading the analytic situation as the reproduction of a mother-child relationship, is nevertheless eventually led to emphasize the role of the father as symbolic Other in her attempt to grasp the meaning of the patient's defense or resistance to talking about her anxiety. Which is no doubt why her solution of analyzing the patient's resistance eventually leads somewhere. According to Lacan, what Anna Freud calls "analyzing the patient's defense against her affects"—the defense against talking about her anxiety, for example—is nothing other than Anna Freud's own partial understanding of the situation; it is "but a stage of her own comprehension and not of the subject's comprehension" (Seminar I, 80/67). Had she immediately introduced the symbolic dimension, she would not have needed this additional hypothesis and this extra step.

This is why Lacan introduces a notion that may seem paradoxical at first blush: the notion that "there is no other resistance to analysis than that of the analyst himself" (E 595). Resistance arises, according to Lacan, when the analyst refuses to adopt a symbolic position and situates herself instead on the imaginary axis. The analyst does not want to hear or see certain things, or misses them because she is looking for confirmation of her preconceived notion regarding where she is situated in the transference, and she thus essentially resists the process of symbolization. As we saw in chapter 1, this does not mean that Lacan believes there is no such thing as resistance on the analysand's part; nevertheless, he thinks it would be helpful for practitioners to realize that they are very often the ones who introduce resistance into the therapy.

Lacan repeatedly tells us that Freud usually perceived the symbolic dimension far more clearly and situated himself on the symbolic axis more decisively. As we saw in chapter 1, Lacan does, nevertheless, point out in Seminar IV the specific instances with Dora and the young homosexual woman in which Freud failed to perceive it, thinking that certain things in the analysis were directed at him when they were not.

One of the consequences of this is that, with her emphasis on the ego and its functions, Anna Freud neglects, both in her theoretical and clinical work, the importance of the symbolic dimension, situating herself in the position of the imaginary rival instead of that of the symbolic Other. (She presumes the analysand will situate her in the position of the analysand's mother, that is, in the imaginary position of a' on the L schema in Figure 1.6.) To neglect the unconscious is thus tantamount to neglecting the symbolic.

The reader may, perhaps, be wondering about the relevance of this critique: Can there still be anyone who ignores the symbolic situation, after all this time? As a clinician practicing in the United States, I would suggest that the notion is extremely widespread that the patient has elaborate defenses against his or her affect that have to be analyzed before anything else. It is so widespread that it permeates psychotherapy from coast to coast, and it is canonized in the pop psychology formulation that we have to help our patients "get in touch with their feelings." The general idea here is that we have feelings that are repressed—an idea that already runs counter to Freud's most often repeated claim that it is representations that are repressed, not affects—and that we have to remove the defenses that keep us from "feeling our feelings." This is not a joke: It could be argued that this is what the ego psychology notion of analyzing the defenses against affect has led to.

Excursus on Affect

On the subject of affect, I would like to briefly address the accusation sometimes made that Lacan ignores the importance of affects and their role in the analyst/analysand relationship. It should be kept in mind that Lacan takes it upon himself to emphasize what he thought other analysts practicing at his time were leaving out, not what they were already attentive to. Certain analysts at that time assumed (and many today still do) that every affect that is manifested in a session is caused directly or indirectly by the analyst, involving the analyst either directly as a living, breathing person with his or her own personality (that is, as an ego) and unconscious impulses or else indirectly insofar as the analyst becomes associated with a parental figure (a maternal or paternal imago, to use Lacan's early terminology). Like Anna Freud, these analysts saw transference simply as the reproduction of an earlier affective situation. Lacan, instead, emphasized the symbolic backdrop or framework, indicating that the affective dimension is very complex and is not to be immediately associated with the here-and-now relationship between the analysand and the analyst.

Using the example found in Margaret Little's article "Counter-Transference and the Patient's Response to It," which I discussed in chapter 1, Lacan indicates that we must take into account not only the here and now of the imaginary relationship, replete as it is with affects that are bound to be mutual, but also the symbolic axis. We must consider the symbolic relationship before we proffer an interpretation at the level of affects, as if we could somehow work on affects directly (Seminar I, 40–43/30–33).

What, in effect, is affect, and how is it supposed to be distinguished from the intellectual? Affect is essentially amorphous—an amorphous quantity or substance, we might say metaphorically. It is common to hear patients say that it was only on Monday that they realized they had spent the entire weekend in some sort of depressed state, indicating thereby that the signifier "depressed" was only added to the state or attached to it three days into it. The state itself, if we can even speak in such a way, is often indefinable, indeterminate, and it does not come with a preset label. The attachment to it of a ready-made label like "depression" may have little effect at all on the state, especially when it is provided by someone else, whether a well-meaning friend or a mental health professional. It is, in fact, a sign of improvement when the patients themselves are able to put some kind of label on it and to say "I was in a bit of a funk over the weekend and I think it was because of *x, y,* or *z.*" In this latter case, the process of symbolization has already begun.

Lacan's view is that "[t]he affective is not like a special density which would [somehow] escape an intellectual accounting. It is not to be found in a mythical region beyond symbol production which supposedly precedes discursive formulation" (Seminar I, 69/57). In other words, affect is not something beyond thought, something that is somehow more real than thought. We must give up "the notorious opposition between the intellectual and the affective—as if the affective were a sort of coloration, a kind of ineffable quality which must be sought out in itself, independently of the eviscerated skin which the purely intellectual realization of the subject's relationship would consist in" (69/57). Although "intellectualization" on the analysand's part can sometimes serve the purpose of "defense and resistance" (303/274), the intellect is nevertheless involved in the all-important symbolization of experience.

Affect is often taken by contemporary therapists to be something that is more real than speech, something that is on the other side of "the wall of language" (E 282, 291, 308, 316, and Seminar II, 286–88/244–46), something that gives us immediate—that is, *unmediated*—access to the subject's reality. In fact, however, affect in isolation gives us access to nothing whatsoever, since we cannot work on affect directly. Even dance and certain of the plastic arts and music deal with affect by codifying it: Certain movements on the stage become associated with despair, others with celebration; certain instruments and ways of playing with sadness, others with joy. It is of little value to us to provoke obvious displays of emotion in analytic sessions unless we are able to help the patient proceed to the work of symbolization at the same time or immediately afterward. The emotion may be a catalyst to symbolization, but if it is not, its effect is limited to that of a momentary discharge of emotion, a catharsis that may be pleasurable but is hardly therapeutic in the long run.

Like the idiomatic expressions and plays on words that are often imminent in dream images, the symbol is imminent in affect. Most radically stated, affects are not necessarily the same in all cultures or linguistic groupings; it can be argued that they are not universals, transcultural, or transhistorical. Certain authors have discussed the transition from a shame culture to a guilt culture, from Greek times to modern times, but such observations could be extended much further. Just as a language colors what one perceives, and just as one sometimes needs to learn or invent a new language to perceive differently, a language colors what one feels, and different languages allow one to feel different things and somatize in different ways: Each language has its own symptomatology.

Ernst Kris, or Why We Should Not Analyze the Subject's Defenses: The Case of the Man Who Craved Fresh Brains

Let us turn now to a somewhat more complicated clinical example, Ernst Kris's analysis of the man who accused himself of plagiarism, whose favorite dish was fresh brains (in "Ego Psychology and Interpretation in Psychoanalytic Therapy"). This case is quite well known among Lacanians, having been discussed at some length by Lacan in Seminars I and III and in two different texts in Écrits: "Response to Jean Hyppolite's Commentary on Freud's 'Verneinung'" and "The Direction of the Treatment."[20] I will summarize it instead of quoting it at great length, but I will take up all four of the different readings Lacan gives it in these different texts. Note right from the outset that Lacan's analysis of this case shifts from admiration in Seminar I to contempt in "The Direction of the Treatment," suggesting a further shift in Lacan's conceptualization of the analytic situation between 1954 and 1958.

The case is that of a scientist who is unable to advance in his academic career because he cannot publish his work. It is not a question of writer's block; it is that he believes that he steals all his good ideas from others, and in particular from a colleague whose office is right down the hall from his own and with whom he talks a lot. He manages, in the end, to finish writing a text, but one day comes across a treatise in the library which, he claims, contains the same ideas as his text, and which he must thus have plagiarized because he had read the treatise some years before.

Kris apparently discusses the two texts with the patient at great length and concludes that there is very little overlap between them. The treatise in the library does not state the patient's thesis; it simply supports it. The patient has "made the author say what he wanted to say himself." Kris now tells us that

> [o]nce this clue was secured, the whole problem of plagiarism appeared in a new light. The eminent colleague [down the hall], it transpired, had repeatedly taken the patient's ideas, embellished and repeated them without acknowledgment. The patient was under the impression he was hearing for the first time a productive idea without which he could not hope to master his own subject, an idea which he felt he could not use because it was his colleague's property. ("Ego Psychology," 22)

Kris concludes that the patient is not a plagiarist but would like to be one. For if he were a plagiarist, that would prove that there is someone—a father figure—who has good ideas to steal from. Kris suggests that "the projection of ideas to paternal figures was in part determined by the wish for a great and successful father (a *grand*father)." In other words, the patient's belief that he was plagiarizing a man's ideas was a way of propping up his own father, an unproductive man who lived in the shadow of his own highly creative and productive father, the patient's grandfather.

This propping up of his father was apparently the boy's solution to his oedipal rivalry with his father: At an early age there had been a competition between them to see who could catch the biggest fish, and later the competition extended to books (which the boy stole as an adolescent, along with sweets) and ideas. Here it would seem that, as part of his chosen resolution of the oedipal conflict, the boy had opted to withdraw from the competition and take a back seat or yield to his father's superiority, attempting to make his father into a grandfather.[21] His own ideas could not be worthwhile; only his father's ideas could be worthwhile, and the way to prove that they were was by stealing them. Hence, he enacted a scenario whereby he believed he was stealing ideas from different father-like figures.

We need not accept all the details of this interpretation, of course: We may well think that this supposed retreat or withdrawal from the competition with his father and staging of stealing of ideas from other men has other possible motivations than those mentioned by Kris. The patient's supposed wish for a *grand*father, a father with ideas worth stealing, may simply be a veil for his rivalry with his father, a way of not admitting his own wish to be superior to his father or to beat his father at his own game.

In any case, Lacan does not focus on this aspect of the case; he homes in, rather, on the patient's reactions to Kris's interpretations.

Kris does not tell us exactly what he said to his patient to convey these conclusions (that the patient was not a plagiarist and that he was, instead, enacting a wish for a *grand*father), but he writes that during the session in which he made these interpretations, the patient fell silent for a while, and then,

> as if reporting a sudden insight, he said: "Every noon, when I leave here, before luncheon, and before returning to my office, I walk through X Street [a street well known for its small but attractive restaurants] and I look at the menus in the windows. In one of the restaurants I usually find my preferred dish—fresh brains." ("Ego Psychology," 23)

Kris takes this to be a confirmation of the well-foundedness of his interpretation, and Lacan, in Seminar I, says that "[t]he interpretation is indisputably valid." He even goes so far as to say that the comment made by the analysand about going out after each session in search of fresh brains is the kind of "response elicited by an accurate interpretation," such an interpretation being "a level of speech that is both paradoxical and full in its signification" (72/60). This is certainly high praise from Lacan.

Note that Lacan incorrectly states in Seminar I that the patient made this comment at the next session—that is, at the session following the session in which the interpretation was made by his analyst—and that Lacan thus seems to think that it was due to this interpretation that the patient went off in search of fresh brains. According to Kris's account, however, the patient made this comment in the same session, right after the interpretation was made, and told Kris that his search for fresh brains had been going on every day for some time.

Kris in Seminar III

Lacan takes up the case again briefly in 1956 (Seminar III, 92–93/79–80). Here he demonstrates that he has interpreted something Kris says in a way that makes it obviously fall outside of an analytic manner of proceeding. What Kris tells us is that his patient's

> paradoxical tone of satisfaction and excitement [about finding his idea in the treatise in the library] led me to *inquire* in very great detail about the text he was afraid to plagiarize. In a process of extended scrutiny it turned out that the old publication contained useful support of his thesis but no hint of the thesis itself. ("Ego Psychology," 22 [emphasis added])

The text is a bit ambiguous as to exactly how and where this inquiry and scrutiny took place, but the most obvious interpretation is that Kris questioned his patient about the two texts in some detail during one or more sessions. Lacan, however, assumes that this means that Kris went to the library, read the treatise, and then told the patient directly that the treatise did not contain the patient's own original idea. He comments that "[s]uch people seem to consider that an intervention like that is part of analysis" (Seminar III, 93/80).

In any case, Lacan's critique here seems to bear first and foremost on the fact that Kris approaches the question of plagiarism from the perspective of reality instead of from the symbolic perspective: The question Kris asks himself is "Did the patient really plagiarize or not?" Ego psychologists justify their adopting such an approach on the basis of their understanding of the ego as mediating between and erecting defenses against three enemies: (1) the id, (2) the superego—these two constituting "internal reality"—and (3) "external reality." Since a defense is a defense, they consider it just as legitimate to analyze a defense against something related to external reality as it is to analyze a defense against an id impulse.

Whether Lacan is right and Kris went to the library or whether Kris simply asked the patient about the texts is ultimately only a question of degree, then, for in both cases Kris's concern is with how things stand in reality: Did he or did he not really plagiarize, and thus is there or is there not an ego defense against seeing that he in fact does not plagiarize?

The result, as Lacan sees it in Seminar III, is that by approaching things from the perspective of what is real and what is not, when Kris tells the patient that he is not *really* a plagiarist, that he just wants to be one, the patient acts out. In other words, Lacan thinks that it is due to Kris's reality-based interpretation that the patient goes off in search of fresh brains. Lacan refers to Kris's comment as "a premature symbolization," suggesting that such premature symbolizations often lead to acting out (93/80).

He suggests that Kris should have approached things *not* from the perspective of reality but from the perspective of the symbolic. To do so, he would have to have realized that "plagiarism does not exist. There is no such thing as symbolic property" (93/80). Had he realized that, a different question would then have arisen: "why things at the symbolic level took on such an accent, such weight" for the patient (93/80).

The acting out, according to Lacan, would suggest that if an analyst tries to prove something to a patient—for example, that he is not really a plagiarist—he proves to the analyst what is at stake "in making [the analyst] eat fresh brains" (93/80). He does not do so consciously or deliberately, but his symptom gets renewed: It takes on a new form in response to such a reality-based intervention.

Kris in "Response to Jean Hyppolite's Commentary on Freud's 'Verneinung'"

By the time Lacan writes up his Seminar I discussion of Kris's case in his "Response to Jean Hyppolite," published in 1956,[22] Lacan has taken a closer look at Kris's text and corrects a number of his earlier misinterpretations. While he still claims here that Kris reads the treatise in question, he at least realizes that the patient's quest for fresh brains has been occurring regularly prior to Kris's interpretation of the patient's belief that he is plagiarizing different people.[23] Lacan even apologizes to his readers for "following the text step by step," presumably because he considers it too boring and stupid to give it that kind of detailed reading.

In this write-up, the critique of Kris's approach is taken quite a bit further. Lacan tells us that Kris attempts to invert the formulation whereby we must attempt, as Freud did with Dora (SE VII, 35–36), to lead the beautiful soul *(belle âme)* to see the part she plays in the chaotic or disorderly world she complains of—a process Lacan refers to in "The Direction of the Treatment" as "rectification of the subject's relations with reality" (E 598) and as "subjective rectification" (E 601). Kris tries, instead, to show a patient who says he feels guilty that *in fact* he is not guilty—which is precisely the opposite of what Freud tells us to do: Freud says that we must accept the patient's self-imposed verdict, even though we realize that his guilt may actually be displaced (see, for example, SE X, 175–76). Kris does the exact opposite, attempting to show his patient that *in fact* he is not guilty. How does he do so? By using Kris's own assessment of the real situation (Lacan still claims here that Kris reads the texts in question), which is based on Kris's own beliefs about what constitutes plagiarism and what does not.

Lacan tells us that "[i]f there is at least one bias a psychoanalyst should have left behind thanks to psychoanalysis, it is that of intellectual property" (E 395). Note that the word "bias" here, *préjugé,* is the same word Lacan uses in his "Presentation on Transference" to define the analyst's countertransference as the "sum total of the analyst's biases [*préjugés*], passions, and difficulties, and even of his inadequate information" (E 225). This bias is thus situated by Lacan as part of Kris's own belief system and hence as part of his countertransference.

In a word, Kris is led to examine the situation on the basis of his own ego. "This analysis of the subject's behavior patterns amounts to inscribing his behavior in the analyst's patterns" (E 397). In other words, Kris tries to get the patient to see things as Kris himself sees them, in accordance with Kris's own thought patterns, belief system, and so on. Lacan goes on to say that "Kris attacks the subject's world in order to reshape it on the model of the analyst's world, in the name of the analysis of defense" (E 398). Once the patient comes to see the world as Kris sees it, all will be well. This suggests an internalization or introjection of a part of the analyst's ego by the patient, an identification by the subject with the "healthy" part of the analyst's ego. We might call this the injection of a new dose of fresh brains.[24]

This is obviously what Lacan means by Kris's "infatuation with normalizing analysis," for after Kris has analyzed enough people, everyone will have the same "normal," standardized ideas about intellectual production and intellectual property as Kris has. "Kris' ideas about intellectual productivity thus seem to me guaranteed to be suitably standardized [or "to receive the Good Housekeeping Seal of Approval": *garanties conformes*] for all of America" (E 398). This is "the New Deal of ego psychology," as Lacan calls it (E 393): Just as President Franklin D. Roosevelt tried to regulate the economy, control businesses, and standardize the quality of certain human services, Kris sets out to give ego psychology its "official status" as a normalizing process, a regulating and standardizing procedure.

Kris in "The Direction of the Treatment"

Let us turn now to Lacan's further discussion of the case in "The Direction of the Treatment." Note that this is Lacan's fourth discussion of the case and his second discussion of the case in writing, and that there thus seems to be something particularly striking to Lacan about this case that keeps him interested in it from 1954 to 1961! Here Kris is said to be "a first-rate author who, by virtue of his background, is particularly attuned to the dimension of interpretation." This is, of course, to set him up as a straw man: "The bigger they come, the harder they fall," as they say.

Lacan takes a still-closer look here at what Kris says and corrects another one of his earlier interpretations: He says that "Kris looks at the evidence" instead of claiming that Kris goes to the library and reads the treatise. Nevertheless, we might say that Lacan's interpretation is still quite creative: He claims that Kris tells the patient he wants to be a plagiarist "in order to prevent himself from really being one." According to Lacan, the id impulse here is the patient's "attraction to others' ideas," and the defense would then seem to be the belief that he is a plagiarist.

Kris never says exactly that, according to my reading of the text. He agrees with the patient's former analyst, Melitta Schmideberg, that the patient was characterized by "oral aggressiveness" and its inhibition ("Ego Psychology," 23), and he tells us that his goal "was to establish how the feeling, 'I am in danger of plagiarizing,' comes about" ("Ego Psychology," 24). The drive would then seem to be the impulse to devour and destroy other people's ideas, the defense being his fear of plagiarizing that stops him from writing and publishing. Since Kris tells us that he was aiming "mainly at uncovering a defense mechanism and not at an id content," Lacan refers to this whole procedure as "analyzing the defense before the drive" (E 599).

Lacan's terse summary of this procedure is corroborated by a passage from an article by Hartmann and Kris where they claim that "interpretation should start as close as possible to the experience of the patient—'from the higher layers'—and elucidate the structure of the 'defenses' before they proceed to what stems from the id" ("The Genetic Approach," 15). Lacan claims that this idea means that "defense and drive are [understood as] concentric" (E 599), the defenses presumably forming a circle or sphere around the smaller circle or sphere of the drives. It suggests a whole topography or model of the psyche, the id being a sort of inner circle or sphere and the ego being a sort of outer circle or sphere that envelopes it (see Figure 2.1). Lacan implicitly characterizes this inner/outer model as overly simplistic and as nowhere to be found in Freud's work (see, for example, SE XXII, 78, where Freud provides a far more complex model of the psyche).

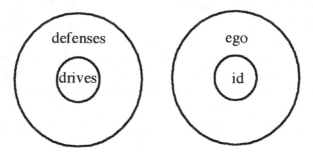

Figure 2.1. Lacan's interpretation of Kris's topography

The fact that the patient repeatedly goes in search of fresh brains after his sessions suggests to Lacan that fresh brains "had been sorely lacking" during the session—that is, that the analyst's interpretations were leading nowhere, bringing up no fresh, new ideas. No new material was being elicited by Kris's analysis of the patient's defenses.

It is of note that in "The Direction of the Treatment" Lacan does something he had not done in any of his previous discussions of the case: He makes a major interpretation of his own. He tells Kris (addressing him in the second person):

> It's not the fact that your patient doesn't steal that is important here. It's that he doesn't . . . Not "doesn't": it's that he steals *nothing*. And that's what you should have conveyed to him.

Contrary to what you believe, it's not his defense against the idea of stealing that makes him believe he is stealing. It's that he may have an idea of his own which never occurs to him or barely crosses his mind. [. . .]

You treat the patient as if he were obsessed, but he throws you a line with his food fantasy, giving you the opportunity to be a quarter-of-an-hour ahead of the nosology of your time by providing a diagnosis of anorexia nervosa [anorexie mentale]. [. . .]

Anorexia, in this case, concerns the mental realm. (E 600–601)

Lacan is, as usual, somewhat cryptic in his commentary here, but my sense is that it is related to his overall critique of ego psychology, which is that the work undertaken by ego psychologists essentially aims at eliminating the subject's desires, reducing them to something else. When Lacan says that the subject here has "an idea of his own which never occurs to him or barely crosses his mind," my sense is that this means he has a desire that is, for all intents and purposes, unconscious. Either it never comes to mind at all, or it flashes through his mind at times the way repressed fantasies, aggressive thoughts, and dream elements do.

Lacan does not tell us what this repressed desire is but suggests that the subject believes he steals ideas precisely because a desire has been repressed. In other words, the belief that he steals would seem to be a displacement or an inversion of the repressed desire. It could, in the most classical terms, be displaced from the wish to steal the mother from the father, or to steal the phallus from the father. In any case, the point is that Lacan seems to conceptualize the case in terms of desire and repression instead of in terms of a drive and a defense against it.

Kris, on the other hand, does not think in terms of unconscious thoughts, wishes, or desires. According to Lacan, Kris is one of those analysts to whom human desire is simply too unwieldy and unmanageable to deal with. Lacan puts the following words in the mouths of such analysts: "Oh, these neurotics are so fussy! What is to be done with them? These people are incomprehensible, upon my word" (E 637).

According to Lacan, ego psychologists refuse to take stock of the symbolic dimension, the only dimension that accounts for the paradoxes of human desire—such as the fact that we ask for things we do not want, only want what we cannot have, and no longer want what we ask for the minute we get it. Such analysts take it upon themselves to make their patients more reasonable, more pragmatic, less flighty and fussy. And the best way to do so is to eliminate desire altogether or, as Lacan puts it, to "wipe desire off the map" (E 602), or to take it off the menu, in the case of Kris's patient (carte means both "map" and "menu"), so that he cannot even think about ordering it—that is, about bringing it up in a session.

Lacan understands Kris to be engaged in a process of reducing the patient's desires to demands, and understands the patient's acting out by going in search of fresh brains to be a protest: "Desire has to stay on the agenda, it has to remain on the analytic menu." The more usual form of anorexic refuses food in order to keep her desire alive; rather than saying that *she does not eat anything,* Lacan would have us say that she eats nothing, the nothing as an object that causes her desire, keeping her desire alive. Eating satisfies needs, biological needs; and responding to the subject's demands by bringing her food reduces her desire to needs pure and simple, crushing the desire budding within demand. She refuses the food precisely in order to maintain some space for her desire, some room for desire to subsist in.

Can we understand Kris's patient along these lines? If we think of the patient's concern with coming up with original ideas as related to a demand placed on his father by his grandfather and by his father on him, we could understand his refusal to have his own ideas as a protest against this demand. To have original ideas would be to comply with his father's demands and thus to crush or close down the space of his own desire. There would be no room for desire for him were he to become intellectually productive. Thinking nothing is the way for him to maintain a protected space for desire (just as eating nothing is for most other anorexics).

What then of stealing? According to Kris, stealing ideas is designed to prop up the patient's father, to show that his father has original ideas—that is, that his father complies with the grandfather's demand that he have original ideas. To steal nothing could then, perhaps, be understood as maintaining a position of protest for his father too: It would amount to asserting that his father has no ideas to steal because he too refuses to reduce desire to demand and satisfy his own father's demands. Here, we would see the sense in which the patient's desire is the same as the Other's desire, the Other here being represented by his father. What of the "content" of this desire? Insofar as this desire seems to be constituted by a refusal of the Other's demands, it would seem to be "simply" a desire to keep one's desire alive, a desire for an unsatisfied desire, a desire for desire itself.

Lacan's remarks about the patient's anorexia nervosa are so laconic that I cannot at all be sure that this is what he had in mind, but I have tried to suggest how we might try to approach Lacan's interpretation here. My suggestions at least have the virtue of fitting in with Lacan's criticisms elsewhere in "The Direction of the Treatment." For example, he criticizes analysts like Kris for trying "to bring the patient back to sound principles and normal desires, those that satisfy true needs. Which needs? Why, everyone's needs, my friend" (E 624). In this parody, Lacan has analysts like

Kris emphasize "normal needs," needs that can actually be satisfied, unlike desire, which is structurally unsatisfiable.

Similarly, Lacan claims, in his discussion of the butcher's wife a bit further on in the text, that when faced with the paradox of desire,

> psychoanalysts stopped responding a long time ago, having themselves given up pondering their patients' desires; analysts reduce their patients' desires to demands, which simplifies the task of converting them into the analysts' own demands. (E 626)

For if the analyst can get the analysand to stop running around pursuing that will-o'-the-wisp known as desire and get him to focus on his demands (say, his demands that the analyst help him get over his fear of plagiarizing and advance in his university career), it will not be so hard for the analyst to get him to embrace her demands instead (say, that he become an analyst). The whole question of his desire will be skirted or circumvented thereby, and he can simply "get down to work."

Lacan's interpretation of Kris's patient is more suggestive than specific and brings up the usual problem of attempting to reinterpret a case on the basis of someone else's two-page account. Had Kris provided us with a great deal more detail and Lacan given us more than a few vague lines, I might feel a bit more confident about my commentary here. Indeed, much of the Lacanian literature is characterized by a dearth of in-depth case studies, which alone allow us to examine an analyst's praxis in detail. In any case, it is on the basis of such two-page clinical discussions by Anna Freud and Ernst Kris that Lacan builds his case against ego psychology as a practice.

Before concluding, I would like to add that Lacan's diagnosis of anorexia nervosa, pretty as it is, does not seem to me to be the best possible diagnosis for Kris's patient. For even though the patient did not, in fact, steal ideas at the time of his second analysis, he did steal sweets and books as an adolescent. And he seems to have had plenty of ideas—in other words, we cannot say he "thought nothing" like the anorexic who "eats nothing." He just did not recognize his own ideas as worthwhile until he heard them repeated or enunciated by someone else. This leads me to view his case in the terms Lacan himself applies to the obsessive, when he qualifies the obsessive's objects as each bearing "the mark [. . .] of origin of its object—contraband" (E 633; cf. Seminar VIII, 306, and my discussion of contraband in chapter 1). Ideas became attractive and intriguing to him only insofar as they were not his own, insofar as he would be stealing them were he to use them. Contraband seems to be a very common characteristic of the obsessive's objects, and might explain why the subject felt obliged to make his colleague or someone else's treatise say what he himself had thought: in order to make his own thoughts taboo and hence desirable.

Conclusion

In concluding my discussion of Lacan's critique of ego psychology as both a theory and a practice, I want to try to say a few words about how Lacan situates ego psychology in the logic of the evolution of psychoanalysis. I do not think he ever really situates it himself, but we might say that ego psychology is the tendency within analysis that lops off the entire symbolic dimension that Lacan sees as Freud's greatest contribution, emphasizing instead the imaginary ego-to-ego relation and the relationship to reality. Lacan obviously takes it upon himself to provide a corrective thereto. In that sense, ego psychology would not turn out to be one of various circuitous routes to the unconscious followed by the different strains of psychoanalysis but, rather, a way of circumventing the unconscious altogether. In this respect, Lacan seems to view it differently than he views Klein's work and object relations theory, both of which he criticizes for different reasons but which he does not seem to view as involving wholesale rejections of the unconscious as such. This perhaps explains why ego psychology remains an important whipping boy for Lacan for so many years. Klein is nevertheless taken to task for overly stressing the imaginary dimension in psychoanalysis, and object relations for focusing on the object-relation in order to gauge the amount of reality involved in it, in other words, to gauge the patient's "reality contact." The former overemphasizes the imaginary, the latter the real.[25]

When Lacan outlines what he calls "the topography of [the analytic] movement" in "Function and Field of Speech and Language" into three directions, he suggests that all three "have one thing [. . .] in common with the vitality of the psychoanalytic experience that sustains them. It is the temptation that presents itself to the analyst to abandon the foundation of speech" (E 242–43). All of the different analytic currents have thus, according to Lacan, forgotten to greater or lesser degrees the symbolic dimension, "the only dimension that cures."

Perhaps Lacan's intention (albeit unfulfilled) to psychoanalyze psychoanalysis was motivated by one of the goals Lacan lists for the individual analysand in "Function and Field of Speech and Language": to rewrite the history of one's own life in such a way that everything that once seemed like a mistake—a wrong turn, a wasted year, a whole decade spent with a partner one came to despise—now seems necessary in order for the analysand to be what he or she is in the process of becoming—in other words, a sort of subjectivization by psychoanalysis of the whole history of the psychoanalytic movement.

3

Reading "The Instance of the Letter in the Unconscious"

Commenting on a text is like doing an analysis.

—Lacan, Seminar I

Lacanian Rhetoric

"The Instance of the Letter in the Unconscious, or Reason since Freud," opens with astonishing rhetorical opacity. The first two pages are devoted to situating the text in what seems to be an unsituable manner—between writing and speech—and the first sentence is utterly inscrutable. The paper opens as follows:

> While the theme of the third volume of *La Psychanalyse* commissioned
> *[commandait]* this contribution by me, I owe this deference to what
> will be discovered here by introducing it in situating it between writing
> *[l'écrit]* and speech—it will be halfway between the two.
>   Writing is in fact distinguished by a prevalence of the *text* in the sense
> that we will see this factor of discourse take on here—which allows for
> the kind of tightening up that must, to my taste, leave the reader no other
> way out than the way in, which I prefer to be difficult. This, then, will
> not be a writing in my sense of the term. (E 493)

Lacan suggests that the theme of the third issue of the journal, "psycho-analysis and the sciences of man," required, demanded, or commanded *(commandait)* that he make this contribution or that it ordered this con-tribution from him. But let us note that, as he himself tells us (E 497), he is the one who chose the theme (or at least, he and his colleagues at the Société Française de Psychanalyse; the royal we, *nous,* he uses could be either). If this theme required such a contribution from him, it was, he claims, out of deference for "what will be revealed herein," for "what will be discovered here by [or on the basis of or through] introducing it in [or by] situating it between writing and speech—it will be halfway between the two" (E 493).

We might first be tempted to try to understand the latter part of this sentence straightforwardly: Lacan gave a talk to a group of philosophy students with a literary background (as he tells us later), and this is the more or less unadulterated transcription of the talk. This straightforward interpretation is, however, immediately belied by the very density of the text; and a comparison of this text with the seminars Lacan gave at around the same time shows there is a very different level of construction, metaphor, and syntax (not to mention footnotes and references) between them. Thus, if the idea is that "Instance of the Letter" is as much like a talk as it is like a paper, the talk itself was more like the public reading of a written paper than most of Lacan's other talks: The talk would seem to have been mostly written out in advance. Moreover, we know that the talk was given on May 9, 1957, and that the actual writing of what we have before us, *la rédaction,* took place May 14–26, 1957, that is, over the course of almost two weeks, beginning five days after the talk itself; this suggests that Lacan worked the text over quite extensively after giving his spoken address.

A number of other texts included in the *Écrits* were also first given as lectures and then written up, but Lacan does not qualify any of them as lying midway between writing and speech. Moreover, Lacan tells us in the published version of "Instance of the Letter" about the occasion of the address itself, which he surely did not do in the course of his spoken address. All of these circumstances suggest that the straightforward interpretation of this work as a transcription of a spoken text is probably not the most fruitful line of thought.

Writing

> I am less implicated as an author in my writing than people
> imagine, and my *Écrits* is a title more ironic than people
> think, when what is at stake are either presentations designed
> for conventions or, let us say, "open letters" in which I lay
> out a portion of my teaching.
>
> —*Lacan, "Lituraterre"*

His writing is different from his speech, Lacan seems to suggest, because the former is "distinguished by a prevalence of the *text* [. . .] which allows for the kind of tightening up that must, to my taste, leave the reader no other way out than the way in" (E 493). Lacan seems to be suggesting that, in writing, he can close up all of the holes in his discourse, leaving only one point of entry, only one hole or orifice, so to speak; the reader can either enter and leave by the same opening or not enter or leave at all. The wish for a certain control over the reader seems quite plain here.[1]

Situated in the context of Lacan's comments on analysts' use and abuse (mostly abuse) of Freud's texts, we might assume that Lacan deliberately attempts to write in such a way that his work cannot be co-opted by any form of psychology, ego psychology, or anti-intellectual reductionistic psychoanalysis. He wants to write in such a way that we either crawl right up into his head or belly or anus (we can probably take our pick) and follow his every theoretical gyration, or we throw his book down in disgust within a few minutes, which is, in fact, what happens with a great many readers: They read him either for years or not at all.

The way in and the way out must be one and the same: The womb metaphor seems fairly obvious, and the phrase that follows, "which I prefer to be difficult" (E 493), makes it clear that we are talking about labor: Only hard labor will get us in or out of that one small opening.[2] That is what real writing can achieve, Lacan seems to suggest.

But writing, even this kind of writing, has its dangers too: The reader might be inclined to take a given text as a system or a doctrine and pick it apart, or "deconstruct" it. The reader might get it into his or her head to take the *text* out of *context* and read it the way people have been reading texts for years: in terms of the internal consistency or inconsistency of the ideas laid out, the arguments made, and the rhetorical strategies employed.

This is dangerous to Lacan for at least two reasons: (1) His work is declarative rather than demonstrative, and the reader is hard pressed to find an argument in it to sustain any one particular claim, Lacan leaving the task of supplying arguments to the reader.[3] (2) He has a tendency to want to avoid being pinned down to any one particular formulation of things and prefers to answer questions about earlier formulations by referring to newer formulations. I will return to the first reason when we come to what Lacan declares to be the "Saussurian algorithm" at the root of all modern linguistics; here I want to take up the second reason.

In "Subversion of the Subject," in the midst of an already-challenging formulation on object *a*'s lack of alterity or specular image (E 818), Lacan includes a footnote to tell us that he has since "justified this by means of a topological model borrowed from surface theory in an *analysis situs*"! There are many other examples of such diversionary tactics as well. There is a sort of endless slippage or *fuite en avant* here: Each new system is better than the old one, and Lacan seems to want to ensure we know that what we have in front of us is not the best he has to offer. Nor does he explain his new formulation, for that might lead us to try to take the new formulation as a system and judge it on the basis of *its* theses and arguments (when arguments are supplied). Instead, he tantalizes us, suggesting that if we just read one more text, read one more seminar, we will get the answer we are looking for—whether we are trying to understand what he means by the fundamental fantasy, the divided subject, or what have you.

Those who have been reading Lacan for some time know how frustrating it can be to locate a particular thesis about, say, anxiety, and build on it and attempt to apply it clinically.[4] Is this a neurotic strategy on Lacan's part: avoidance? Is he avoiding being pinned down because that would require him to take a stand, to put it all on the line with a particular thesis and argument, and thus expose himself to castration (that is, limitation, critique, and the like)?[5] I do not think neurotic avoidance can be ruled out so easily, and yet it hardly seems to be the whole story. Indeed, to classify this avoidance as neurotic presumes that providing a concrete thesis is a worthy goal, in and of itself. In other words, it would be to adopt an obsessive standard for theory: Theory has to produce a discrete, discernible object (a turd of sorts) for us to examine (admire or scorn).

A great deal of theoretical writing adopts this very presupposition, which is essentially an obsessive bias associated, for the most part, with what we might cavalierly call "anal male academic writing." Why should this be the yardstick by which Lacan's writing is measured? Perhaps we should admire, rather, not the final *product* but the flow or process of Lacan's writing: its twists and turns, recursive style, and movement. Consider what Lacan values in Saussure's work: He refers to the *Course in General Linguistics* as "a publication of prime importance for the transmission of a teaching worthy of the name, that is, that one can stop only on its own movement" (E 497). To Lacan's mind, a teaching worthy of the name must not end with the creation of a perfect, complete system; after all, there is no such thing.[6] A genuine teaching continues to evolve, to call itself into question, to forge new concepts.

In a word, we can adopt an obsessive stance and say that Lacan is avoiding giving us the (anal) gift we want so that we can size him up and see if he is worthy or not; or we can adopt a more hysterical stance—one perhaps closer to Lacan's own—and say that Lacan himself does not view his own texts as constituting any kind of a finished theory or system. His way of presenting the *Écrits* when it was published in 1966 leaves little doubt as to its status as a work in progress.[7] Consider, in particular, the remarks he makes in 1973 about Jean-Luc Nancy and Philippe Lacoue-Labarthe's reading of "Instance of the Letter,"[8] which Lacan claims is the best reading anyone has ever done of his work to date (Seminar XX, 65/69). He thinks that they err, in the second half of the book, when they assume that he has a system; they even provide a highly complex diagram of the system.

Lacan, instead, sees his own work the way he sees Freud's work: We cannot, he tells us again and again, accept the late Freud and discount the early Freud (E 267). Freud's work must be grasped at the level of its twists and turns, reformulations, and new topographies.[9] Freud's later formulations do not invalidate or annul his earlier ones: They build on them in a kind of *Aufhebung* (a simultaneous maintenance and suppression in overcoming). It is not so much by grasping the id/ego/superego topography that we really come to understand Freud, but by seeing how he invents successive topographies to deal with specific theoretical and clinical problems, why he becomes dissatisfied with them, and so on. Indeed, an important part of Lacan's critique of psychoanalysts' work since Freud's time has to do with the way they read Freud, thinking they can extract a concept here or there, put it to work in a foreign context, and leave behind everything else that surrounded it in Freud's writing.

Lacan thinks that it is a mistake to read Freud in that way and that Freud's deceptively simple and accessible writing perhaps fostered such a superficial reading.[10] He does not want his own work to be read in that way and deliberately tries to thwart such a reading. He sees his own work as grappling with certain problems and as trying ever anew to forge new concepts and schemas by which to get a handle on the Freudian Field, and he does not want his terms to be taken out of context and put to foreign uses.

That is impossible to control, of course, and the history of literary criticism and social theory in the United States shows that even the most difficult writer's work can be co-opted and taken out of context.

The larger issue here, it seems to me, is that Lacan wants to draw a distinction between psychoanalysis and philosophy. Lacan does not view his work as a philosophy: It is not a system and is not meant to be evaluated like one. The "problem" is that psychoanalysis does not exist in a vacuum and is, for better or for worse, held to the same standards as other disciplines: Science expects psychoanalysis to produce "empirically verifiable hypotheses," and philosophy expects psychoanalysis to provide internally consistent arguments. Freud provides far more arguments than Lacan does, and scientists and philosophers have tried to prove or disprove, reconstruct or deconstruct his arguments. Lacan, especially in his written texts (not so much in the seminars), provides very little indeed for scientists and philosophers to latch onto; while Lacan's strategy has stopped scientists (I know of no attempt thus far to empirically validate or invalidate any Lacanian thesis), it has not stopped philosophers from taking his work as a system and trying to reconstruct and deconstruct it. Indeed, it is very difficult to convince scientists and philosophers that psychoanalytic practice and theory cannot be held to the same standards as their disciplines, that psychoanalysis is structured in a fundamentally different manner than their fields are. Their response is often simply that, in that case, it is no more than *poetry*.

Speech

Let us turn now from writing to speech. Speech apparently leaves more holes than writing. It does not allow one to "tighten things up" quite as much: It is looser, easier to wiggle in and out of, easier to pick holes in, perhaps, and easier to turn to one's own purposes. It is not as strict or tight-lipped; it does not "cover its ass" as well.

Yet Lacan is clearly enamored of speech in many ways, and privileges his spoken work over his written work whenever the occasion presents itself.[11] Lacan sees his own oral teaching as an important part of training: To his mind, his seminars contribute to the training of analysts far more than his writings ever could (even though they too strive to achieve certain training effects). Since Plato's time, it has been clear that oral transmission engenders love and that love and knowledge are not unrelated. Lacan's seminars provide a transferential context, engendering love in the students, love that puts them to work. The student at Lacan's seminar is inspired to work, much as is the analysand in analysis. There is more to it than that, of course: Lacan was, from many accounts, a fine and charismatic speaker who made a great impression on his audience. He also seemed to crave and genuinely thrive on the transference love he inspired in his students. He worked for that love, just as they worked for him.

The distance from the audience implied by publishing means that many of the effects of speech—charisma, tone, flourishes, and accompanying gestures—fade or disappear altogether. It seems to be more difficult to generate transference love textually than orally, hence Lacan's sense that his speech is richer in training effects than is his writing. And hence, perhaps, his concern in this paper to bring in the speech context of this paper—reminding us that there was more to it than meets the eye: "I gave this talk orally, designing it specifically for this particular audience, hoping to influence them." Perhaps he hopes that by telling us this, we will "hear" the paper differently, as if it were being spoken, with all that implies (because so many French words are homonyms, it immediately implies greater polyphony than the written text does).

Despite this discussion of writing and speech, part of the obscurity of Lacan's opening remarks remains. For Lacan states, in the third sentence of the text, "This, then, will *not* be a writing [or a written text] in my sense of the term" (E 493 [emphasis added]). This sounds like a classic denial, like "the woman in the dream is *not* my mother" (Freud, "Negation," SE XIX, 236). Why mention writing in the first place only to deny that it is writing? Why write for us—his readers, for he certainly did not include this particular sentence in his spoken lecture—that this written text before us is not writing? Lacan is no doubt aware of the paradox here: We were not at his talk; all we have is the written text in front of us; how else are we to take it than as a written text?

Lacan seems to want us to be exposed *either* to his raw speech—with all the charismatic and transferential effects he can conjure up—*or* to his tight-orifice writing that makes us work so hard to get in and out (if we ever get out!). He sounds particularly touchy about this piece that is neither fully the one nor the other, and yet he celebrates it in a certain way: "[I]t will be halfway between the two" (E 493), unlike any other text, presumably; he certainly does not qualify any of his other publications in this way.

What can we hope for from a text that is midway between the two, that is neither altogether one nor the other? Is this not, in essence, the exact nature of the analysand's discourse, as Lacan depicts it? The latter is speech, insofar as it is spoken in the analytic setting to the analyst, and yet it is based on or dances around a kind of writing: the inscription of the subject's past and desire in the unconscious. Were we to transcribe on paper the analysand's discourse, we would lose all the hesitations, intonations, risings and fallings in volume, and increases and decreases in speed. The force of specific words or phrases would be lost, the sense of conviction would evaporate, and so on. But were we to view it as pure speech with no interference from the writing of the unconscious—the written text that is the unconscious, the series of inscriptions that the unconscious consists of—we would be missing a great deal. Indeed, we would fall back into phenomenological psychology.

Hence my tentative thesis about what Lacan is up to here: By situating his discourse midway between speech and writing (between heaven and hell, between head and toe—the insistence of the womb again?—or, as the French say, *entre cuir et chair*), Lacan is situating his discourse here as an analysand's discourse, which he does elsewhere in his work as well (for example, in the first class of Seminar XVIII, on December 2, 1971; in Seminar XIX on March 8, 1972; and on the first page of Seminar XX: "I can only be here in the position of an analysand"). The analysand's discourse is thus midway between writing and speech.[12] Lacan is, of course, an unusual kind of analysand, if we consider the discourse he proffers here. In any case, this would be a generous way of pointing to the unfinished nature of his analysis: His analysis continues in speaking and writing for us, putting us to work as analysts trying to decipher it (thereby training us) and as analysands mulling it over and associating to it (thereby encouraging us to go further in our own analyses).[13]

Note that the small opening Lacan provides in his writing—the way in and the way out—might then correspond to the opening of the unconscious, which Lacan describes as fleeting: "[T]he unconscious is what closes as soon as it has opened" (Seminar XI, 131/143; see also 29–32/32–33).

The seemingly speculative connection I am making here between situating a text between writing and speech, on the one hand, and the analysand's discourse, on the other, may find confirmation in the following passage from "Function and Field of Speech and Language":

> [The analysand] then grasps the difference between the mirage of the mono- logue whose accommodating fancies once animated his bombast, and *the forced labor of a discourse that leaves one no way out [sans échappatoire],* on which psychologists (not without humor) and therapists (not without cunning) have bestowed the name "free association." (E 248 [emphasis added])

The analysand's discourse, characterized by "free association," leaves one no way out. One might even add here that it leaves one no way out other than the way in: the analytic rule—that is, the fundamental rule of psychoanalysis *de tout dire,* to say anything and everything that comes to mind.

If I am right here in thinking that Lacan is deliberately situating his discourse in "Instance of the Letter" as an analysand's discourse, then it marks a turning point in Lacan's approach to teaching: Teaching, and consequently training, are not to be dispensed along academic or professional psychiatric lines (which Lacan probably never fully followed anyway).[14] Teaching analysts—and enlisting those trained in other disciplines in the analytic cause, thereby creating a new audience of analyst/philosopher/ literary critics—requires a different kind of teaching discourse, a discourse that aims not at providing answers but, rather, at putting the audience to work.[15] "Instance of the Letter" perhaps marks Lacan's explicit realization that he has left behind the IPA's traditional approach to teaching and training, and has perhaps even left behind Freud's own still somewhat didactic approach. The shift in Lacan's writing style is hard to date exactly, but might be understood as beginning with "The Freudian Thing" (1955–56) and as being theorized by Lacan in "Instance of the Letter" (1957). We might view Lacan as having understood in "Instance of the Letter" that he is no longer situating his writings in any sort of preexisting university discourse but, rather, in what he later formulates as the analyst's discourse, a discourse that aims to bring out the split in the subject.

I hope this at least makes some sense of the rhetorical flourish found in these first two pages. Let me try to elucidate just one more detail of this rhetorical flourish: Lacan mysteriously claims here that, although he has primarily aimed at presenting new material every week at his seminar, it is now urgent for him to give up that aim momentarily and write the paper we are about to read ("For the urgency that I am now taking as a pretext for leaving that aim behind . . ." E 493). Why it is urgent for him to do so he does not say, but a few paragraphs later he mentions "a new tack concerning symbolization and language in the *International Journal of Psycho-Analysis*" (E 494), which might suggest that other analysts are beginning to encroach upon "his turf." And if we look back to Seminar IV, we see that Lacan indicates there that in the December 1956 issue of the *International Journal of Psycho-Analysis,* Loewenstein referred to Saussure and to the signifier and the signified (Seminar IV, 188). The urgency would thus seem to be that Lacan now feels that he had better hurry up and publish his own work on the subject or people will accuse him of borrowing from the likes of Loewenstein![16] Although Lacan may, as he tells us in a note to "The Direction of the Treatment," be content to have his ideas enter French psychoanalytic circles by "infiltration" (E 601, note 1), he is not content to let others upstage him in the international theater—certainly not his former analyst.[17]

But if this is, in fact, the source of the urgency, one wonders why Lacan reveals it to us. Perhaps his urgency is not all strictly subjective; perhaps it is also strategic. We always have the option of psychoanalyzing Lacan, of assuming that what bothers us in his work is a product of his own neurosis—that the first few sentences of "Instance of the Letter," for example, display a particularly nasty compromise formation (writing, being, as he himself tells us, "the return of the repressed" [Seminar XIX, December 15, 1971]). But we have to be careful, in doing so, not to project too many of our own biases and neuroses onto him. Lacan's sense of urgency here may also stem from the concern that, because language is being taken up in psychoanalysis in the sense of communication theory, if he does not act swiftly, the insights of linguistics will soon be subsumed within the banalities of sender, signal, and receiver (as happens in Charles Rycroft's article, "The Nature and Function of the Analyst's Communication to the Patient," in that same issue of the *International Journal of Psycho-Analysis*).[18] Lacan may well be feeling the urgency of preventing linguistics from being co-opted by the most trivial forms of analytic theory. And, as Lacan himself teaches us, human knowledge is generally produced in a kind of rivalry and competition with others.[19]

Figures of Speech

Given the highly theoretical nature of "Instance of the Letter," which may seem to be only tangentially related to, if not altogether divorced from, psychoanalytic practice, I want to turn next here to some of the immediate clinical applications of what Lacan provides us in this article. I will point first to a passage near the end of the article:

> This is why an exhaustion of the defense mechanisms. [. . .] turns out to be the other side of unconscious mechanisms. [. . .] Periphrasis, hyperbaton, ellipsis, suspension, anticipation, retraction, negation, digression, and irony, these are the figures of style (Quintilian's *figurae sententiarum*), just as catachresis, litotes, antonomasia, and hypotyposis are the tropes, whose names strike me as the most appropriate ones with which to label these mechanisms. Can one see here mere manners of speaking, when it is the figures themselves that are at work in the rhetoric of the discourse the analysand actually utters? (E 521)

In his typical fashion, Lacan does not elaborate on this, neither here nor anywhere else, to the best of my knowledge (cf. E 268). But the passage contains an important thesis: If the unconscious functions in accordance with the mechanisms Freud lays out in *The Interpretation of Dreams*— condensation and displacement, associated by Lacan here with metaphor and metonymy, designed to disguise unconscious thoughts—the analysand's discourse functions in accordance with a plethora of other mechanisms designed to keep the unconscious down. These mechanisms can be associated with what Freud called the defense mechanisms: The analysand spontaneously employs well-known rhetorical figures to keep from saying certain things and to keep certain ideas from surfacing. He or she eventually fails in this endeavor: Things do slip out, and the analyst, trained to detect these rhetorical ploys, learns where to intervene in order to undo them.

Let me begin with an example. When a person mixes a metaphor, it is often because one of the words in that metaphor is disturbing to that person. If the metaphor is "stop beating around the bush," and there is a certain sadistic or masochistic thought about beating that the person wants to keep out of sight and out of mind, he is likely to replace "beating" with a different term, "circling," for example: "stop circling around the bush." Or if the term "bush" seems too sexually charged or likely to bring up sexual thoughts he wants to avoid, he might substitute "issue" for "bush": "stop beating around the issue."

This is very common. Of course, at times it can simply imply that the person does not really know the expression he is half-using, but most native speakers know many of the idiomatic expressions they use by heart, and they can be immediately made to wonder why they changed the wording simply by repeating their own changed wording back to them. In everyday speech, "beating around the issue" would be termed a *mixed metaphor*, since it is a compromise formation between "beating around the bush" and "skirting the issue." In rhetorical terms it might be called *catachresis*, which designates a misuse of words. In either case, it suggests to the attentive clinician that *something is being avoided*.

It may suggest, alternatively, that another train of thought is interfering with the completion of the initial train of thought. One of my analysands, in describing a relationship she had been in, came out with the following: She had "unzipped her soul." At a poetry reading, we might simply enjoy the formulation and make nothing further of it. But as analysts we must also recall that the commoner metaphor would be to "bare one's soul." And because the soul, in Western cultures, is most often associated with the heart or chest area, the unzipping might suggest a drifting of thought from the bosom to the genital region: She had "unzipped her pants." Here we might emphasize the avoidance of "baring" or the combination of "unzipping" and the "soul."

Let us consider some of the other tropes Lacan mentions in the passage I quoted above. Litotes, also known as understatements, are used constantly in sessions and are often preceded by a slight pause. The analysand is about to say, "I really lust after my best friend's wife," and he tones it down by saying, "I don't find her unattractive." The pause, short as it may be, combined with the highly constructed double negative, suggests that something is going unsaid: a certain thought is being circumvented because it has been judged unacceptable ("How can I be so low as to lust after my best friend's wife?").

Ellipsis, where some portion of a description or phrase is left out, is one of the most common ways in which the analysand avoids saying something that has come to mind. The omission may be made with the supposed intent to "achieve a more compact expression" (as the definition of "ellipsis" in rhetoric would have it), but often it is simply intended to suppress something that seems inappropriate or overly revealing to the analysand, and sometimes the sentence that is actually uttered is nonsensical, too much of the grammar having been elided. There may be no pause at all that would alert us to the elision, or there may be a lengthy one.

On one occason, an analysand of mine was discussing an organization of which he was the director, and although he intended to tell me that some of his actions were designed "to avoid being controlled by fools," what he actually uttered was "to avoid control by fools." His analysis of the ellipsis was that in the attempt to avoid referring to everyone else in the organization as fools, he had ended up calling himself a fool, since he himself was the person "in control."

Here is an example of what might be understood as a pleonasm from a session I had with an analysand: In a dream, he was being followed by a "female person." Had he been talking about animal species at any point in our work together, the addition of "person" after "female" might not have seemed redundant, but that not being the case, it struck me, and it struck him too after I repeated it. He admitted, in effect, that he was not sure it was a woman, and the first person who came to mind was a somewhat effeminate man he had met the night before. The association between this man and the dream had not occurred to him before, even though he had given the dream a good deal of thought prior to the session. Here it is hard to say whether the redundancy was, in fact, designed to reveal or conceal!

Periphrasis is the technique of verily and truly beating around the bush or skirting the issue. An example from my practice was provided by an analysand who was ashamed of using certain direct language related to his anus and employed ever more elaborate circumlocutions to refer, in particular, to the "butt plug" he used during masturbation. Such roundabout references are often designed to gloss over the activity in question and to ward off any "probing" on my part into sensitive subjects.

Digression is, of course, a very common way to *noyer le poisson,* or change the subject without anyone noticing: The analysand starts telling so many background stories to a dream that his train of thought moves ever further from the dream, in the "unwitting" design of never returning to it. It is, of course, the analyst's job to attempt to distinguish useful associative material from *des échappatoires,* "escape routes," and to reroute the analysand to the dream itself.

Retraction too is an everyday affair in analysis: "I think my mother sorely neglected me," the analysand states, only to take it back the next moment, "Well, I'm sure she took care of me the best she could." We must be vigilant not to let the more powerfully charged retracted statement slip by in favor of the rationalization. Like a classic Freudian slip, where the patient says, "I wanted to kill my brother" instead of "I wanted to kiss my brother," it is the "mistake" that we take more seriously than the correction.

Irony is, of course, a classic way to deny the importance of the very thing one is saying: "Of course I hated my father—isn't that what Freud says we all do?" That does not stop the irony from serving as a front, a way of minimizing the scope of one's own speech and experience.

I hope these various examples have sufficed to make it clear to what extent these figures of speech are not "mere manners of speaking," and that "it is the figures themselves that are at work in the rhetoric of the discourse the analysand actually utters" (E 521). Freud noted that when the analysand falls silent, he is thinking about something connected with the analyst; and as we can see here, there are silences that may imply elisions, diversions, and defenses of all kinds that are designed to avoid seeming to the analyst to be a certain kind of person. The unconscious at work in dreams employs metonymy and metaphor, and the analysand in talking about his dreams employs virtually all of rhetoric's figures and tropes. *To the analyst, nothing is ever "just a figure of speech."* The analyst's mode of reading attends to both what is presented and what is not presented, to both speech and writing, to both what is enunciated and what is avoided. In essence, it reads all speech as a compromise formation, as produced by competing forces.

We are, of course, entirely justified in suspecting that there is more than meets the eye when we encounter such figures in written texts as well. I did not bother to mention *negation* here, since Freud himself and Lacan too discuss it in such great detail. But consider this comment from Nancy and Lacoue-Labarthe's analysis of "Instance of the Letter": "Our intent here is not to attack Lacan or to play a trick on the text" (*The Title of the Letter*, 89). Here we can justifiably underscore or highlight the word "not," just as we might in an analytic session; and although Nancy and Lacoue-Labarthe are not here to tell us their associations, we need but notice that the next forty pages of their book are devoted precisely to an attack on Lacan and to playing a trick on his text!

So too when Lacan says this "will not be a writing" (E 493), we are justified, as I mentioned earlier, in wondering why he bothered to bring it up only to deny it.

Section I: The Meaning of the Letter

> The letter is in the real and the signifier is in the symbolic.
> —*Lacan, Seminar XVIII, May 12, 1971*

Having looked at the very beginning of the text and the very end, let us turn now to section I: *"Le sens de la lettre"* (E 495), rendered in the English version as "The Meaning of the Letter," though we shall see that "meaning" is not necessarily the only suitable translation in this context. Lacan's primary thesis here is that the unconscious is *not* merely the seat of the instincts or drives, as many analysts have claimed it is; indeed, it may not be the seat of the instincts at all. Rather, it is the seat or locus of the whole structure of language. Here we have to distinguish between the unconscious and the id.

What does it mean to say that the entire structure of language is headquartered or located in the unconscious? This is not immediately obvious, nor is it immediately clear what the "structure of language" entails or what it has to do with the Freudian conception of the unconscious.

A Litter of Letters

As usual, instead of explaining this thesis, Lacan introduces another concept: that of the letter ("But how are we to take the letter here?"). Let us note that the letter is introduced nowhere prior to this in the text except in the title of section I ("The Meaning of the Letter"). Presumably, there is some connection between the structure of language and the letter, but if there is, it is up to us to find it. Here is what Lacan tells us about this newly introduced concept: "How are we to take the letter here? Quite simply, literally *[Tout uniment, à la lettre]*" (E 495). While this is quite lovely in French, it is hardly informative.

The text continues: "By 'letter' I designate the material medium *[support]* that concrete discourse borrows from language" (E 495). What exactly is it that concrete discourse—also known as speech—borrows from language? Something material known as the letter, according to Lacan. This may strike one as a bit counterintuitive: Speech obviously borrows its lexicon and grammar from language and presumably borrows the phonemes it employs from the set of phonemes available in the language spoken, but where exactly does the letter come in?

We know what language is not: It is "not to be confused with the various psychical and somatic functions that serve it in the speaking subject" (E 495); that is, it is not the physiological and neurological systems involved in the process of speaking (or hearing). It is a different kind of system that "exists prior to each subject's entry into it at a certain moment in his mental development" (E 495); indeed, it might be said to exist outside of or apart from any given set of human subjects. For a newly discovered form of writing, found on parchments in the desert somewhere, that no one can yet decipher is still considered to imply the existence of a language. It may well be a dead language that no one speaks anymore, or even a language no one understands at all anymore. That does not stop it from having its own lexicon and grammar, its own rules and laws. The *signifier* remains intact; the signified, however, is completely enigmatic. Language here consists in all the signifiers employed in the text (note that Lacan often refers to the whole battery of signifiers in a language simply as "the signifier") and the rules regulating their combination (which may not be known).

Presumably, then, speech borrows its signifiers and grammatical rules from language. Perhaps what Lacan refers to as the letter is simply the signifier here. Confirming this would be the fact that what Saussure qualifies as "material" is the *image acoustique,* "sound-image" or "sound pattern," which he goes on to equate with the signifier.[20] Note that Saussure says that the *image acoustique* is material in only one specific sense: It is not sound itself as a pure phenomenon of physics (that is, sound waves) but, rather, the impression or stamp of the sound on the psyche: *l'empreinte psychique de ce son* (*Cours,* 98). Is this what Lacan, in his "Seminar on 'The Purloined Letter,'" means by the famous "materiality of the signifier" (E 24)?

The letter is mentioned again three paragraphs further down in "Instance of the Letter": "The deficits of aphasia [. . .] prove, on the whole, to be distributed between the two aspects of the signifying effect of what I am calling here 'the letter' in the creation of signification" (E 495). We know from Jakobson's paper on aphasia that it seems to affect either the subject's metaphorical ability or her metonymic ability, and thus Lacan is suggesting here that metaphor and metonymy are "two aspects of the signifying effect of [. . .] 'the letter,'" two aspects of what the letter does in creating signification. The letter would here seem to be equated with the signifier (in its meaning-making function) insofar as it has signifying effects. Thus, up to this point, it does not seem that there is any real difference between the letter and the signifier.

Let us examine the only other concrete mention of the letter in this text, which occurs several pages further on:

> [The most basic] elements [of speech], the decisive discovery of linguistics, are *phonemes;* we must not look for any *phonetic* constancy in the modulatory variability to which this term applies, but rather for the synchronic system of differential couplings that are necessary to discern vocables in a given language *[langue].* This allows us to see that an essential element in speech itself was predestined to flow into moveable type which, in Didots or Garamonds squeezing into lower-cases, renders validly present what I call the "letter"—namely, the essentially localized structure of the signifier. (E 501)

Here the letter might seem to be the written manifestation of the phoneme. Or it might be the structural position or place of a phoneme, the part that is written in one or more characters (or pieces of movable type). For example, the letter *s* does not correspond to some specific phoneme that is always pronounced the same way by the same speaker or by all the speakers of the same language or by all the people who speak the same language over the course of history. The letter *s* corresponds, rather, to a particular differential element in that language, which may be pronounced differently at different times by one and the same speaker, by different speakers, and by speakers from different centuries, but which nevertheless occupies a place in a "synchronic system of differential couplings that are necessary to discern vocables in a given language" (E 501). That synchronic system could be limited to my own personal way of speaking the letter *s*, which, if I lisp, for example, could be quite unusual, but different enough from the way I pronounce other phonemes for my interlocutors to recognize it as a distinct differential element, an element that allows them to tell the difference between different words I pronounce. The letter might thus be understood as a specific place within a word, a place that may be temporarily occupied by a variety of different phonemes.

Consider, for example, the place occupied by the characters *o, u, g,* and *h* in the word "through"; it is not the fact that "threw" is a homonym of "through" that I wish to emphasize, for that is a contingent fact of current pronunciation and could, in theory, change over time. The characters *o, u, g,* and *h* here might be understood as occupying the place of *one letter* and different spellings could alternatively occupy that place, as long as they allow us to distinguish "through" from "throw," "thorough," and so on. The letter here is not the phoneme per se, but the place that can be occupied by a variety of phonemes.

In a hundred years, "drizzle" might be pronounced *dritszel,* but that will be of no importance as long as the *place* occupied by the consonant in the middle of the word is filled by something that allows us to continue to differentiate the word from other similar words in the English language, such as "dribble." The letter here might then be understood as half of what Lacan calls a "differential coupling"—a coupling such as that between *p* and *b* in *nipple* and *nibble,* which allows us to distinguish between those two words at a particular moment in time, that is, within a synchronic system. Alternatively, we might think of it as a place or position in a word into which one phoneme or another is inserted at a particular moment in the evolution of a spoken language.

Lacan claims that the discrete units (which presumably make up these differential couplings) were "predestined" to be represented by discrete marks. These marks, made on small pieces of lead set into lines of type by a compositor, all in a specific typeface (Didot, Garamond, Times Roman, Courier, or what have you), all "render validly present what I call the 'letter'—namely, the essentially localized structure of the signifier" (E 501). These "characters," as we call them now in computer lingo, "render validly present" or embody what Lacan calls the letter. These characters—which can only be combined in certain ways in any given language (based on spelling rules, such as *i* before *e* except after *c,* with their myriad exceptions)— are avatars of the letter, the latter being the "essentially localized structure of the signifier" or the micro- or nanostructure of the signifier, as it were.

The *definition* of the letter thus provided in this paper seems to lie somewhere between the signifier and its microstructure (which is materialized or re-presented by type or printed characters without being equated with them), somewhere between the signifier and the position within a word that remains the same despite the variability of the phoneme that occupies that place at any particular moment in time. But is this the *meaning* of the letter? Or is that the wrong question: Is this the direction or directionality *(sens)* of the letter? Note that the notion of the "materiality of the signifier" (E 24), made much of by Jacques Derrida and by Lacoue-Labarthe and Nancy, plays no role in "Instance of the Letter," written just one year after "The Seminar on 'The Purloined Letter.'" Here Lacan suggests only that the letter is materialized in type. But that which is materialized would not *seem* to be material itself. Lacan's "definition" of the letter ("By 'letter' I designate the material medium *[support]* that concrete discourse borrows from language"[E 495]) continues to insist in its opacity, assuming the material medium in question is something other than the ink on paper referred to in Lacan's often-repeated comment about the "kilos of language" contained in the "piles of books and mountains of paper" around us (Seminar VIII, chapter 2; see also Seminar II, 232/198; and E 282).[21]

The Algorithm That Grounds Linguistics

Let us turn now to what Lacan calls the algorithm that grounds linguistics, the algorithm that is the foundation of linguistics as a modern science (E 497): $\frac{S}{s}$. Note, first, that this algorithm can be found nowhere other than in Lacan's text, never having been provided by a linguist. It is radically different from Saussure's depiction of the sign (*Cours,* 99; see Figure 3.1).

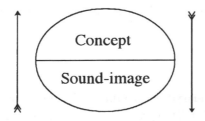

Figure 3.1. The Saussurian sign

According to Saussure, the signifier and the signified, the sound-image (or sound pattern) and the concept, are indissolubly tied together. As Saussure says, "the two elements [concept (or signified) and sound-image (or signifier)] are *intimately united*" (99 [emphasis added]); they seem, in the image he provides for the sign, to form a whole due to the line drawn around them. This is an encapsulated sign, a sign in which the signifier and signified do not seem to slip away from each other, forming instead a yin-yang-like configuration. Lacan unceremoniously abolishes the enclosure, eliminating the apparent harmony of the image and the seeming totality it forms.

The reciprocal arrows on either side of the diagram seem to suggest a kind of mutuality of concept and sound-image, a mutuality of the order of the signifier and of the order of the signified; that is, the effects each order may have on the other order are comparable. There is some debate as to whether the arrows in Saussure's diagram were introduced by the editors or by Saussure himself, but since my intent here is simply to emphasize what Lacan *subtracts* from this way of conceptualizing, visualizing, or representing the sign in Saussure's text, what is most important to us is the fact that he, once again, unceremoniously eliminates them.

According to Lacan, there is no mutuality between signifier and signified, no reciprocal penetration or determination of the one by the other. They are not *intimement unis et s'appellent l'un l'autre,* "intimately united, with each calling the other to mind" (*Cours,* 99 [my translation]).[22] Lacan insists, instead, on "the independence of the signifier and the signified" (Seminar III, 258/227).

Note next that Lacan reverses what he himself makes into dominant and subordinate positions by situating the signifier on top and the signified on the bottom. The signifier dominates the signified without the signified ever having a chance to dominate the signifier.

I have already pointed to three major changes Lacan makes to Saussure's representation of the linguistic sign, and yet Lacan nevertheless credits Saussure with this formalization. He even goes so far as to give the bar between signifier and signified a thoroughly new meaning, that of "a barrier resisting signification" (E 497), a meaning quite contrary to Saussure's notion that the sign is "a two-sided psychical entity *[une entité psychique à deux faces]*" (*Cours,* 99), that is, that signified and signifier are like two sides of the same coin.

With these four major changes, we see that Lacan has utterly subverted the Saussurian sign. In effect, he no longer even refers to it as a sign; rather, he calls it an algorithm or formalization. Nevertheless, he attributes it to Saussure. Why would he do such a thing? No argument is here to be found. Perhaps this claim is simply prescriptive: It is as if Lacan were saying that this algorithm *should* henceforth serve as the foundation for all modern linguistics. In any case, no demonstration is given here of why this particular algorithm grounds all modern linguistics, nor of why we should prefer this formalization to Saussure's diagram.

Instead, a number of points of view (for example, logical positivism) are ridiculed and a number of assertions are made, the most important of which seems to me to be that *the signifier does not serve the function of representing the signified*. This assertion is repeated in many of Lacan's seminars (for example, "the signifier is posited only insofar as it has no relation to the signified" [Seminar XX, 32/29]) and counters a functionalist or instrumentalist view of language that takes language as a tool designed to express human thought.[23] Human thought—that is, the signified (or concept)—is taken by certain theorists to exist prior to or independently of language, language serving merely to help us express it to others. Lacan does not *demonstrate* his opposing point of view to us by means of any kind of conventionally recognizable argument; rather, he *performs* it by showing, in his own use of language, just how far beyond any register of functionality his own language can go. *Lacan's writing style, here as elsewhere, is performative, not demonstrative.* He does not argue, in any usual sense of the term, that the signifier and signified do not have complementary, reciprocal relations. Instead, he provides an example that confuses us as to where the signifier is located in the first place.

First he turns Saussure's tree diagram (which some believe Saussure's editors made up; *Cours*, 99) on its head (see Figure 3.2), and he then supplies his own diagram (Figure 3.3) that immediately renders irrelevant any one-to-one correspondence theory of language or any "point and speak" theory of language acquisition.

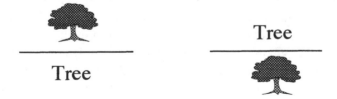

Figure 3.2. Saussure's "Tree" (left) versus Lacan's "Tree" (right)

For in Saussure's pictorial diagram we might still be tempted to see a thing (or the image thereof) being pointed at by an index finger, and a word being pronounced, the idea being that if this is repeated often enough with different trees, the concept or signified, tree, will be formed or learned by a child in association with its sound image or signifier, "tree." Whenever the word "tree" is pronounced, it will indissociably conjure up the image of a tree, and whenever a tree is seen it will ineluctably conjure up the signifier "tree." (I am not saying that this is Saussure's argument; rather, I am noting that one might be tempted to misunderstand the tree diagram in this way.)

Such a view is rendered extremely problematic due to the duplication of signifiers that Lacan introduces in the "Gentlemen and Ladies" example, especially given the counterintuitive "concepts" or "signified" he draws below them (Figure 3.3).

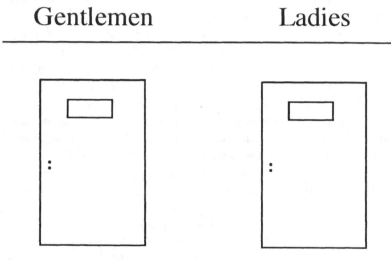

Gentlemen　　　　Ladies

Figure 3.3. Gentlemen and Ladies

He does not provide little stick figures representing men and women, like we find on many restroom doors. Instead, he provides pictures of the doors themselves, complete with little plaques on which are undoubtedly found the same signifiers Lacan writes above the bar (the writing on the plaques is presumably too small to be seen in the picture he provides). Here the signifier enters the signified quite literally—it is included right in the no-doubt tongue-in-cheek representation of the "concept"—and "the squinting gaze of a nearsighted person might be justified in wondering whether it is indeed here [on the plaques on the doors themselves] that we must see the signifier" (E 500). In other words, if we are shortsighted, we might be tempted to see the signifier *in* the signified itself.

These two doors hardly seem to qualify as a simple "concept" in Saussure's sense, symbolizing instead something far more complex, like "the private stall offered Western man for the satisfaction of his natural needs when away from home, [and] the imperative he seems to share with the vast majority of primitive communities that subjects his public life to the laws of urinary segregation" (E 500). As we shall see, the signified here is actually far more complex still.

According to Lacan, Figure 3.3 deals "a low blow" (E 500) to the nominalist debate over whether or not abstract concepts stand for objectively existing entities, presumably because this highly abstract idea exists not in the doors themselves but, rather, in their juxtaposition. (I suppose we could say that Lacan's figure catches nominalists with their pants down.) And its form "is not immaterial" (E 500) in both senses of the term: not unimportant, and not without materiality or substance, since it is printed on the enamel plaques on the doors. It simultaneously seals the fate of the signified: The signifier's primacy or victory is celebrated here, and the signified is laid to rest, as we pay our last respects to it, filing in separate male and female lines down from the upper (k)nave of a church or down the main aisle. (I assume the reader is following along in Lacan's text with me.)

We find throughout this article that the signifier behaves very badly: It does not "respect boundaries" (allegedly Saussurian boundaries, at least) and certainly does not keep in step with or allow itself to be regulated by the signified.

The signifier enters the signified, or, as Lacan puts it sixteen years later, "[T]he signifier stuffs the signified" (Seminar XX, 37/37). The term Lacan uses there, *truffer,* is a culinary term, the one used to refer to stuffing the Christmas goose with chestnuts, sausage, bread crumbs, and the like. The context there is Joyce's *Finnegans Wake,* where we find phrases such as "How bootifull and how truetowife of her."[24] The signifier "bootifull" contains "boot," "booty," and "full" and sounds a lot like "beautiful" (indeed, some children pronounce "beautiful" that way). The signified of such a signifier is chock-full or stuffed full of all the meanings of each of these. I suspect that it is in that sense that "the signifier stuffs the signified," makes it overfull and overflow: It enters the signified and makes it swell or blow up like a balloon. The more closely we examine any particular signifier, not just Joyce's, the more its meaning inflates.

Trains of Thought: A Difference without Any Signification (but with Plenty of Significance)

Lacan now moves from this brief allusive discussion of his subverted Saussurian diagram, wherein a surprising amount of meaning is generated by the simple juxtaposition of the two signifiers, "Gentlemen" and "Ladies," to a story told him by his wife (as the grapevine would have it) about a little boy and a little girl looking out a train window as the train pulls into a station. They each conclude that they are at "Gentlemen" or "Ladies," based on where they are sitting and thus their particular line of sight out of the train window; and they each seem to take seriously the idea that "Gentlemen" and "Ladies" could in fact be the names of this particular town or train station! (Had they been written in a foreign language, the latter might have seemed more plausible.)

The signifier here is, in effect, the juxtaposition of what is written on those very restroom door plaques just outside the train window (note that this was the signified in Figure 3.3), the juxtaposition of this "couple" of terms, and the signifier must somehow cross the rails—which "materialize the bar in the Saussurian algorithm" (E 500)—and come up the steps and down the train-car corridor. To do what? "To impress its curves upon the ducts by which [. . .] indignation and scorn hiss on this side" (E 501)—"on this side" presumably meaning inside where the brother and sister are sitting. And in doing so, the signifier must not "carry any signification with it." "It can reveal only a signifying structure in this transfer" (E 501).

What is transferred seems to be indignation and scorn as opposed to any specific signification. The signifier here—the juxtaposition of these two binary terms—generates "Dissension" (E 500), inspiring the two children to fly off in divergent directions, without telling us what Gentlemen are and what Ladies are. *It is the opposition itself that is crucial, not its meaning.*

In the elaborate lists Claude Lévi-Strauss provides of oppositions in specific cultures—sacred and profane, raw and cooked, and so on—it is the structuring effect of the oppositions themselves that takes precedence over any particular signification they may carry. Indeed, among the questions we spend the most time talking about in our own analyses are, What are men? What are women? What does it mean to be a man? What does it mean to be a woman? We are well aware that there is a difference, but the difference carries with it no specific signification. A good deal of time is spent in sessions puzzling over *the missing signification* here. The signifier in this context creates an opposition that is ever ready to take on meaning but that brings with it no particular meaning of its own. We might view it as a signifier without a signified.

The missing signified or signification here suggests that the relationship between the signifier and the signified is problematic, even nonexistent. This recalls the nonrelation between man and woman, Lacan's famous *Il n'y a pas de rapport sexuel* ("There's no such thing as a sexual relationship"; see, for example, Seminar XX, 17/12, 35/34). The relationship between Gentlemen and Ladies, between man and woman, is mediated by the phallus,[25] and, indeed, on my reading of "Subversion of the Subject," the phallus is the very "relationship" between the signifier and the signified (see chapter 4). In other words, the phallus is the missing relationship between them. Note that Lacan refers to the phallus as "the signifier that has no signified" (Seminar XX, 75/81). Note too that he asserts that the phallus is not unrelated to the bar between the signifier and the signified (40/39). In that sense, we might say that the phallus is the signifier of the barred relationship (or missing relationship) between the signifier and the signified (hence, the missing sexual relationship).

Whereas according to Saussure, the signifier and the signified are "intimately united," according to Lacan there is no intimacy here: The relationship between the signifier and the signified cannot serve us as a model for sexual relationships! Although one is on top and "stuffs" the one on the bottom—"the signifier stuffs the signified" (37/37)—the relationship seems to be a culinary relationship, not a sexual one. The bar, however, serves as an insistent reminder of that missing sexual relationship.

The "Technical Specifications" of the Signifier

Lacan now turns to some technical notions about the signifier: Its smallest differential elements are phonemes, which we have already discussed, and its largest units, we might say, are entire sentences. Lacan does not exactly say that here (he says, "Such are the structural conditions that define [. . .] the order of the signifier's constitutive inclusions up to the verbal locution as the lexicon" [E 502]), but he does so in Seminar XX. There he indicates that the expression *à tire larigot* (figuratively, "by the bucketful" or "by the shovelful") must be taken as a single signifier (just like the American English expression "How do you like them apples?" must be taken as a single signifier), since its meaning is not in any way built up out of smaller meaning units: It is only the phrase as a whole that carries a particular meaning. The same is true, he says there, of proverbs. The meaning of a proverb like "A stitch in time saves nine" is not entirely self-evident from its constituent parts and has to be learned. Personally, I originally thought it had to do with sewing up time somehow, no doubt on the basis of Madeleine L'Engle's children's book *A Wrinkle in Time;* but that did not stop me from learning the meaning of the proverb as a whole, in other words, as one single signifier.

Lacan next brings in the chain metaphor, which he borrows from Saussure (*Cours,* 103). Specific beginnings of sentences, specific subjects and verbs, for example, require us to continue a sentence in a certain way (this is less true in English than in languages where adjectives and pronouns have to agree in gender and number with the nouns they refer to). In the French "Elles se sont dites qu'il fallait qu'elles le fassent" ("they told themselves they had to do it"), the form of the verb *dire* is dictated by the feminine plural pronoun *elles* and the reflexive, the first *que* is dictated by the verb *dire* (*parler* does not take *que,* for example), the tense of the second verb is dictated by the tense of the first verb, and the tense of the third verb is dictated by the verb chosen, *falloir,* and the tense of the prior verbs. There are thus multiple links between the words in the sentence, and they form a kind of chain. When in English I begin by saying "On the one hand . . . ," I pretty much have to continue at some point with "but on the other hand . . ." This is the basis of the notion of the signifying chain: a necklace make up of links, those links connecting each necklace "onto a link of another necklace made of links" (E 502).[26]

When we want to know the signification of a particular locution, like *à tire larigot* (Seminar XX, 23/19) or "How do you like them apples?" we have to look at their usage—that is, we look at the larger linguistic context within which they are employed. As Lacan says here, we look at "contexts just one degree above that of the units in question" (E 502).

Thus far, Lacan has discussed grammar (the signifier's "constitutive encroachments" [E 502], that is, the way it forms links between all of the elements within a sentence and even between the elements in one sentence and those in the next sentence) and the lexicon (which includes entire phrases or even sentences, such as proverbs). Here he goes on to say that "[i]t is not because grammatical and lexical approaches are exhausted at a certain point that we must think that signification rules unreservedly beyond it. That would be a mistake" (E 502).

What exactly lies "beyond" the point we have reached is not clear, but the idea seems to be that while grammatical and lexical considerations do not exhaust the signification of what we say, it is not signification itself that calls the shots beyond them. Lacan begins by introducing the way the beginning of a sentence makes us anticipate what is to come. For example, if I am talking with someone and I say, "The fact remains that . . . ," my interlocutor knows that I am about to disagree with him or introduce a counterargument of some kind, and if I pause after saying so ("The fact remains that [pause] . . ."), the meaning he anticipates may be all the more weighty and "oppressive"—presumably because he does not know what my argument is going to be or because he fears the worst.

Lacan implies thus that the signifier here carries much more weight, is heavier with signification, than might be gleaned from a simple analysis of the grammar and lexicon of these few words. The same is true, claims Lacan, in the line "I am very dark, but comely" (Song of Solomon 1:5). The word "but" here, which Lacan qualifies as a *recul,* a "postponement" (E 502), momentarily delays the arrival of the adjective "comely," lending it more weight. If the sentence read, "I am very dark and comely," the signification would be quite different: There would be no opposition—the beauty would not be set off, highlighted, or showcased as much without the contrast with "dark" created by the word "but." Just as a woman with light-colored hair might wear a dark blouse to set off her hair to good advantage, or vice versa, the use of the word "but" generates a heightened awareness of what is to follow because of its difference from what preceded.

In the second example Lacan alludes to, "the poor, but honest woman" (E 502), the woman's honesty is all the more significant due to its contrast with her poverty. The implication here is that rich people can afford to be honest, but poor people cannot (this is the argument made by Eliza Doolittle's father in *My Fair Lady:* He claims he cannot afford bourgeois values and respectability). Imagine the different effect that would be produced if we simply characterized the woman here as "poor and honest." There would seem to be little virtue in being poor *and* honest, yet there is quite a bit in being poor *but* honest.

This brings us to what I take to be one of the important "conclusions" of this section: "Whence we can say that it is in the chain of the signifier that meaning *insists,* but that none of the chain's elements *consists* in the signification it can provide at that very moment" (E 502). All of the implications of the word "but" that I just mentioned insist in the simple phrase, "poor, but honest," but none of the elements of the phrase "consists in" these significations. What exactly would it mean for an element of a phrase or sentence to consist in the signification it can provide? Would it mean that it somehow would be confined or limited to the particular signification that it transmits, evoking or suggesting nothing else? It may help here to juxtapose this sentence with one from Seminar IV: Hans's phobia allows Hans

> to manipulate this signifier ["horse"], drawing out of it possibilities for development that are richer than the possibilities it contains. In effect, the signifier does not in advance contain within itself all the significations that we make it take on; it contains them rather by the place it occupies, the place where the symbolic father should be. (401)

The point here seems to be that meaning grows out of *the place* in which we situate the signifier, the structure within which we make it operate. Meaning insists in a sentence or series (chain) of sentences, without our being able to localize exactly which element gave rise to the meaning: It is their combination in a certain way and order, which includes temporal aspects that do not fall under the heading of grammar, that gives rise to a meaning that we cannot attribute to any one of its parts.[27] In other words, the whole (meaning) is greater than the sum of its parts (the meaning of each individual element). The meanings any particular signifier carries may also be highly individual: "Horse" does not carry the same meanings for most of us as it does for Hans!

The "Sliding of the Signified"

According to Lacan, this brings to the fore the notion of "the incessant sliding of the signified under the signifier" (E 502), a somewhat cryptic phrase that has given rise to a great deal of misunderstanding, in my view. Lacan never claims, either in this text or anywhere else as far as I know, that there is no discernible signified of a signifier; he never proceeds as if we cannot truly interpret psychoanalytic texts like those of Freud and Kris because we cannot be sure what they mean, or as if we cannot interpret the analysand's discourse during the session because what the analysand says can mean anything and everything (as certain of Lacan's commentators seem to have concluded on the basis of this phrase).[28] As we shall see in a moment, Lacan repeatedly emphasizes the multiple meanings in discourse: the fact that it is virtually impossible to say anything that is devoid of all ambiguity and that does not play off all the resonances that individual words and expressions have in the language one employs and in one's cultural environment. The well-known shift in Lacan's emphasis from meaning to nonmeaning, which has already begun in "Instance of the Letter," is not motivated by a frustration on Lacan's part with locating a discernible meaning in the analysand's discourse: He indicates that there is only too much meaning there and that such meaning has mesmerized analysts, blinding them to the fact that the pursuit of meaning leads to the further alienation of the subject in the Other's meaning and the Other's desire, whereas it is only nonmeaning or nonsense that can separate the subject from these latter (I return to this at the end of this chapter).

Having provided such a preamble, let us consider what Lacan means by "the incessant sliding of the signified under the signifier" (E 502). He asserts that Saussure illustrates this sliding with a drawing in his *Cours,* the schema found on page 156 (see Figure 3.4).

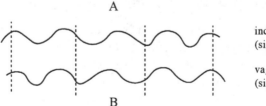

A

indefinite plane of jumbled ideas (signified)

vague plane of sounds (signifier)

B

Figure 3.4. Saussure's subdivision schema

Now Saussure states that the upper curve is the indefinite plane of confused ideas and the lower is the no less indeterminate plane of sounds. Language, he says, is "a series of adjoining subdivisions simultaneously imprinted both on the plane of vague, amorphous thought (A), and on the equally featureless plane of sound (B)" (*Cours*, 155–56). He goes on to say that "[a] language might also be compared to a sheet of paper. Thought is one side of the sheet and sound the reverse side. Just as it is impossible to take a pair of scissors and cut one side of the paper without at the same time cutting the other, so it is impossible in a language to isolate sound from thought or thought from sound" (*Cours*, 157). As arbitrary as the associations may be between a particular thought and a particular sound, they do not seem to slide in any sense here: The thought does not slip or drift ever further away from the sound. To the best of my knowledge, signifier and signified are not tectonic plates moving in different directions in Saussure's perspective.

Lacan, in any case, continues by saying that psychoanalytic experience shows that thought and sound are tied together, such that they cannot slip apart, at certain crucial points that he refers to as *points de capiton* (E 503). I translate the French here as "button ties"; Russell Grigg translates it as "quilting points" in his translation of Seminar III, where the term is first introduced. These are points at which *the potential sliding of the signified under the signifier is stopped*. Note that certain versions of the button-tie diagram found in "Subversion of the Subject" can be seen as modifications of Saussure's drawing here (which I have simplified in Figure 3.5).

Saussure   Lacan

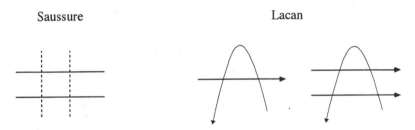

Figure 3.5. Saussure's subdivisions and Lacan's button tie (simplified)

In these modifications, Lacan seems to implicitly take Saussure's drawing to imply a temporal unfolding of sound, as if the sounds made in speaking were inscribed in the left-to-right movement of the waters in the drawing, the signified "flowing" along with the unfurling of the signifier (E 502–3).[29] (Unlike Saussure, Lacan again places the signifier on top and the signified on the bottom.) He suggests that this indicates Saussure endorsed a notion of "linearity": that both speech and thought can be recorded or inscribed as straight left-to-right lines, each bit of sound corresponding to the concept conveniently located just below it (E 503).[30] I have not been able to find anything in Saussure's work that would corroborate this, but in any case the button-tie diagram is designed to show that meaning is *not* constructed in that way, because elements that come late in a sentence retroactively determine the meaning of earlier elements (see my further discussion of this in chapter 4). In other words, the latter part of a sentence *puts a stop to the sliding of meaning* (that is, to the sliding of the signified), that sliding being equivalent here to the listener's uncertainty as to which of a number of possible meanings should be preferred.[31]

If I say that "Dick and Jane were exposed, when they were young children and in a repeated manner, to . . . ," the listener does not know how to understand "exposed" until I finish the sentence with "harmful radiation," "foreign languages," or even "their uncle the exhibitionist" (not the best English construction, but this sort of thing is heard all the time). The end of the sentence determines how the listener understands or "rereads" the beginning of the sentence; the end of the sentence fixes the meaning(s), putting an end to the sliding (without necessarily reducing multiple meanings to one single meaning). And I may well play with my audience by generating assumptions early on in my sentence that I go on to undermine later in the sentence; indeed, much of humor works in this way.

Here we might say that, if we are attentive listeners, upon hearing the word "exposed" we already prepare ourselves to understand it in a number of different ways, each of the possible ideas evoked being situated on a different stave (see Figure 3.6).

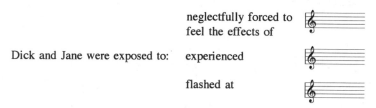

Figure 3.6. Discourse aligned along the several staves of a musical score I

"All discourse," Lacan says, "is aligned along the several staves of a musical score" (E 503). And each word or phrase here could be broken down similarly: "Dick" and "Jane" remind us of our elementary school primers, "Dick" is also slang for "penis," and "Jane" might evoke the movie *GI Jane*. Indeed, every signifying chain "sustain[s]—as if attached to the punctuation of each of its units—all attested contexts that are, so to speak, 'vertically' linked to that point" (E 503). Every extant meaning or usage of a word or expression can be written on one of these staves, and thus all contexts that can be attested to in some way (dictionary, literature, Internet, and so on) form a sort of vertical line beginning from it (see Figure 3.7).

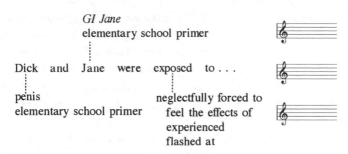

Figure 3.7. Discourse aligned along the several staves of a musical score II

Lacanian "Citations"

Lacan gives as an example all the attested contexts of *arbre*, taking his lead from the entry under *arbre* in the Littré dictionary, one of the most complete French dictionaries of his time (E 504). These contexts run the gamut from the Bible's "tree of the cross" to Paul Valéry's twentieth-century poem "Au Platane" ("To the Plane Tree"). When we read *arbre*, in whatever context, all of these possible contexts must be kept in mind—a useful reminder when reading Lacan in the original, for his usage of a word is far more likely to refer to its least-common usage than to its most common.

The verses by Valéry—slightly misquoted, as is often true when Lacan cites people—are "organized according to the same law of the parallelism of the signifier, whose concert governs both primitive Slavic epic poetry and the most refined Chinese poetry" (E 504). I assume that the reference to Slavic poetry is to Jakobson's "Slavic Epic Verse" (1952);[32] as for the Chinese poetry, I am not so sure where to look. The "law of the parallelism of the signifier" presumably implies that whereas the signifiers here work in parallel, the signified does not. (I do not profess to understand Lacan's claims about the poem and so I will not dwell on them here.)

Lacan next raises an objection we might have to expect: that all these signifiers do not operate on their own—they have to be present in a subject if they are to have any effect (E 504). He "answers" the objection by assuming the subject has moved or dropped to the level of the signified. For the subject need know nothing of the workings of the signifier. Like the signified itself, the subject here is an effect of the signifier.

Language Allows Me to Convey the Exact Opposite of What I Say

With words I can convey something altogether different from what I, in fact, say (E 505): If I tell a friend that I am going to Cracow, I may convey the exact opposite, precisely because he knows that I always try to mislead him. I can say that so and so "is the most wonderful human being I have ever met," but my tone of voice can indicate the precise opposite. Or, like Jonathan Swift, I can tell an elaborate story about a made-up land in order to allegorically criticize my own government. The many will see only the story; the few will see the savage critique in the allegory as well. How do I concoct such stories? By using two fundamental mechanisms: metonymy and metaphor.

By means of metonymy, I may replace, for example, a minister with some insignia of his office or clothing (his briefcase, say), or with a word that is close in sound, say, "muenster" (as in cheese). That will considerably alter the outward appearance of my political story. By means of metaphor, I may replace, for example, the word "election" in my story with the phrase "stink contest" and describe a stink contest to see which of my muensters has the most knock-'em-dead smell (the winner being given prominent supermarket shelf space).

To turn to Lacan's examples (E 505), ships and sails are often associated in speech and thought,[33] and the displacement from the one to the other is based on the *"word-to-word* [that is, metonymic] nature of this connection" (E 506). On the other hand, a man and his sheaf *(gerbe)* are not often associated in either speech or thought, the one not immediately evoking the other—that is, there is no metonymic connection between them in the language we speak (unless we are, of course, well versed in French poetry). Nevertheless, Victor Hugo is able to get us to think of the man by substituting his sheaf for him in his poem "Booz endormi" (E 506). The concept sheaf does not disappear in the process: When we hear the word "sheaf," we think both sheaf and Booz. Hugo manages thereby to condense the two, to evoke the two meanings with one signifier. It is this substitution of one signifier for another that Lacan considers to be the essence of metaphor.[34]

According to Lacan, it is not the mere juxtaposition of two highly disparate images that creates metaphor's poetic spark (as certain surrealists and Walter Benjamin would have it) but the replacement of one signifier by another: the use, for example, of "stink contest" for "election" in a political allegory, or of "sheaf" for "Booz" (E 506–7). Here we have *"one word for another"* (E 507), one word put in the place of another, the latter disappearing while its meaning is preserved, in some sense, in the former.

Lacan suggests that the poem "Booz endormi" operates by negating miserliness and hatred ("His sheaf was *neither* miserly *nor* hateful"), which is easier to do when it concerns an inanimate natural object than a human being, since such an object "knows neither our reserve nor our rejections, and even in its accumulation remains prodigal by our standards" (E 508). Booz, the occulted signifier, cannot easily return to the place the sheaf has usurped because he has been "ejected [. . .] into the outer darkness where miserliness and hatred harbor him in the hollow of their negation" (E 507). Miserliness and hatred have not disappeared altogether: Negating them simply moves them to a different level, and it is the same level at which the occulted "Booz" is situated. However generous he may be, he will always be less generous than his bountiful sheaf.

The Mysterious Signifier of Paternity

It would seem, however, that by allowing himself to disappear behind his gift, to disappear in the very act of giving the gift of his sheaf, Booz is rewarded: He is to become a father late in life. Lacan claims that this process—the process by which the man's proper name is abolished by another signifier—"reproduces the mythical event through which Freud reconstructed the path along which the mystery of paternity advances in the unconscious of every man" (E 508). We are, of course, left to reconstruct what Freud said about the mystery of paternity and what it has to do with the poem here.

To begin to do so, let us consider a passage from "On a Question Prior to Any Possible Treatment of Psychosis," where Lacan criticizes a view put forward by Ernest Jones:

> Concerning the state of beliefs in some Australian tribe, [Jones] refused to admit that any collectivity of men could overlook the fact of experience that—except in the case of an enigmatic exception [the Virgin Mary]—no woman gives birth without having engaged in coitus, or even be ignorant of the requisite lapse of time between the two events. Now the credit that seems to me to be quite legitimately granted to human capacities to observe reality is precisely what has not the slightest importance in the matter.
>
> For, if the symbolic context requires it, paternity will nevertheless be attributed to the woman's encounter with a spirit at such and such a fountain or at a certain rock in which he is supposed to dwell.
>
> This is clearly what demonstrates that the attribution of procreation to the father can only be the effect of a pure signifier, of a recognition, not of the real father, but of what religion has taught us to invoke as the Name-of-the-Father.
>
> Of course, there is no need of a signifier to be a father, any more than there is to be dead, but without a signifier, no one will ever know anything about either of these states of being. (E 556)

At least one of the points being made here is that while it is always immediately obvious who the mother of a newborn child is, since we can see the child come out of its mother's body with our own eyes, paternity is a more abstract or distant relationship, one that has to be reconstructed. And it can only be reconstructed on the basis of the ability to count and to divide time into countable units, that is, on the basis of the signifier. And just because members of a culture can count up to nine months does not automatically mean that they attribute paternity to the man who had intercourse with the child's mother nine months earlier. Depending on the system of beliefs in the culture, paternity may be attributed to fountain spirits, a particular god, and so on. A name is given to the father that may not be the name of any particular man, such as Booz. The Name-of-the-Father may be Zeus, Vishnu, or even sheaf, but it involves the substitution of a name (which might simply be "father") for one's proper name.

One reference to Freud here would be to a footnote in the case of the Rat Man (SE X, 233) where Freud says that "[a] great advance was made in civilization when men decided to put their inferences upon a level with the testimony of their senses and to make the step from matriarchy to patriarchy." The "mystery of paternity" is also discussed by Freud in the case of little Hans (SE X, 133–35), for little Hans feels that "his father must have had something to do with little Hanna's birth," since the father calls Hanna *his* child, but Hans does not know what his father contributed or did in order to become her father. Recall that Hans's mother and father seem to refuse to answer his questions about all of this, or they defer to the old stork story. This question preoccupies Hans greatly and leads to a great deal of conscious and unconscious speculation about sexuality, the role of the penis, and so on. Hans's predicament suggests that, even in modern culture, paternity is not self-evident to each new individual who ponders it and requires a sometimes long and difficult thought process. This is why the father is a symbolic function.

On Metaphor

While we have been inquiring into the mystery of the "mystery of paternity," Lacan has already moved on to the structure of modern metaphor and "love in a dimension that I have said strikes me as tenable" (E 508)—a glancing reference to his discussion of "Love is a pebble laughing in the sun" in Seminar III, which must have been utterly and completely mysterious to his Sorbonne audience that day if he, in fact, mentioned it there. I will not take up the discussion of love here, since all we get in "Instance of the Letter" is this passing allusion and I discuss it at some length in chapter 6.

Lacan goes on to say, however, that metaphor is situated where "meaning is produced in nonmeaning" (E 508). I presume that the nonmeaning here has to do with the absence of a preexisting word-to-word connection between Booz and sheaf: There is nothing self-evident or obvious about their relationship. Meaning is produced by substituting the one for the other. This involves, Lacan seems to suggest, the crossing of a certain river (the Rubicon, perhaps) or boundary.

When that river is "crossed in the opposite direction" (E 508), presumably by producing nonmeaning in meaning, we find ourselves in the realm of jokes or witticisms. A joke introduces something nonsensical (or at least devoid of meaning on the face of it) into meaning, that is, into the story as we are expecting it to be told. It is by subverting an expected meaning that we create a pun or joke. Heinrich Heine's audience is expecting him to say that the Baron Rothschild treated him with familiarity, but instead he says the baron treated him with famillionairity. This seems, in fact, to produce a surplus of meaning rather than nonmeaning, strictly speaking, but Lacan does not elaborate on it here. Consider, however, the following passage from "Function and Field of Speech and Language":

> For, however little interest has been taken in it—and for good reason—
> *Jokes and Their Relation to the Unconscious* remains the most unchal-
> lengeable of [Freud's] works because it is the most transparent; in it, the
> effect of the unconscious is demonstrated in all its subtlety. And the vis-
> age it reveals to us is that of wit *[l'esprit]* in the ambiguity conferred on
> it by language, where the other side of its regalian power is the witticism
> *[pointe]*, by which the whole of its order is annihilated in an instant—the
> witticism, indeed, in which language's creative activity unveils its abso-
> lute gratuitousness, in which its domination of reality is expressed in the
> challenge of nonmeaning, and in which the humor, in the malicious grace
> of the free spirit, symbolizes a truth that does not say its last word. (E 270)

Lacan thus associates witticisms with the challenge of nonmeaning.

Before turning to section II of "Instance of the Letter," note that it would seem that while the Lacanian letter has no proper meaning, it is directional: *Le sens de la lettre* is a *sens* not of meaning but, rather, of directionality, a directionality of subversion, a subversion of the place of meaning itself.

Section II: The Letter in the Unconscious

In section II of "Instance of the Letter," Lacan makes it abundantly clear that his reading of Freud on dreams is certainly not a Jungian reading: Freud is not to be understood as interpreting dreams on the basis of the universal symbols they contain or of the images found in them that relate to the cosmology and mythology of myriad peoples. Freud himself lapses, at times, into such sweeping generalizations as claiming that going up stairs in a dream is always a symbol or displaced representation of intercourse. These are the kinds of lapses that were picked up on by Carl Gustav Jung and others who read an entirely different approach to dream interpretation into Freud's work, that different approach being a prepsychoanalytic approach—that is, the very approach Freud criticizes in the first part of *The Interpretation of Dreams,* one that has been around for millennia.

Lacan, instead, picks up what we might call the predominant strand, the one found in so many of Freud's early works: We read what the analysand says of his dream (the "text" of the dream) *à la lettre.* For example, if in a dream the analysand sees the former U.S. vice president Al Gore rhythmically dancing the Macarena, this could well be the way in which the dream is able to represent the word "algorithm."

An analysand of mine, after a number of sessions in which he talked about how he felt like a fraud, untrustworthy, and lacking in credibility, dreamt of a rail leading off in two different directions. No associations came to him about the rail or the opposite directions (and no, he had not been reading "Instance of the Letter"), but when I spoke the word "liar" to him, the palindrome of the word "rail," he burst out laughing. We need not take that as confirmation of the "soundness" of the interpretation—an interpretation's soundness being found only in the new material it produces (E 595)—but it does suggest the possibility that the dream, being unable to represent a liar (a fairly abstract concept that a simple image cannot render) resorted to representing something easier to depict. This is part of the reason why Lacan recommends that analysts do crossword puzzles (E 266) and cryptograms (E 511). For the unconscious, in attempting to translate thoughts into images, plays with words until it finds homonyms, anagrams, or other combinations of the words composing the thought that allow of easy visual representation (see especially SE V, 339–49, "Considerations of Representability").

This, of course, does not mean that every rail in every analysand's dream refers to liars and lying. Rather, it means that each analysand's account of his or her dream must be read at the level of the letter of his or her discourse. We do not engage in "decoding" (E 510), as if there were a one-to-one correspondence between the images of the dream and the dream thoughts. Rather, we "decipher" (E 511).

Analysts who are more or less bilingual may be familiar with a maneuver dreams commonly employ, which is to find a name or word in one language whose different pronunciation in another language serves as a suitable disguise for the thought in question. The analyst here has to look at the spelling of the name in his or her mind's eye and then pronounce it in the other language the analysand speaks to get the analysand to see that the latent dream thought is not about a famous movie actor, for example, but rather about the analysand's own father. The analyst who does not speak the same languages as the analysand is obviously at a disadvantage here, and has to be vigilant about asking if such names have different pronunciations and meanings in the analysand's other (usually mother) tongue.

Paying attention to the letter does not, Lacan says, excuse us from having to be familiar with all aspects of the analysand's cultural and literary background:

> Must we make a career out of "antidoted fanfreluches"?
>
> Indeed, we must resolve to do so. The unconscious is neither the primordial nor the instinctual, and what it knows of the elemental is no more than the elements of the signifier. (E 522)

"Antidoted fanfreluches" is from Rabelais's *Gargantua* (chapter 2) and constitutes a fairly obscure literary reference that one of Lacan's analysands (or Lacan himself when he was an analysand) probably brought out during a session. Lacan suggests that analysts have to be consummately familiar with the elements of the signifier that constitute the analysand's particular, perhaps quite idiosyncratic or foreign, cultural background—a tall order in many cases! Otherwise they will not be able to read the analysand's discourse on "the several staves" of the musical score on which it is written.[35]

Lacan takes a few pages in this section to review some basic material from Freud's *Traumdeutung,* which Strachey entitles *The Interpretation of Dreams* but which Lacan here renders as *la signifiance des rêves* (E 510), which in my view emphasizes the degree to which dreams are signifiers that need to be taken *à la lettre,* decomposed into their smallest literal components, in order to be read correctly. Dreams are characterized by their nature as signifiers, by their signifier-*ness,* not by their meaningfulness or their significance. Of course, they are full of meaning and significance once we explore all the latent content. But first and foremost, they are signifiers: texts to be deciphered. The meanings we are able to draw out of them rarely exhaust all the meanings of which they are capable.

Despite the clarity with which Freud adumbrates his language-based method in the *Traumdeutung,* Lacan suggests that analysts continue to slip into interpreting dreams as if they were based on "a symbolism deriving from natural analogy" (E 510), reading dream images as though they were coffee grounds forming patterns that look like birds, planets, or other parts of the natural environment. In other words, they look at dreams as though they were images traced in a nondescript, homogeneous medium—as if in the sand on a beach or with finger paints on a glass surface—instead of signifiers made up of letters. They act as if the dream image could be transmitted somehow from analysand to analyst, the articulatory medium of speech and language counting for nothing in the process. But all we know of the analysand's dream is what he or she says of it.

To once again dispel any illusion we might entertain that dreams involve a form of "natural expression," Lacan suggests an analogy: Dreams are like the game charades, in which by means of gestures and codes, one player has to get the other players to guess a saying or the name of a movie, person, or book (E 511). This means that the signifiers making up that saying or name are immanent in the gestures: They are the motor force behind them. An image of a man standing under a line may have nothing to do with the idea of being below a certain standard, but everything to do with "understanding." (I assume the reader is familiar enough with the *Traumdeutung* to skip the particulars of secondary revision here.)

Lacan's point in this section is to show that Freud recognized "the constitutive role of the signifier" in unconscious productions such as dreams, fantasies, and slips *right from the outset* (E 512). His interpretations of them demonstrate the importance of words, idiomatic expressions, writing, homophonies, and so on. Lacan suggests that analysts failed to see this because it was so radically different from anything they had ever seen before and because linguistics had not yet caught up with Freud, failing to provide him with the necessary scientific justification for his work in this area. The other reason why analysts misunderstood Freud's emphasis on the signifier was, Lacan says, because they were so captivated by the specific significations psychoanalysis brought to the fore: the Oedipus complex, the ambivalence of affect, and so on (E 513).

Lacan goes on to provide a brief reminder here that what Freud means by the unconscious is not all of the psychical processes that occur without our being aware of them—that is, beyond the pale of consciousness (E 514). In other words, he distinguishes between what is nonconscious and what is, strictly speaking, unconscious (that is, repressed). This distinction is made in much greater detail in "Position of the Unconscious" (E 830–31).[36]

The Topography of the Unconscious

We have finally arrived at the point at which Lacan proposes "to define the topography of this unconscious" (E 515). He claims that it is defined by "Saussure's algorithm," which, as we saw above, purportedly founds modern linguistics. This is immediately transformed or generalized as

$$f(S)\frac{1}{s}$$

which might be read, though Lacan does not say as much, as "The signified *(s)* is a function of the signifier (S)." Note here, again, that there is nothing reciprocal about the relationship between signifier and signified: He does not add that the signifier is a function of the signified.

Lacan goes on:

> It is on the basis of the copresence in the signified not only of the elements
> of the horizontal signifying chain but also of its vertical dependencies,
> that I have demonstrated the effects, distributed in accordance with two
> fundamental structures, in metonymy and metaphor. (E 515)

In the "Gentlemen and Ladies" story above, we saw an example of the (co)presence in the signified of the signifiers "Gentlemen" and "Ladies" on the plaques on the restroom doors. In the phrase "Dick and Jane were exposed . . . ," we saw what Lacan means by "vertical dependencies": all of the attested contextual usages of a signifier, appended, as it were, above or below the word in a written sentence. Lacan now tells us that it is on the basis of these things that he has demonstrated the effects (of what?) in metonymy and metaphor. He does not tell us where he has demonstrated these effects, but we know, because some of his seminars eventually began to circulate in published and unpublished forms, that it was in chapters 17 and 18 of Seminar III and chapter 22 of Seminar IV. Note, however, that the formulas he provides here were never apparently given in the same form in those seminars.

Metonymy is symbolized as follows (E 515):

$$f(S \ldots S') S \cong S (—) s$$

This might be read as stating that metonymy is a function of the word-to-word connection that allows for displacement or slippage (written ". . .") from sail (S) to ship (S'), and leads to (or amounts to or is congruent with) the maintenance of the bar between signifier and signified. This means, at least in part, that the signifier does not enter or *stuff* the signified here: By a simple displacement from minister to a sign of his office, his briefcase, for example, I manage to convey "the same signified"—if not to the many, at least to the few. I manage in this way to skirt the censor and tell my political tale by way of allegory. But I do not manage to create a new meaning altogether; I cannot stuff something new into the signified by means of metonymy. I simply tell "the same story" in different words (or so Lacan seems to argue here).

Lacan also suggests another way of reading the bar in parentheses in the "algorithm" for metonymy: it is a kind of minus sign, for it symbolizes the *lack* of being *(manque de l'être)* the signifier instates in the subject's object-relation. Lacan is especially laconic here, saying only that the signifier uses "signification's referral value to invest it with the desire aiming at the lack that it supports" (E 515).

Let us use the Fort-Da binary (SE XVIII, 14–17) as an example of the signifier here; note that it both renders present and annihilates what it signifies: It makes it possible to talk about the mother in her absence, thus making her present even *in absentia,* and to think of her as absent even in her presence. This means that the mother is never again present the way she was before: A certain kind of immediate presence is rendered impossible by the ability conferred on the child by the signifier to imagine her absent even when present and, indeed, to worry about her going away whenever she is there. His relation to her as an object that is present, his object-relation, will never be as "full" as it was prior to his coming to be in language: Henceforth it will always and inescapably be felt to be lacking in some respect, and the child will come to desire to make good the lack (this is the child's "lack of being"). It is an impossible task to make good this gap in presence instated by the signifier, but the child will nevertheless look to each new object as a possible way of compensating for it. Hence his desire is induced or guided into the eternal slippage from one object to the next, in the hope that the next one will do a better job of filling the gap than the last one. As Lacan puts it here, the enigmas of desire are based on the fact that "instinct [. . .] is caught in the rails of metonymy, eternally extending toward the *desire for something else*" (E 518). Biological instinct is transformed into human desire by its insertion into language and, in its attempt to fill the lack in being (or lack of being), is ineluctably led from one object to the next, to the next, to the next.[37] This is a rough-and-ready gloss, and other more nuanced ones incorporating concepts from Lacan's later formulations, such as object *a,* could be provided.

Note that, as I mentioned in chapter 1, Lacan says in "The Direction of the Treatment" that "the ego is the metonymy of desire" (E 640). We are now in a position to elucidate this: The metonymic slippage that is part and parcel of desire is equivalent to the ego insofar as the ego is precisely what is constructed to cover over our lack of being. In the mirror stage, the ego is precipitated due partly to the tension owing to a lack of unity and coordination in ourselves. We sense that we are *not* beings like the other unified beings we see around us; there is as yet nothing we can point to as a discrete, total being (something that can be counted as a One). Instead, there is a conspicuous lack of being; being as such is missing prior to the anticipatory action of the mirror stage (which creates a One where there was none). This is why Lacan tends to associate the ego with false being (Seminar XV, January 10, 1968). The lack of being or failure to be—in other words, the failure to come into being—persists at another level, that of the unconscious. The lack at the level of the unconscious is static: It is forever the same. At the conscious or ego level, however, that lack is in constant motion, always moving on to something else.

Let us turn now to the formula Lacan provides for metaphor (E 515):

$$f\left(\frac{S'}{S}\right)S \cong S\,(+)\,s$$

This might be read as stating that metaphor is a function of the replacement of one signifier (for example, "Booz," written S) by another ("sheaf," S'), the former nevertheless remaining present (this is indicated by the repeated S before ≅), leading to (or amounting to or congruent with) the crossing of the bar between signifier and signified and the creation of a new signification.

$$f\left(\frac{\text{sheaf}}{\text{Booz}}\right)\text{Booz} \cong \text{Booz}\,(+)\,s$$

The + here is both a cross (a crossing of the bar)[38] and a plus sign (indicating an extra signification, that is, "the emergence of [a new] signification," E 515). Metaphor, Lacan tells us elsewhere, is "a substitution that simultaneously maintains what it takes the place of" (Seminar IV, 378).

Subject of the Signifier or Subject of the Signified

> For the symptom *is* a metaphor, whether one likes to admit
> it or not, just as desire *is* a metonymy, even if man scoffs at
> the idea.
>
> —*Lacan, "Instance of the Letter"*

Metaphor is of concern to us, not only because of its creative, poetic effects but also because it has something to do with the place of the subject, unlike metonymy, which concerns the ego. According to Lacan,

> This crossing [of the bar in metaphor] expresses the condition for the passage of the signifier into the signified, whose moment I pointed out above by provisionally conflating it with the place of the subject. (E 515–16)

Lacan presumably conflates this metaphorical moment (the crossing of the bar) with the place of the subject earlier on in the essay. Looking back, we note that Lacan said,

> But all this signifier can only operate, it may be objected, if it is present in the subject. I answer this objection by assuming that he has shifted to the level of the signified. (E 504)

There is no real explanation of what he means by this, and the French is typically ambiguous (*il*, translated here as "he," could equally well refer back to "signifier"); but he reformulates the point he wants to get at as follows:

> Is the place that I occupy as subject of the signifier concentric or eccentric in relation to the place I occupy as subject of the signified? That is the question. (E 516–17)

I apparently occupy a place as subject of the signifier and another place as subject of the signified, and the question is whether or ne'er the twain shall meet (see Figure 3.8).

eccentric   concentric

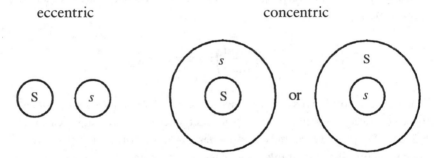

Figure 3.8. Concentricity or eccentricity of the subject of the signifier (S) and the subject of the signified *(s)*

The point is not to know, he says, whether what I say about myself corresponds to what I am, that is, whether my speech (or thought) corresponds to my being. The point is, rather, "to know whether, when I speak of myself, I am the same as the self *[celui]* of whom I speak" (E 517). When I speak of myself, I am presumably the subject of the signifier, whereas the person of whom I speak is presumably the subject of the signified. Is there any overlap at all between these two?

It would seem that this is the exact same question that Lacan raises in Seminar XI (192/211), with his Venn diagrams of meaning and being, and that he raises again and again in the 1960s, culminating in his lovely answer to Descartes's "I am thinking, therefore I am": "Either I am not thinking or I *am* not" (Seminar XV, January 10, 1968). We find a similar formulation here: "I am thinking where I am not, therefore I am where I am not thinking" (E 517). The unconscious has no being—it is where I *am* not—but it does plenty of thinking. I find my being where this unconscious thought does not occur, that is, in the ego as false being.

Descartes seems to have believed that man was situated in the zone where being and thinking overlap, or in the area that we might say signifier and signified have in common (see Figure 3.9).

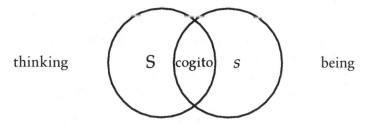

thinking   S   cogito   s   being

Figure 3.9. The Cartesian cogito

But being and thinking, like signifier and signified, are not situated in the same plane, "and man was deluding himself in believing he was situated in their common axis, which is nowhere" (E 518). Descartes's cogito would seem, according to Lacan, to be situated in the intersection between the realms of the signifier and the signified, whereas for Lacan that intersection is empty[39] (see Figure 3.10).

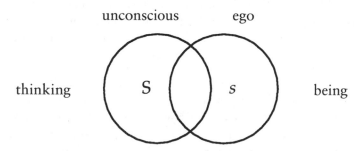

unconscious   ego

thinking   S   s   being

Figure 3.10. Lacan's empty intersection

Figure 3.10 illustrates that the unconscious is not a subset of the ego. As we saw in chapter 2, Lacan denied any validity to Kris's apparent topography (Figure 2.1), whereby the drives are a subset of or are subsumed within the system of the ego defenses, and he uses the same term, "concentric," in both discussions (E 517 and 599). This means (if we momentarily equate the id and the unconscious, as we should not generally) that working with the ego will never get us to the unconscious: We cannot move from the "higher layers" of the ego to the id, as Kris would have it, since there is no overlap between the two. Working at the level of the ego and working at the level of the unconscious are two radically different kinds of projects, according to Lacan.

Metaphor and the Symptom

Let us consider, in this context, a passage from "The Direction of the Treatment":

> To get [the analysand] to refind himself [in the signifying flow constituted by his discourse in analysis] as desiring is the opposite of getting him to recognize himself therein as a subject. [. . .]
>   Desire merely subjugates what analysis subjectivizes. (E 623)

To get the analysand to refind himself as desiring in what he says in analysis is thus to encourage the continued *metonymy* of his desire, which, as we have seen, Lacan equates with the ego. Here, by fostering the further displacement or metonymy of the analysand's desire, the analyst helps prop up the neurotic's ego, which Lacan characterizes as itself a symptom, "the mental illness of man" (Seminar I, 22/16). Since, "in analytic experience, the ego represents the center of all resistances to the treatment of symptoms" (E 118), the analyst must pursue a different path if she is to treat the neurotic's symptoms.

That different path is the opposite of getting the analysand "to refind himself as desiring"; it involves "getting him to recognize himself [in his discourse] as a subject," for only this latter project reaches the level of the symptom. As Lacan indicates in "Instance of the Letter,"

> [m]etaphor's two-stage mechanism is the very mechanism by which symptoms, in the analytic sense, are determined. Between the enigmatic signifier of sexual trauma and the term it comes to replace in a current signifying chain, a spark flies that fixes in a symptom—a metaphor in which flesh or function is taken as a signifying element—the signification, that is inaccessible to the conscious subject, by which the symptom may be dissolved. (E 518)

A symptom is a metaphor (E 528), for in a symptom, something presents itself in the place of the (subject of the) unconscious, some *thing* (represented here by S_1, an isolated signifier that dominates the subject, whether in the guise of a facial tic, a spider phobia, a limp, or what have you) presents itself instead of the subject:

$$\frac{S_1}{\mathcal{S}}$$

The subject has to come into being where it (that thing) was. How do we affect the subject at the level of the symptom, in the register of metaphor? Lacan suggests that it is by working not so much in the realm of meaning *(s)* as in that of nonmeaning—namely, by working with the nonsensical, nonmeaningful facet of the signifier (S), by working with its "'literating' structure" (E 510), or literality, with its signifier*ness (signifiance)*.

4

Reading "The Subversion of the Subject"

"The Subversion of the Subject and the Dialectic of Desire in the Freudian Unconscious" is one of the most difficult papers in *Écrits*. Like so many of Lacan's texts, one either works the text over and over or one gets virtually nothing out of it. Lacan seems to suggest that this is related to the very nature of knowledge: "One has but to look to see that, wherever one does not come by such knowledge by pounding it into one's head by tough experience, it falls flat. It can neither be imported nor exported. There is no information that stands up unless it is shaped for use" (Seminar XX, 89/97).

Whether that tough experience will seem worthwhile is a question one has to answer for oneself. As Lacan says regarding knowledge in Seminar XX, "[T]he jouissance of its exercise is the same as that of its acquisition" (89/97); if the jouissance of acquiring this knowledge is so abominable, how much can we expect to enjoy exercising it? This remains to be seen.

Part of the difficulty of this specific text stems from the fact that it builds on ideas developed over many years in Lacan's work. To provide but one example, the concept *point de capiton,* which I translate as the "button tie," is first introduced in Seminar III, *The Psychoses,* and the graph Lacan presents in four parts in this article is constructed over the course of Seminars V and VI and mentioned repeatedly in Seminar VIII. And since

"Subversion of the Subject" was never published prior to 1966, it is quite possible that the material on castration at the end was added in 1966—in other words, after Seminar XIII.

The Subject's Relationship to Knowledge

There are several trajectories running through the article—and their very multiplicity tends to lead the reader astray at times—but the one I want to begin with is that of the subject's relationship to knowledge. For Lacan says right at the beginning of the article that Hegel tries to "situat[e] the subject: on the basis of a relationship to knowledge," and the question is how psychoanalysis situates the subject.

First we need to see what Lacan is excluding in talking about knowledge: He is not talking about the *state of mind* in which knowledge is acquired, that is, the different possible states of consciousness *(états de la connaissance),* such as states of enthusiasm (en-*theos,* having the god within, as in the case of Socrates and his daemon), the state of *samadhi* in Buddhism (a state of "deep contemplation" of an object in which the subject/object distinction is at first preserved and then, at a later stage, all distinctions are absorbed or abolished), or the *Erlebnis* (experience) of using hallucinogens. According to Lacan, Hegel says that while these states may be objects of experience, they are not *epistemogenic* (E 795). It is not because one is in a certain state of mind or receptivity that knowledge can be produced. Lacan characterizes the attempt to investigate the unconscious in such states or via hypnosis (or even in the hypnoid states characteristic of some forms of hysteria) as a form of "rape" *(ravissement),* or taking by force. He situates the subject not on the basis of some *experience* or *state of consciousness* but on the basis of a logic that "is already operative in the unconscious" (E 796).

This logic that is "already operative" reminds us of the logic Claude Lévi-Strauss discovered, the logic already operative in the rituals and activities within the tribes he studied, a logic that operates unbeknown to tribal members. The latter may well offer explanations that account for the effects more or less completely, but not as completely as the subjacent logic the anthropologist uncovers. In this sense, Lacan already seems to introduce the subject in question here—the subject of the unconscious—on the basis of *inscience:* Knowledge is inscribed in some way and in some place in the subject, but the latter does not know what he is doing. (When asked why he is doing what he is doing, he concocts a rationalization, much like the neurotic who contrives a reason for acts motivated at the unconscious level.)

In fact, if we catalog the main things Lacan says about the subject who is at stake here, we find: (1) "He did not know he was dead"—a reference to a dream Freud recounts (E 802; SE V, 430; SE XII, 225–26). (2) He does not know what he wants. In analysis this subject asks the analyst, "What do you want from me? Tell me what you want so I will know what to do" (for example, whether to comply or refuse to comply) (E 815). (3) "He does not even know he is speaking" (E 800). The essential feature of the subject here is thus that *he does not know.*

This is not, I think, related to what Lacan refers to as his own "Je n'en veux rien savoir" ("I don't want to know anything about it") (Seminar XX, 9/1). For that is the battle cry of the ego, refusing to know what has been repressed, refusing to know about the why and wherefore of jouissance. This is thus not a deliberate or intentional inscience but, rather, a constitutional inscience. Whereas philosophy—at least Hegel's philosophy—situates the subject on the basis of a relationship to knowledge, psychoanalysis situates the subject on the basis of her lack of knowledge, her inscience. This, in its own way, seems to be a relationship to knowledge via negation.

What this immediately implies is that *the subject at stake for Lacan here has no self-knowledge, no self-consciousness.* She is excluded from the ego/ego-ideal dialectic by which self-consciousness can be explained, in Lacan's view.

According to Lacan, self-consciousness arises in the following manner: By internalizing the way the Other sees one, by assimilating the Other's approving and disapproving looks and comments, one learns to see oneself as the Other sees one, to know oneself as the Other knows one. As the child in front of the mirror turns around and looks to the adult standing behind her for a nod, recognition, a word of approval or ratification—this is the reformulation of the mirror stage in Seminar VIII (chapters 23 and 24) presupposed here—she comes to see herself as if from the adult's vantage point, comes to see herself as if she were the parental Other, comes to be aware of herself as if from the outside, as if she were another person (see Figure 4.1).

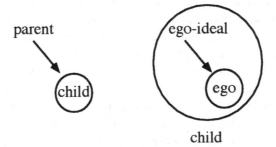

Figure 4.1. Internalization of the Other

In other words, I (ego-ideal) see myself (ego) as an object, just as the Other does, which is what allows for the Cartesian "I think." Otherwise, we would have to simply say "there is thinking," as Nietzsche does. This is, Lacan tells us here, the key to "self-consciousness": The consciousness "in which the ego assures itself an indisputable existence [. . .] is in no way immanent in the ego, but rather transcendent, since consciousness is based on the ego-ideal as unary trait (the Cartesian cogito does not fail to recognize this)" (E 809). The Cartesian ego assures itself that it exists due to a consciousness that stands outside the ego, that transcends the ego: a consciousness of consciousness or a consciousness raised to the second power—in short, self-consciousness. If we consider the publications that continue to come out on the issue of self-consciousness, we see that Lacan's explanation remains completely ignored—no wonder, perhaps, given that it is so laconic and that it is buried in such a difficult text.

In any case, there is clearly no such reflexivity or self-awareness when it comes to the subject: The subject may be dead and not know it, want something and not know it, and even speak without knowing it. Whatever the subject is, it does not take itself as an object. There is no self-knowledge at the level of the subject of the unconscious, for there is no self there.

The unconscious is not something *one* knows but, rather, something that is known. What is unconscious is known *unbeknown to* the "person" in question; that which is unconscious is not something one "actively," consciously grasps but, rather, something that is "passively" registered, inscribed, or counted. It is written in the subject without the subject being conscious of it. This unknown knowledge is locked into the connection between signifiers—it consists in this very connection.

This is what Lacan refers to as *the subject of science*. We might also refer to this unknowing subject as the Lévi-Straussian subject, and it is certainly a subject we deal with in psychoanalysis in the form of the subject of the unconscious. It is the subject of structuralism: the subject that can be exhaustively accounted for in scientific terms, exhaustively formulated on the basis of a combinatory with a finite number of terms (in theory, at least).

Tying Together the Regimes of Knowledge and Truth

In taking up the question of knowledge, and of situating the subject through a relationship to knowledge, Lacan mentions Freud's "Copernican step" and then takes a step back to discuss Copernicus himself (E 796).

Let me first point out something Lacan says again and again: Copernicus, *even if* we credit him with removing the earth from the center and instating the sun there, left the whole structure of center and periphery intact and continued to rely on the use of epicycles to explain things—a bias based on the supposed perfection of the sphere (Seminar XX, 42/42). The persistent theme of the sphere and its importance as a metaphor in so many realms is discussed by Lacan in Seminar XX and in other places as well (see, for example, Seminar VIII, chapter 7). Lacan also takes Copernicus to task for leaving the door open to the continued split between knowledge and truth, between *scientific savoir* and *Revealed Truth* (E 797). Knowledge, in Copernicus's work, becomes something with no real impact, just a game—like epicycles. Copernicus situates the earth at the center in order to simplify calculations. This move has no effect, in his view, on Scriptural Truth. It is just a device for more easily predicting where the various heavenly bodies will be at any given time. Here knowledge is divorced from truth.

Lacan asserts that the question for psychoanalysis is *how to tie the regimes of knowledge and truth together.* Jumping the gun a bit, I would suggest that we already have here the fundamental distinction we find throughout Freud's and Lacan's work—namely, representation and language *(savoir)* versus affect, libido, and jouissance (truth as jouissance).

Hegel, according to Lacan, has his own explanation of the relation between knowledge and truth, which involves a necessary teleology: Man by his very nature, by the very nature of consciousness, will come to understand everything. Consciousness, which is already perfect (or perfected), is the guarantee of absolute knowledge (E 797–98), which man cannot but achieve. In other words, there is an inevitable convergence between man's knowledge and truth, not a fundamental hiatus or disjunction.

According to Lacan, however, the history of science does not obey the Hegelian dialectic, in which absolute knowledge is obtained sooner or later. Convergence is not what we find in scientific theories but, rather, detours (despite the fact that the special theory of relativity is subsumed within the general theory of relativity) (E 798). Hegel's subject is thus absolute (always already perfectly approaching perfection), whereas science tries to absolutely abolish any subject other than the Lévi-Straussian subject mentioned earlier. The latter has little if anything subjective about it: It is strictly *Other.* The pure subject of science is, in the final analysis, nothing more than the Other inscribed in the living being, the knowledge of a tribal member's culture that the tribal member manifests, unbeknown to himself. Science is willing to look at the Other in this being, but at nothing pertaining to subjectivity, which is more than just the inscription of the Other in a *Homo sapiens.*

Nevertheless, as Lacan mentions in "Aggressiveness in Psychoanalysis," even the "hard sciences" are never able to completely eliminate all aspects of subjectivity:

It cannot be objected to us that [the analyst's] subjectivity must be null and void, according to the ideal physics lives up to—[the latter] eliminating it by using recording devices, though *it cannot avoid responsibility for human error in reading the results*. (E 102 [emphasis added])

Science tries to eliminate any subjective element, to suture it, as if subjectivity were a kind of thorn in science's side, pricking it, as if the wound had to be sewn up or sutured (E 861).

Now what is this subjectivity that science sutures? And how is it structured? Lacan attempts to answer these questions with his "Graph of Desire."

The Graph of Desire

To provide a thorough commentary on the Graph of Desire, we would ideally need to examine Seminars V and VI in detail, as well as later commentaries on the graph in Seminar XVI (December 11, 1968, and January 8, 1969) and elsewhere. I will not do so here, but it should nevertheless be kept in mind that Lacan worked and reworked the graph for some time, and that its gradual development and transformations are at least as important as the written form we have in "Subversion of the Subject."[1]

The original impetus for the Graph of Desire seems to be Lacan's dissatisfaction with Saussure's models of the relationship between the signifier and the signified. As we saw in chapter 3, Lacan seems to interpret the schema Saussure provides (*Cours*, 156; see Figure 4.2) of the "indefinite plane of jumbled ideas" (the signified) and the "vague plane of sounds" (the signifier)—or perhaps of the "delimitation" schema (*Cours*, 146; see Figure 4.3)—as indicative of an unfolding of sound in time, leading to a corresponding temporal unfolding of the signified.

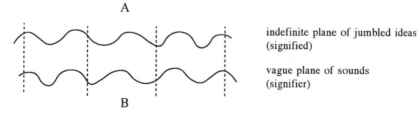

A

indefinite plane of jumbled ideas (signified)

vague plane of sounds (signifier)

B

Figure 4.2. Saussure's subdivision schema

Lacan inverts the upper and lower terms (at least, in his mind) and speaks of the "incessant sliding of the signified under the signifier" (E 502), but it is not clear exactly what "sliding" refers to here. It seems to have often been interpreted by Lacan's commentators as referring to some constant slippage or change in meaning of signifiers (as in the catchphrase "the slid-ing of signifiers"), which is certainly not what Saussure emphasizes in the synchronic systems he studies (in Saussure's view, meaning changes occur diachronically, that is, over time). The "incessant sliding of the signified under the signifier" would seem, in a Saussurian context, to have nothing to do with some kind of hypothetically shifting or slippery signification of signifiers.

Lacan's own use of language is, for the most part, very closely linked to etymology and classical French usage (as obscure as his sources may be), and does not at all rely on some supposed "stretching" or sliding of the meanings of signifiers. He emphasizes the way that metaphor can add new meanings to a word and how a signifier's place in a larger structure can supply different significations, but he does not emphasize any other "slid-ing" than that attributable to metonymy (associated with displacement). There does not seem to be any evidence of a "dangerous divergence" of signifier and signified in either Saussure's or Lacan's work.

Rather, the "incessant sliding of the signified under the signifier" re-fers (as I mentioned in chapter 3) to Lacan's interpretation of Saussure's schemas as implying that the signified unfolds contemporaneously with speech, meaning being accretive or additive in nature, each later part of a sentence adding a portion of the meaning to the portions already provided at the beginning of the sentence (see Figure 4.3). Lacan seems to interpret the schemas as suggesting that clause A gives rise to meaning a, clause B to meaning b, and clause C to meaning c, and that the meaning of the three clauses taken together in a particular order is none other than a + b + c. Here the signified can be thought of as unfolding or "sliding" along with the signifier (or "under" the signifier, due to the $\frac{S}{s}$ algorithm), the signifier being the sound-image (or sound pattern) produced by the enunciation of the three clauses.

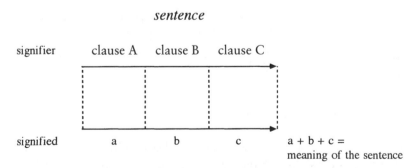

Figure 4.3. Modified Saussurian "delimitation" schema (*Cours*, 146)

Lacan wants to argue, against this particular interpretation of Saussure's work, that the signified is not additive in this way. There are moments, according to Lacan, at which a certain meaning precipitates out, or crystallizes, so to speak, either by anticipation or retroaction. As we saw in chapter 3, the clause "On the one hand . . ." leads us to anticipate more than the signifiers themselves imply, strictly speaking. It leads us to anticipate "but on the other hand . . . ," for example. And when clause C is "harmful radiation," clauses A and B, "Dick and Jane were exposed, when they were young children and in a repeated manner, to . . . ," retroactively take on a particular meaning. More specifically, the meaning of "exposed to" is *tied down* when clause C is provided; its meaning is narrowed down from its other possible meanings (such as "experienced" or "flashed at"). Signifier and signified are, as it were, *tied together* at that moment.

Lacan likens this tying together of signifier and signified to the attaching of a button to fabric (and perhaps to the padding underneath the fabric) with an upholsterer's stitch known in French as a *point de capiton* (*point* here means "stitch," and the verb *capitonner* means "to quilt" or "sew things together"). A mattress maker might use such a stitch to attach buttons to the mattress filling and outer fabric at regular intervals (see Figure 4.4).

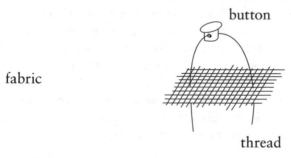

Figure 4.4. Upholsterer's stitch known as a button tie

The closest equivalent in English I have been able to find in upholstery books for *point de capiton* is "button tie." Alan Sheridan translated it as "anchoring point," but a button tie has a sort of *independent suspension* belied by "anchoring point": A button tie holds things in place while not exactly anchoring them to anything—they are simply tied to each other. The signifier and the signified are not anchored to anything outside of themselves, any "external reality" or "referent."

In "Subversion of the Subject," Lacan generalizes this schema—through which a particular signifier and signified become tied together, leading to an undisplaceable meaning, a meaning that cannot be altogether uprooted—to account for the meaning-making process in general. The fabric in Figure 4.4 becomes the temporal unfolding of signifiers in speech as, for example, when one enunciates a sentence. (Lacan abbreviates this in his Graph 1 as S and S', which stand for "a signifier" and "another signifier," located at the points where the two vectors intersect; I retranslate them in Figure 4.5 as S_1 and S_2, based on Lacan's later mathemes.) The thread in Figure 4.4 becomes the meaning-making process itself, which proceeds from the end of the sentence (S_2) to make sense of the beginning of the sentence (S_1).

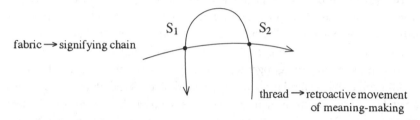

Figure 4.5. Lacan's *point de capiton*

Since meaning is not simply automatically registered beneath each part of a sentence (as it was in Lacan's interpretation of Saussure's "delimitation" schema) and since a retroactive movement is required to grasp the meaning of the sentence, how is that movement made? Or better still: who or what makes the movement? As Lacan puts it, "Where is the upholsterer here?" "Where is the mattress maker?" (Seminar V, 14). Or more broadly stated: Where is the subject who is engaged in the meaning-making process? Who and what is this subject? These are among the questions Lacan tries to address in constructing his Graph of Desire.

Commentary on Graph 1

The form of the complete Graph of Desire is based on certain schemas found in group theory and the study of combinatories. It can be understood as growing out of a pure combinatory, the one worked out in the "Suite" to the "Seminar on 'The Purloined Letter'" (E 57).[2] Lacan constructs it in stages, introducing the subject right from the outset. Figure 4.6 presents the first stage (or "elementary cell" [E 805]) of the graph.

The left-to-right vector is that of speech, and the horseshoe-shaped vector is that of subjectivity. The triangle where the vector of subjectivity begins stands for the human being as a living organism *(le vivant)*, a physical, biological, or animal being: It represents our prelinguistic, presubjec-

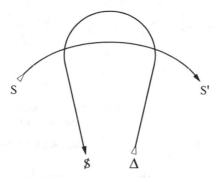

Figure 4.6. Graph 1

tive, vegetative state, so to speak. The endpoint of the vector of subjectivity is the specifically human subject *split* by her use of language. In this very simple model, through some kind of as-yet-to-be-determined process of speech, we move from a biological member of the species, *Homo sapiens,* to a particular human subject determined by language. The subject as so determined is fixed, tied down, or pinned down in the process. We might, perhaps, say that the subject becomes *fixated* here, or subjected to something else. It is a limiting, delimiting process.

As we saw earlier, the button-tie schema can be used to illustrate the meaning-making process in general by designating S_1 as the beginning of the sentence and S_2 as the end (Figure 4.5). If the beginning of the sentence contains a slip of the tongue, we can see that if the analyst interrupts the analysand immediately after the slip, he disrupts the usual meaning-making process engaged in by both speaker and listener in which they mentally replace the slip with what they believe the S_1 was supposed to have been (at least at one level) on the basis of the context, S_2, glossing over the slip in order to "get to the point"—the intended meaning, or intended *point de capiton.* Interrupting the analysand stops her from enunciating the intended S_2 (which might be understood here as the context), impeding thereby the retroactive meaning-effect that had been intended. The slip (S_1) is thereby "taken out of context," allowing other possible S_2s (or contexts) to come to mind which can retroactively give a different meaning to S_1. This tends to frustrate the analysand at first, but it is one way to get beyond meaning making, which is situated in the lower half of the Graph of Desire, what we might refer to as the imaginary half.

The button tie has essentially the same structure as Lacan's later formulation of the master's discourse, as can be seen by comparing Figures 4.7 and 4.8.

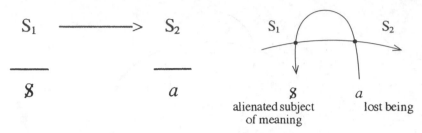

Figure 4.7. Master's discourse   Figure 4.8. Button tie

In the master's discourse, in the movement from one signifier to another, the subject is determined, congealed, or fixated as meaning (*$\mathcal{S}$*), whereas his being *(a)* is lost or sacrificed. The person is forced to give up some of his being, and here we can refer to this being as that of the living being, the life of the body, our animal existence, and thus the immediate pleasure taken or obtained from the body. To put it in terms that are as general as possible, we lose much of our animal being in order to come into being as "social" animals. (Bears do not come into being in this way: They may have a personality—be friendly or affectionate—without there being what Lacan refers to as "subjectivity.") This is essentially what Lacan calls "alienation" (see, for example, Seminar XI, chapter 16).[3]

Commentary on Graph 2

The bottom half of Graph 2 essentially maps the mirror stage (see Figure 4.9).

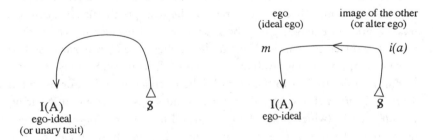

Figure 4.9. New start and end points

The terminus of the vector of subjectivity (the horseshoe-shaped vector) is different in Graph 2 than in Graph 1: The terminus, I(A), is the ego-ideal, the Other's ideal that the subject internalizes.[4] The matheme I(A) can be read as "the ideal given by (or received from) the Other," "the ideal of the Other," or "the Other's ideal." It can also be understood as the subject's identification with the Other's ideals. The subject comes into being here insofar as she identifies with the Other's view of her (replete as it is with the Other's ideals and values); in other words, she internalizes the ideal for her that the Other has, what she would have to be in order to be ideal in the Other's eyes: the ego-ideal. As I mentioned above, the ego-ideal is essentially a point outside of the ego from which one observes and evaluates one's own ego as a whole or totality, just as one's parent observes and evaluates it. The ego is denoted as *m* on the graph, for *moi* (ego), and is located opposite *i(a)*—the little other like oneself (or "semblable") who serves as a matrix or mold for one's own ego—such that the two mirror each other.

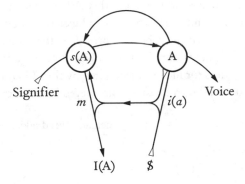

Figure 4.10. Graph 2

Even though there seem to be two possible pathways indicated on Graph 2 (Figure 4.10) by which to get to I(A), Lacan excludes one of them as a short circuit:

> [The] imaginary process, which goes from the specular image to the constitution of the ego along the path of subjectification by the signifier, is signified in my graph by the $\overrightarrow{i(a).m}$ vector, which is one-way but doubly articulated, first as a short circuit of the $\overrightarrow{\$.I(A)}$ vector, and second as a return route of the $\overrightarrow{A.s(A)}$ vector. This shows that the ego is only completed by being articulated not as the *I* of discourse, but as a metonymy of its signification. (E 809)

Lacan can be seen to be already suggesting here that the ego requires a relation to the Other in order to be "complete." The imaginary relationship, represented by the $\overrightarrow{i(a).m}$ vector, may suffice to precipitate the first form of the ego in a rivalry with one's semblable, but it is not sufficient to finalize or complete the ego. The ego-ideal has to be established for such completion to occur; completion here implies that, with the instatement of the ego-ideal, the ego is no longer subject to disintegration, the kind of disintegration we quite commonly see in psychosis.[5] For the ego-ideal provides a vantage point or a fixed point (even a *point de capiton*) outside of the ego that gives the ego its unity, tying the ego together, in a sense (see Figure 4.1).

It should be kept in mind that the Graph of Desire is designed to depict the advent of the subject through language. In it, we see the transformation of need into *need addressed to another person,* a person who is not as helpless as oneself (that is, who is not a semblable) but who is, instead, considered to be qualitatively different, capable of satisfying one's needs (Figure 4.11). Lacan refers to need addressed to this Other (or simply the addressing of the Other) as demand, and what the subject is demanding is not self-evident in and of itself. It must be interpreted by the Other, and the matheme for the Other's interpretation of the subject's demand is $s(A)$, which can be read as the signified (or meaning) supplied by the Other. It is the meaning of the subject's demand or request as interpreted by the Other.

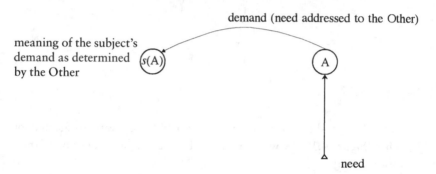

Figure 4.11. Demand as need addressed to the Other

A disjunction is introduced at the moment at which need turns into demand: Due to the fact that we must express ourselves in language, need is never fully expressed in demand. *Our need is never completely expressed in the request or demand we make of another; that request or demand always leaves something to be desired.* There is always a leftover—a leftover Lacan calls "desire"—and it is here that the upper level of the graph comes into play (see Figure 4.12).

Our demand, as interpreted, does not exhaustively account for or cover everything we want. Nor do the objects the Other provides in response to our demand fully satisfy us. A young bear is given honey to eat by its mother, gorges itself, and lies down for a nap, sated. We receive the blanket we demand from our mother and then dream about cars and dolls and

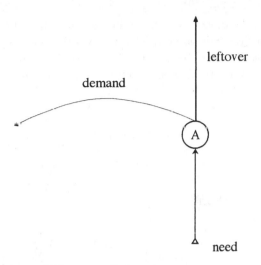

Figure 4.12. Need never completely expressed in demand

world domination. For us there is always something more to be desired. We find ourselves to be wanting something more, but what is it that will fill that want, make good that lack? These questions lead us to Graph 3.

Commentary on Graph 3

Lacan's first answer to these questions seems to be that what I want, as a subject, is recognition by the Other, and this recognition takes the form of being wanted: *I want to be wanted*. In order to be wanted, I try to figure out what the Other wants so I can try to be it and thereby be wanted. I desire the Other's desire for me. Object *a* in the matheme for fantasy, at one level, can be understood as the Other's desire for me; thus, in my fantasy, I imagine myself in relation to the Other's desire for me.

How can I get the Other to want or desire me? Perhaps if I can figure out what the Other (for example, my parents) wants, I can try to become it. What do my parents want? This question leads me to continually investigate and sound the Other's desire. Not content to figure out my own desire (whatever that might be), I ask the Other, "What do you want?" This, I believe, would help me answer the questions "What should I do?" and "What should I be?" in order to be wanted.

This attempt to discover what the Other wants often occurs in analysis as well, and the analyst has to turn the question back onto the subject. Not that it does any good at the outset. Desire being the Other's desire, what does it mean to ask the subject what he wants, as if it could be anything other than what the Other wants? Nevertheless, it is a sort of calculated

attempt to shift the subject away from the ego-ideal, I(A). The analyst raises the question "What do *you* want?" ("Chè vuoi?" in Graph 3) in order to
separate the two, in order to separate what the subject wants (upper half of
Graph 3; Figure 4.13) from what the Other wants of him (Graph 2, or the
lower half of Graph 3).

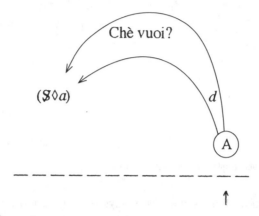

Figure 4.13. Upper half of Graph 3

The shift to the upper half of the Graph of Desire marks out a path
beyond demand and beyond alienation in language. Demand, for example,
no longer appears at the top of the graph, at least not nakedly so. It is the
realm of desire (*d* on the graph) that comes into play, desire that introduces
a gap or space between the subject and the Other.

Whereas the subject is constituted in the form of the Other's ideals at
the bottom of Graph 2, being constituted through an identification with
the Other, I(A), the top half of Graph 3 suggests another possible pathway.
Indeed, I would suggest that Graph 3 inclines us to think that the path
generally followed by the neurotic in the complete graph is from A to *d* to
fantasy ($\mathcal{S}\Diamond a$) to S(A̸); see Figure 4.14.

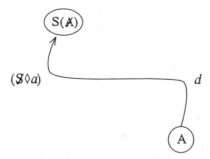

Figure 4.14. Trajectory in upper half of the complete graph

For the essential movement here (*d* to *$◊a*) is motivated by the subject's own question: What does the Other want? In what is the Other lacking? Thus, where do *I* fit in?

The Other is not eliminated in any sense at this intermediary level between (*$◊a*) and *d*. Desire is the Other's desire or desire for the Other's desire: Desire and fantasy come from the Other (as Lacan puts it in "Freud's *Trieb* and the Psychoanalyst's Desire" [E 853]) and are bound up with the Other.

In the lower part of the graph, the subject identifies with what the Other wants and tries to be it directly: to be what the Other says she wants him to be. In the upper part of the graph, the subject has to face the fact that the Other often seems to want something quite different from what she says she wants, that the Other, too, is split between conscious wishes and unconscious desires. The Other is fundamentally lacking in some respect and does not know what she really wants; the subject's attempt to be what she wants is thus doomed to failure: He cannot be the phallus for her, the phallus understood here as the signifier of her desire. Using Lacan's own terms developed two or three years later, in Seminar XI, the move from the lower half of the graph to the upper is the move from alienation to separation, separation from the Other's desire, separation from the ill-fated attempt to be the final signifier of the Other's desire ("final" in the sense that it would completely satisfy that desire and thereby put an end to it).

Commentary on the Complete Graph

The first point encountered in the upper line of the complete graph (Figure 4.15) is S(Ⱥ), and one of the first places Lacan discusses it in detail is in his commentary on Hamlet in Seminar VI.[6]

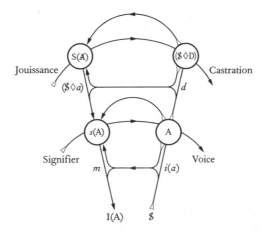

Figure 4.15. Complete Graph of Desire

Hamlet is trying to discern, according to Lacan, where he himself fits in his mother's desire, what he means to her, how important he is to her. In other words, Hamlet discerns desire in the form of lack in his mother and wants to know the name of that lack, the signifier she attaches to that lack. But Gertrude continually answers Hamlet's questions by talking *not* about what she is missing—a third term—but about herself. Lacan puts the following words in her mouth: "I'm the kind of woman who needs to be getting it all the time, I'm a true genital personality; I know nothing of mourning" (Seminar VI, March 18, 1959).[7] Lacan situates her answer at $s(A)$ on the graph. In other words, her answer brings Hamlet back to a meaning about the Other, a meaning supplied by the Other. In fact, since the Other determines the meaning of the subject's question, Gertrude turns Hamlet's question into something quite different, into a question about herself as she already understands herself. She does not respond by saying, "I don't know what I feel for your father anymore" (that is, indicating that *she has no answer* to his question), or by saying, "I want to honor your father's memory but I cannot help myself" (that is, indicating that she is a split subject with contradictory desires). She gives an answer rather than indicating that she does not have all the answers, rather than intimating that the Other is lacking. Gertrude thus fails to answer Hamlet at the level at which he can confront $S(\cancel{A})$, the signifier of a lack in the Other or the lack of a signifier that can tell Hamlet who he is, define him, take him under its wing, and tell him what he is supposed to do (see Figure 4.16).

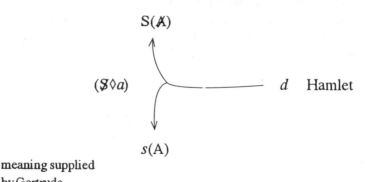

Figure 4.16. Hamlet's predicament

In "Subversion of the Subject," Lacan describes the matheme $S(\cancel{A})$ in more abstract terms: It designates the fact that there is no Other of the Other, no guarantee (or guarantor such as God) of what the Other says—whether the familial, juridical, religious, or analytic Other. No statement has any other guarantee than its very enunciation, he suggests. "Objective reality" is not the guarantor of what the analysand says in analysis (Freud was initially concerned with events that "really occurred" and would interview all of a patient's family members to see if any of them recalled a particular event his patient had recounted, but early in his career he gave up this practice; see SE XII, 141), for example, nor is God the guarantor of what a scientist says. The only guarantee is found in the discourse itself: "Truth draws its guarantee from somewhere other than the Reality it concerns: it draws it from Speech" (E 808). There is, thus, no metalanguage: no discourse outside of discourse, no discourse that is not subject to the ambiguities of language, and so on. Even logic, as a kind of formal symbolism, still has to be talked about to be conveyed, and that makes it subject to speech and its ambiguities. S(Å) thus takes on a multiplicity of meanings and is in some sense the most overdetermined part of the graph.

Note that in the lower level of the complete graph, the Other provides something: meaning, $s(A)$. In the upper level, the Other provides nothing— and this is crucial, for the Other sometimes has to work very hard to provide nothing, not to give an answer, an answer that could only be premature. At the upper level, the Other supplies no explanation for the subject's being or for the subject's enjoyment, no raison d'être, no cause to embrace: The subject has to take responsibility for all that himself. The Other simply points or gestures beyond herself. Lacan suggests that the neurotic is not sufficiently confronted with this, except perhaps in analysis or in an exceptional life event, such as what Hamlet experiences at the end of Shakespeare's play. As Lacan puts it at the very end of Seminar VI, "The neurotic's desire is what is born when there is no God" (June 24, 1959), that is, when no ideal, answer, or guarantee is supplied by the Other. Desire, if it is to be something other than just the Other's desire, requires absence, requires that something be missing (see Figure 4.17) and that this "something missing" be symbolized.

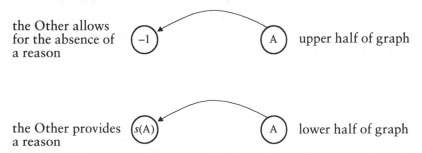

the Other allows for the absence of a reason   (−1)   (A)   upper half of graph

the Other provides a reason   (s(A))   (A)   lower half of graph

Figure 4.17 Something missing allowed by the Other

Lacan, always attempting to figure out how to write or graph or to-
pologize what there is that goes beyond structure in human beings, what
goes beyond the automatic functioning of the signifying order (the latter
being laid out in the diagram that was the basis for this graph in the Suite
to "The Seminar on 'The Purloined Letter'"), places it at the top of this
graph: jouissance (see Figure 4.18). He says, "This place is called jouissance" (E 819). If language is what makes us different from animals, jouissance is what makes us different from machines.

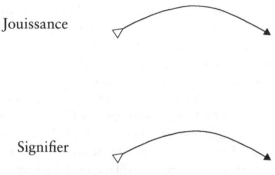

Jouissance

Signifier

Figure 4.18. The enjoying subject beyond language

The two levels of the graph thus correspond to the two all-important
Freudian registers of representation and affect, thought and feeling. The
Lacanian subject here is divided between language and jouissance, between the subject as a purely linguistic machine—a body mortified by
the language it has assimilated, a body subdued by the signifier—and the
remainder of the living being, the part that escapes signification, the part
with no rhyme or reason ("Jouissance is what serves no purpose," Seminar
XX, 10/3).

S(Ⱥ) thus occupies the place in the graph of a logical anomaly—the exception that proves the rule, the signifier that has to be excluded in order
for a class of signifiers to be defined (it is the outside of the treasure trove
of signifiers)—but also of the name of the subject: jouissance, enunciation,
something that is beyond what is said and that is found in the saying, in the
very act of speaking. It is beyond knowing; it concerns enjoying.[8] Recall
that Lacan's announced goal at the beginning of this paper is to situate the
subject through a relationship to knowledge. The top of the graph is what
does not come under knowledge that can be scientifically investigated—it
has to do with a truth beyond such knowledge. (An obvious question
arises: What is the status of the psychoanalytic knowledge of that truth?)

Movement across the Top of the Graph

What of the movement across the top of the graph? The subject as jouis-sance encounters the signifier of a lack in the signifying order as such. We might say that he encounters the signifier of jouissance, Φ, the signifier of the very process by which the signifier dominates and creates the signified (see chapter 5). For what is *not* included in the Other as the collection or set of all signifiers is that which grounds the very functioning of signifiers.

While in the set of all signifiers we find S', S'', and S''', we do not find $\frac{S}{s}$, the process by which the signifier creates the signified (see Figure 4.19).

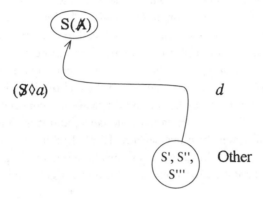

Figure 4.19. What is missing at the lower level is found at the upper level

This means that, in the Other as treasure trove, there is no signifier for the signification process as such, for the way in which the signifier kills the thing it signifies. Now that signifier, according to Lacan, is Φ. The signi-fier of what is lacking in the Other, known as S(Ⱥ), is also known as Φ. (By the time of Seminar XX, however, Lacan dissociates these two mathemes.) Lacan says many things about Φ, as we shall see.

But S(Ⱥ) is also the dead father in the Freudian myth, the father who would turn a blind eye to desires, who does not know he is dead—the father who is apparently slain in the oedipal struggle (E 818). In the seem-ingly never-ending series of equivalences, Lacan also associates S(Ⱥ) with the Name-of-the-Father (E 812).[9] This suggests that it is the paternal metaphor that is at work here: the father's naming of the mother's desire (or of the child's desire for the mother) and the prohibition of jouissance that this naming brings about.

So although the upper left-to-right vector in the complete graph (see Figure 4.20) shows jouissance coming into S(Ⱥ), there seems to be a loss of jouissance (which Lacan abbreviates as minus phi, −φ) that occurs at

Jouissance

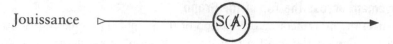

Figure 4.20. Movement across the top line I

S($\cancel{A}$), as well as an effect of Φ.[10] Minus phi (−φ) is the "meaning" of the instatement of the Name-of-the-Father; indeed, it might be referred to as the first meaning. It is a jouissance that is lost, symbolized, and sublated. It is a minus, of course, only insofar as it is named; *otherwise it has no existence as anything.* There is no lack if something is not named. Lack only comes into being by being named. Otherwise it is simply the way an animal experiences hunger: It may be intense and lead to ferocity, but as soon as it is satiated, it is forgotten. But if it is named, it can be re-presented at any time, long after the hunger has been satiated; it can live on, persist.

This loss of jouissance does not mean the end of all jouissance, though it may be taken in that way by the subject, who may consider life no longer worth living. ("This place is called Jouissance, and it is Jouissance whose absence would render the universe vain" [E 819].) But there is still the satisfaction of the drives; while there is a minus (of jouissance) on the left side of the upper horizontal vector, there is a plus on the right (see Figure 4.21).

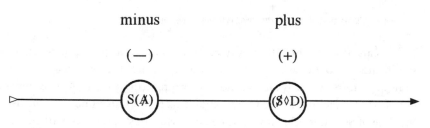

Figure 4.21. Movement across the top line II

On the right we find the formula for the drive, but Lacan tells us that both the subject ($) and the Other's demand (D) disappear here, leaving only the cut: the lozenge or stamp, the cut of castration. And castration is what we see at the end of the arrow running from S($\cancel{A}$) to the drive and beyond it (see Figure 4.22).

Figure 4.22. Movement across the top line III

How are we to understand that? Based on a later comment from Seminar XI, this part of the graph would seem to depict how "a subject who has traversed his most basic fantasy [can] live out the drive" (246/273): how a subject who has gone beyond demand,[11] who has encountered the prohibition of jouissance and the signifier of the lack in the Other, can enjoy. Castration here does not, to my mind, figure an end to enjoyment; rather, it figures an enjoyment of drive satisfaction after or despite prohibition and loss.

Demand might be understood as breaking down into two parts at this level: the impulse toward satisfaction and the addressing (the addressing of that impulse to the Other). The addressing here would seem to fade away: The subject pursues satisfaction without holding the Other responsible for it and without granting the Other the preeminent status of being the only one who can provide it.[12]

Conclusion

While "Subversion of the Subject" begins with the subject as a relation to knowledge and a claim (reiterated in "Science and Truth" [E 858]) that in psychoanalysis we deal with the subject of science—the pure subject of the combinatory, the pure subject of language—we see that the subject of the graph is split between language (the combinatory) and jouissance (a lack of knowledge, an inscience; "acephalous" is the term Lacan uses in Seminar VIII, 254; Seminar XI, 167/184; and Seminar XVIII, June 9, 1971). The subject of science is divorced from the id, which is the enjoying subject, and yet the latter cannot be left out in psychoanalysis. The subject of science is simply the Other, the unconscious. The Graph of Desire might, then, be seen to illustrate *the difference between the unconscious and the id,* which (as we saw in chapter 2) is often collapsed in ego psychology.

Thus, Lacan's term "subversion of the subject" here implies a number of different things: the subject of science is not the consciously cogitating subject but, rather, the unconscious subject. This is the by now well-known Copernican/Freudian decentering cum subversion: If thinking can still be considered to be at the center of the human subject, the "I" of Descartes's "I think . . ." cannot. Rather, thinking happens, or, as Lacan puts it, "it thinks" in the sense in which we say "it's raining." Note, however, that Lacan also mentions subversion in the context of the castration complex (E 820), implying that the subversion in question here is that carried out by the castration complex: the instating of the symbolic (the phallus) where the imaginary was (minus phi). *This is the properly psychoanalytic subversion.*

When it comes to the relationship between psychoanalysis and science, my sense is that Lacan's claim that in psychoanalysis we deal with the subject of science is a polemical one. We deal with a subject as constituted by language, since we work only with her speech—he says this to counter those who would rather read her gestures and body language or even manipulate her body. But we nevertheless have an impact on the subject as drive, the subject as jouissance.

In "Science and Truth," written in 1965, things are formulated a bit differently: The cause—which Lacan says is sutured by science—is where jouissance is situated. It is not the subject who is said to be sutured in that article, for science is said to deal with the same subject we deal with in psychoanalysis; instead, science is said to suture the cause, dealing only with the "nonsaturated" subject (E 863), not with what we might call the "saturated" subject—the latter being the one who is saturated by her cause, that is, the subject we deal with in psychoanalysis. The terms Lacan uses to qualify what is sutured by science in "Subversion of the Subject" are "subjectivity" and "truth"; in 1965, the terms he uses are "jouissance" and "the cause." In both cases, it is the upper level of the Graph of Desire that depicts what is sutured by science or what is *beyond science:* the cause, affect, libido, jouissance.

Why such a graph? Is it helpful to us? Some, including Malcolm Bowie,[13] say it is pointless. But it needs to be viewed in the context of the multifarious attempts Lacan makes to come to grips with the two facets of the subject: language and jouissance, meaning and being. It attempts to tie together the regimes of knowledge and truth. To say, as Bowie does, that it does not give us all the answers is anything but a devastating critique when viewed from Lacan's own perspective: The day Lacan delivers us all the goods, all the answers, is the day he will have put us to sleep and put an end to psychoanalysis. Instead, Lacan always leaves something to be desired.

5

The Lacanian Phallus and the Square Root of Negative One

> It is altogether hopeless to language the phallic instrument.
>
> —Lacan, Seminar XVIII, February 17, 1971

In commenting on Lacan's discussion of the phallus in "Subversion of the Subject," Alan Sokal and Jean Bricmont, in their *Fashionable Nonsense*,[1] admit that they find it "distressing to see our erectile organ equated to $\sqrt{-1}$" (*Fashionable Nonsense*, 27). This is likely to strike the psychoanalytically minded reader as a telling admission in more ways than one. They go on to say that "this reminds us of Woody Allen, who, in *Sleeper*, objects to the reprogramming of his brain: 'You can't touch my brain, it's my second-favorite organ!'" (*Fashionable Nonsense*, 27). We are apparently left to conclude that their penises are their "first-favorite" organs and that it is anxiety-provoking to them to have their penises in any way, shape, or form associated with something as abstract or aseptic-sounding as the square root of negative one—whether it is the "square root" part or the "negative one" that they find the most "distressing" ("deflating"?) is not immediately evident, though perhaps easy to divine.

Of course, that was not exactly what they intended to convey, and I do not intend to psychoanalyze them here. But their comment exemplifies the way in which one always says more than one intends to say (see Seminar V, 18)—an aspect of language that Sokal and Bricmont would rather not have to take into account when it comes to understanding "serious writing." For example, I just claimed that I do not intend to psychoanalyze them here, but that in itself is a classic denial, no doubt indicating that at some level I do intend to analyze them; after all, why would I mention it at all if I had no such intent?

But language, in their view, is designed to communicate an intended meaning, to inform the reader of one specifically premeditated thing, not "to evoke," as Lacan would have it.[2] Serious writing must, in their view, convey clear meanings and that is all; as soon as it does anything else, it becomes poetry. Lacan's explicitly announced goal, on the other hand, is to put the reader to work:[3] to the work of hearing all the different meanings in what people say and write and to the work of deciphering meanings that are not at all evident on the face of things—not to the work of jumping to conclusions about the meaning of things, such precipitated understanding inevitably involving a reduction of things to what we already know.

This goal does not necessarily excuse all the obscurantism that Lacan indulges in and that Sokal and Bricmont justly point out. They seem to neglect, however, that what works in France—talking over the heads of one's audience and seducing them into doing background reading on the authors and technical terms mentioned—does not work quite as well in the English-speaking world. Lacan could easily assume that his faithful seminar public—his audiences numbered up to 700 in the 1970s—would go to the library or the bookstore and "bone up" on at least some of his passing allusions. To spell out every glancing reference and elaborate at length on every analogy (scientific, mathematical, philosophical, linguistic, or whatever) would have put part of his audience off, leaving them with the feeling that they were being talked down to, infantilized—after all, a number of them were accomplished scientists, mathematicians, philosophers, and writers. The English-speaking lecture-going public does not, for the most part, operate in the same way, preferring to be spoon-fed rather than to be left to fill in the demonstration.

As I indicated in chapter 3, much of Lacan's written work is declarative, not demonstrative. Certain of his oral seminars (above all, those prior to the 1970s) are quite demonstrative; in them, Lacan unpacks case histories presented in the analytic literature and provides detailed discussions of topological surfaces such as the Möbius strip, the torus, and the cross-cap (Seminar IX) and incisive commentary on Freud's use of terms in different texts. In his written work, however, Lacan, unlike Freud, rarely if ever makes an assertion and then justifies it with numerous examples. Instead, he leaves the reader the task of coming up with an argument, an argument she should be able to reconstruct after having attended Lacan's ongoing weekly seminar and having read the texts discussed in it or by exercising her noggin. As Lacan himself says, his rhetoric is designed to have "training effects" on his audience (E 493–94, 722).

This is a particular writerly strategy. One may not like it, and most of us—even those of us who devote a lot of time and energy to deciphering Lacan's work—become infuriated with him for it at one point or another; but it cannot simply be dismissed because it is not the kind of writerly strategy that Sokal and Bricmont endorse. Perhaps, in trying to provide the necessary demonstrations, they find their performance lacking?

Stressing the Phallus

Sokal and Bricmont cast a very wide net in taking Lacan to task, and it would require a whole book to adequately explicate all the passages they cite. I would note, however, that they themselves generally provide very little in the way of argumentation, leaving the apparent "absurdity" of the text to speak for itself, which it probably does for those readers who have no idea at all what is being discussed. When these passages are, however, situated in their context—which is far larger than that of the particular text being cited, as Sokal and Bricmont suggest—most of them (I will not say all of them, since I would be hard pressed to explicate them all) convey something quite important that escapes their "hermeneutics." I will illustrate this using the example of the phallus (*Fashionable Nonsense,* 25–27).

Let me first provide a better translation of the initial text they cite from, "Subversion of the Subject." Here is the text provided in my 2002 English translation *Écrits: A Selection:*

> For my part, I will begin with what the abbreviation S($Ⱥ$) articulates, being first of all a signifier. [. . .]
>
> Now insofar as the battery of signifiers is, it is complete, and this signifier can only be a line that is drawn from its circle without being able to be counted in it. This can be symbolized by the inherence of a (–1) in the set of signifiers.
>
> It is, as such, unpronounceable, but its operation is not, for the latter is what occurs whenever a proper name is pronounced. Its statement is equal to its signification.
>
> Hence, by calculating this signification according to the algebra I use, namely:

$$\frac{S \text{ (signifier)}}{s \text{ (signified)}} = s \text{ (the statement)},$$

> with $S = (-1)$, we find: $s = \sqrt{-1}$. (E 819)

This passage, without any further explanation, is obviously incomprehensible. And Sokal and Bricmont's comments make it clear that they have no idea whatsoever what Lacan is up to here. First of all, they claim that the horizontal bar between the signifier and the signified is "an arbitrarily chosen symbol" (*Fashionable Nonsense*, 26). But anyone who has read Saussure's *Course in General Linguistics* is aware that Saussure introduced the bar between signifier and signified, and it has a specific meaning that Lacan extends (or subverts, if you like) in his commentary on it in "Instance of the Letter" (see chapter 3). The bar, in Lacan's work, designates the resistance between signifier and signified—that is, the facts (to simplify) that there is no easy one-to-one correspondence between word and meaning and that it is very difficult to pin down unequivocal meanings of words as used in ordinary spoken languages. Signifier and signified are not complementary; they are not equally weighted in the formation of the sign (this is where Lacan diverges from Saussure); rather, the signifier dominates and creates the signified. (These are just some of the meanings of the bar as Lacan uses it.)

"Instance of the Letter" (especially page 515 in the French edition) makes it clear that Lacan is not using the bar to "denote the division of two numbers" (*Fashionable Nonsense*, 26) and that no known or even unknown form of *mathematical* calculation is being carried out here: Lacan never combines his algorithms (like S(Ⱥ), $, a, and so on) in a way that has anything more than a passing resemblance to mathematical algebra (he even criticizes his students Jean Laplanche and Serge Leclaire when they try to do so).[4] Although he refers to his symbols as forming "*an* algebra," he never lapses into claiming that it bears any relation to algebra as a branch of mathematics. His symbols are designed to abbreviate important psychoanalytic concepts in a way that is easy to write and remember, allowing for a form of psychoanalytic "formalization" that is unrelated to quantification (his formulas, for example, generally do not allow of numerical solutions).

Turning to Lacan's point in the above-cited passage, the reader first has to know that "A" stands for the Other (*Autre* in French), which Lacan defines as the set (or battery) of all signifiers. It is the hypothetical set of all signifiers that make up a particular language, and that set is complete by definition (for Lacan defines it as including *all* the signifiers; he defines it in other ways as well that we need not go into here). The capital letter "S" stands for the signifier and the lowercase, italic letter "*s*" stands for the signified (or meaning). "S(Ⱥ)" denotes the signifier of a lack in the Other—that is, the signifier that points to the fact that the Other is lacking in some respect, even though it is defined as complete. It is still missing something.

Lacan claims that whenever a proper name is pronounced, whether it is the name of someone's father or the name of a province like Saskatchewan, "its statement" (or its enunciated, that is, what is said or stated) "is equal to its signification" (E 819). The name "Saskatchewan" has no other meaning in English than its designation of the province known as Saskatchewan. It signifies no more than what is said. It does not have multiple significations: It does not evoke a hundred things; it simply signifies what is known as Saskatchewan.[5] Saul Kripke says much the same thing when he qualifies proper names as "rigid designators."[6]

Now comes the more difficult part, because we have to assume (or speculate) that signification is being denoted here by Lacan as $\frac{S}{s}$ (the signifier over the signified). This denotation is, I believe, what allows Lacan to write the "statement [of a proper name] is equal to its signification" as follows:

$$signification = statement$$

$$\frac{S \text{ (signifier)}}{s \text{ (signified)}} = s \text{ (the statement)}$$

Signification is not always equated with $\frac{S}{s}$ in Lacan's work, but in at least this context signification seems to refer to the relationship between signifier and signified; in particular, *signification here refers to the process by which the signifier brings the signified into being.*[7]

We have here, in fact, a double equation because Lacan also implies that what is stated when a proper name is pronounced is equivalent to the signified of that proper name; in other words, when a proper name is pronounced, there is no difference between what is stated and its meaning (for a proper name denotes only what is known by that name). This equation between statement and signified is evinced by the fact that he labels both of them "s."

Note that Lacan sets the signifier here—that is, the proper name (for example, Saskatchewan)—equal to negative one. A possible reason why he does so might be because when one names something for the first time, a baby for example, one provides a signifier that is not already part of the existing set of signifiers, at least not usually part of the set that already exists for the namer. This is truer of things than of people: When the term "Internet" was created, it was a new signifier that was not previously part of the set of all existing signifiers (even though it was composed of an already existing word and prefix). We might say that it was missing from that set.

The process of naming shows that the set of all signifiers is missing something: The name of a new town or the name invented for a new device is not, for example, included in any already-existing dictionary or encyclopedia. We could just as easily refer to the new name as a "positive one" instead of a "negative one," but Lacan wants to emphasize the way a proper name points to the incompleteness of the supposedly complete set of all signifiers. In the passage quoted above, he likens that set (or battery) to a circle, the circle being an image of completeness since at least Greek times. The new name, he says, cannot be counted within that circle.

Having set S (the proper name) equal to minus one, Lacan now plays fast and loose with his equation of signification and statement, pretending for a moment that he is working with a real algebraic equation. He reduces

$$signification = statement$$

$$\frac{-1}{s} = s$$

to

$$-1 = s^2$$

finding then that

$$\sqrt{-1} = s$$

His conclusion is that *what a proper name signifies* (its signified or meaning) *is something as unthinkable as the square root of negative one,* known in mathematics as an irrational number. A person's proper name signifies what is unthinkable about him as a subject, not some particular property, not his specific history (though, of course, his proper name may speak volumes about his genealogy). In Lacan's own words: "This is what the subject is missing in thinking he is exhaustively accounted for by his cogito—he is missing what is unthinkable about him" (E 819).

To put it banally, Lacan is harping on his well-known theme that the Cartesian cogito does not account for the whole of the human subject: It leaves out the unconscious; it leaves out the question of the subject's being; it leaves out something that is never covered when someone says "*I* want this" or "*I* am that."

If we have not yet realized that Lacan is using the square root of negative one metaphorically here, we need but read on:

At the risk of incurring a certain amount of opprobrium, I have indicated how far I have gone in distorting mathematical algorithms in my own use of them: for example, my use of the symbol, $\sqrt{-1}$, also written i in the theory of complex numbers, can obviously be justified only if I give up any claim to its being able to be used automatically in subsequent operations. (E 821)

In other words, his use of $\sqrt{-1}$ to talk about what is unthinkable about the subject does not allow it to be put in ordinary equations; it cannot be used "automatically," that is, in the way mathematicians use it. He is using this symbol *for his own purposes,* not as mathematicians use it. It is a way of thinking about things: $\sqrt{-1}$ or i is the meaning of a proper name. *Its meaning is, in that respect, unthinkable.* It is what the subject is that is unthinkable about him.

The unthinkable, however, is not even a thinkable category or concept to Sokal and Bricmont; they say, "[Lacan's] analogies between psychoanalysis and mathematics are the most arbitrary imaginable, and he gives absolutely no empirical or conceptual justification for them (neither here [in "Subversion of the Subject"] nor elsewhere in his work)" (*Fashionable Nonsense,* 36). If one first rules out the concept of the unthinkable, then it is, indeed, difficult to find any sort of "conceptual justification" here.

What Is So Very Distressing about the Phallus?

Now where does the phallus fit in? According to Lacan, the signifier "phallus" is like a proper name in the sense that it is not really included in the set of all signifiers. Rather, *the phallus is the signifier that rigidly (turgidly?) designates the signification process itself; it designates the relationship or, better, the nonrelationship between the signifier and the signified.* Would that Lacan himself had said it so directly! Let us look at (a better translation of) the passage Sokal and Bricmont quote (*Fashionable Nonsense,* 27):

It is thus that the erectile organ—not as itself, or even as an image, but as a part that is missing in the desired image—comes to symbolize the place of jouissance; this is why the erectile organ can be equated with the $\sqrt{-1}$, the symbol of the signification produced above. (E 822)

As always, this requires more than just a little unpacking: The erectile organ is taken here "not as itself" (in other words, not as a real, biological organ) or "even as an image" (not as the visual or sensory image of the biological organ), "but as a part that is missing in the desired image." Here we must recall Lacan's work on the child's image of itself in the mirror, where he suggests that the mirror image of the genital region is problematic. Due to what the child interprets as a castration threat—which can be understood most generally speaking as a threatened loss of pleasure or jouissance due to the parents' prohibition of touching oneself, that is, of masturbation—*the genital region is connoted negatively* in the child's image of itself as desired by its parents ("the desired image" is the image of the child that is valued by the parents and that the child comes to value as well, the child coming to value and desire what the Other values and desires). The child comes to believe that *all* of its genital pleasure is prohibited by its parents, even if that is not what the parents intended to convey—that is, even if what they meant was "Not here," "Not now," or "Not in front of our guests." The genitalia become "negativized" in the child's eyes, a liability, subject to loss (whether through castration, excision, or some other form of deprivation of jouissance).[8]

Lacan's symbol for this negativization of the genitalia is $-\varphi$ (he uses the Greek letter phi to stand for phallus). The symbol is tied to Freud's concept of the castration complex, which applies to both boys and girls, originating in the observation that little boys sometimes express a fear that their penises will be cut off if they do not comply with certain demands and prohibitions. The use of the lowercase form (φ) indicates, given Lacan's conventions, that it is imaginary—the *image* of the penis—and the minus sign indicates that it is the image of the penis as always potentially lost and thus, in a sense, as always already lost; this is why it is negativized. What Lacan here calls the "erectile organ [. . .] as a part that is missing in the desired image" (E 822) is thus $-\varphi$.[9]

How is it that the fear of this castration is overcome, if indeed it is ever completely overcome? By, as little Hans says, the plumber coming by to unscrew the old one and replace it with a new one—or, in more theoretical terms, by the child giving up the imaginary one (the image of the penis as representing a precious but precarious source of jouissance, since it is in danger of being taken away) for a symbolic one (being valued for other things that one is in life, for one's qualities or abilities that are desired by the Other). The "negative" (or minus) image is given up for a "positive" symbol. The child's attachment to the penis (or genitals, more generally) as a source of masturbatory pleasure is a sore point between child and parent, and the child gives it up to retain the parent's approval, displacing some of the value formerly attached to the genital zone to those activities or aims approved of by the parent, the social milieu, or both.

In the highly schematic picture I am painting here, these activities and aims are socially valued: There is a whole discourse in the family and society about their value as status symbols. Other people desire them, the child's parents desire them, and the child (in this scenario) comes to desire them too. The child's qualities or activities that foster these aims are un-equivocally valued: They are viewed positively. (Positive and negative here are obviously not mathematical values but, rather, indicators of social ap-proval or disapproval; they may be read at other levels as well.) The phal-lus, in Lacan's lexicon, the symbolic phallus, is what is socially valued, valorized, desired.[10] The phallus as a symbol—not as an image in a fantasy of it falling off or being cut off—is designated by Lacan as Φ, Lacan using the uppercase or capitalized form of the Greek letter here. It is not what is physically present that is of value, at this level, but, rather, something more abstract, something that is not accessible to sight or touch. It may run the gamut from the child's "charm," "sense of humor," or "intelligence" to his "craftiness" or "intuition."

The (threatened) lack of jouissance becomes a potentially positive quan-tum of jouissance here: jouissance that might possibly be attained through the pursuit of what the Other values. The phallus comes to represent what is desired by the Other above and beyond the child's physical attributes. It comes to represent "the place of jouissance" (E 822), as Lacan puts it: It holds the place of what determines the Other's desire and potential sat-isfaction, becoming what determines the child's own desire and potential satisfaction.[11]

Lacanian "Algebra"

How is the overcoming of castration anxiety formulated here by Lacan? He says,

> The erectile organ can be equated with the $\sqrt{-1}$, the symbol of the signifi-cation produced above, of the jouissance it restores—by the coefficient of its statement—to the function of a missing signifier: (−1). (E 822)[12]

We saw above that the "erectile organ [. . .] as a part that is missing in the desired image" is what Lacan writes as $-\varphi$. Lacan now equates $-\varphi$ with $\sqrt{-1}$, $\sqrt{-1}$ being the signification he had "produced" earlier in the text by equating a proper name with −1 (a signifier missing from the set of all signifiers). In other words, we began with the formula:

$$significaction = statement$$

$$\frac{S}{s} = s$$

Substituting −1 for S, we obtained:

$$signification\ =\ statement$$

$$\frac{-1}{s}\ =\ s$$

Solving that "equation" for s, we saw that s is equal to $\sqrt{-1}$. Since $-\varphi$ is also equal to $\sqrt{-1}$, we can substitute $-\varphi$ for s wherever it appears in the above equation.

$$signification\ =\ statement$$

$$\frac{-1}{-\varphi}\ =\ -\varphi$$

Lacan now continues:

> The shift of $(-\varphi)$ (lowercase phi) as phallic image from one side to the other of the equation between the imaginary and the symbolic renders it positive in any case, even if it fills a lack. Although it props up (-1), it becomes Φ (capital phi) there, the symbolic phallus that cannot be negativized, the signifier of jouissance (E 823).

Φ is obviously being equated with -1 here, and the phallus as a symbol is being designated as the name or "signifier of jouissance."[13] We can thus substitute Φ for -1 in the equation, the symbolic side of the equation being where we find the symbolic phallus, the imaginary side being where we find the imaginary phallus alone.

$$signification\ =\ statement$$
$$symbolic\quad\quad imaginary$$

$$\frac{\Phi}{-\varphi}\ =\ -\varphi$$

We can then "solve" the equation as follows:

$$signification\ =\ statement$$
$$symbolic\quad\quad imaginary$$

$$(+)\ \Phi\ =\ (-\varphi)^2$$

Note that whenever a negative quantity is squared, mathematically speaking, the result is positive. The formula thus suggests that a positivization is achieved by the squaring in question here.

The implication is that *the overcoming of the castration complex requires a shift from the imaginary* (the imagined loss of genital jouissance that is demanded by one's parents or, possibly, the perceived loss of jouissance, in the case of girls, owing to being deprived of a penis considered to be of value by others) *to the symbolic,* from a minus value to a plus that neutralizes the imagined loss. This is, after all, the specific function of the signifier: When a child is not yet able to speak in even a rudimentary fashion, its mother's absence may be experienced as extremely painful; when, on the other hand, it is able to talk about its mother in words, it can make her present even in her absence, thereby alleviating some of the pain.

As we saw in our discussion of the Fort-Da binary in chapter 3, her absence is no-thing in particular until it is symbolized: It is not yet a "loss." Absence cannot even be understood as some *thing* until it is named. Whether naming the absence of the mother or the absence of the penis, language has the power to alleviate the oppressive weight of absence by the very process of naming and signifying it. In naming absence, *language both brings it into being* as something that can be talked about, something that exists in our universe of discourse, *and drains away its onerous charge.* There is a positivization that inevitably occurs whenever a lack or absence is symbolized. Our ability to use the signifier in speech surmounts absence, sublates the loss into something positive.

According to Lacan, *the phallus is the symbol of this very* Aufhebung, *this very sublation or positivization of loss that language performs* (E 692). The phallus, in Lacan's vocabulary, is the name of this very process and power; or, as he puts it in the early 1970s, "What the phallus denotes is the power *[puissance]* of signification" (Seminar XIX, January 19, 1972). The phallus denotes the power of the signifier to bring the signified into being, that is, the signifier's creative power (the signified is not always already there, just waiting to be symbolized). As he says in "The Signification of the Phallus," "[The phallus] is the signifier that is destined to designate meaning effects as a whole" (E 690). It is in this sense that we can also understand the title of this latter paper ("La signification du phallus") as "The Phallus as Signification," for the Lacanian phallus is the signifier of signification itself; that is, it is the signifier of the way in which the signifier makes things signify. Lacan himself later refers to the title of this paper (which is also given in *Écrits* in German as "Die Bedeutung des Phallus") as constituting a pleonasm, asserting that "there is, in language, no other

Bedeutung than the phallus" and that "language derives its structure from the fact that it is constituted by but one single *Bedeutung*" (Seminar XVIII, June 9, 1971).[14]

As such, Lacan conceptualizes the phallus as a signifier that is not included in the set of all signifiers: It is an exception, a signifier that is not like the others. It is in this sense that, at this stage in Lacan's work, the phallus is essentially equivalent to S($\cancel{A}$), for it is the signifier of that which is *not* included in the Other as the set of all signifiers.[15]

This reconstruction of Lacan's point in these several pages of "Subversion of the Subject," if indeed it is correct, seems rich in implications and conceptual power. Those who casually reread the 1977 translation of these several pages from "Subversion of the Subject" may find it hard to believe that such an argument can be extracted and that such conclusions can be drawn from Lacan's text, but I would argue that a close reading of the French suggests otherwise. I admit that it has taken me many years to decipher these formulations and that this may well seem a "distressingly" long period of time to spend deciphering any text to many readers. I hope I have shown, nevertheless, that Lacan is saying something comprehensible here, and that it is, indeed, far more interesting and thought-provoking than anything found in *Fashionable Nonsense*. I think I have at least made it clear that Sokal and Bricmont's distress over seeing "our erectile organ equated to $\sqrt{-1}$" shows they have no idea what Lacan means by either the erectile organ ("a part that is missing in the desired image") or by $\sqrt{-1}$ ("what is unthinkable about" the subject). It would seem that their distress is misplaced, if not indeed displaced.

6

Hors Texte—Knowledge and Jouissance: A Commentary on Seminar XX

Psychoanalysis shares a problem with a number of the social sciences and humanities, although this may not be immediately apparent. Psychoanalysts, in their work with patients, often find that, despite myriad interpretations and explanations—which both analyst and analysand may find convincing and even inspired—the analysand's symptoms do not go away. A purely linguistic or interpretative analysis of the events and experiences surrounding the formation of the symptoms does not suffice to eliminate them. (We shall see further on how this is related to a problem encountered in other fields.)

Freud encountered this problem early on in his work (SE XII, 141–42), and he even formalized it in 1920 by saying that "analysis falls into two clearly distinguishable stages": a first stage in which "the physician procures from the patient the necessary information [. . .] and unfolds to him the reconstruction of the genesis of his disorder as deduced from the material," and a second stage in which change finally occurs, "the patient himself get[ting] hold of the material" in his own manner (SE XVIII, 152). Later, Freud formulated the problem differently, in terms of what he called "an economic factor": A powerful force must be holding the patient's symptom in place; the patient must be deriving considerable satisfaction from it (even if it is, as Freud qualifies it, a "substitute" satisfaction [SE XVI 365]).

This brings up the fundamental distinction Freud makes between representation and affect, briefly discussed in chapter 4. If we hypnotize a patient, we can elicit all kinds of representations from him—we can get him to remember the most minute details of events he cannot remember at all while awake, and we can get him to put into words many aspects of his history—but often nothing changes. When we wake him up from hypnosis, he remembers nothing more than before, and the symptoms that seem to be tied to those events very often remain intact. It is only when the patient is able to articulate his history and *feel something* at the same time—some emotion or affect—that change occurs.

Representation without affect is thus sterile. This is one of the reasons for the sterility of so-called self-analysis: One tells oneself lovely stories about the past, one analyzes one's dreams and fantasies to oneself or on paper, but nothing happens, nothing changes. It is all very informative and interesting, and one remembers all kinds of things about one's past, but there is no metamorphosis. Affect is rarely brought into play without the presence of another person to whom one addresses all of these thoughts, dreams, and fantasies.

Lacan translates Freud's fundamental distinction between representation and affect as the distinction between language and libido, between signifier and jouissance. And much of his discussion of the subject—of who or what the subject is in psychoanalysis—has to do with this fundamental distinction or disjunction.

Freud had already grappled with where to locate representation and affect. He came up with various overlapping topographies of the mind, assigning representation to the ego and affect to the id, affect being discharged through the drives said to be part and parcel of the id. The superego did not quite fit, however, given its use of representations—imperatives, critiques, and so on—combined with a stern moral tone suggesting that the superego derives a little too much satisfaction from berating the ego (SE XXII, 59–67).[1] Freud's earlier attempt to theorize the mind had left affect out of the picture altogether: The conscious-preconscious-unconscious topography suggests that representations can be found at all three levels, but what of affect? Freud is led here, inconsistently, I would argue, to suggest that affects can be unconscious, whereas most of his theoretical work goes in the direction of saying that only a representation can be unconscious.[2]

We might say that Lacan polarizes the representation/affect opposition more explicitly than Freud, though it is not always indicated as such in his work. Although Lacan talks about *the* subject, we might say—following Jacques-Alain Miller's articulation in his unpublished seminar "Donc" (1993–1994)—that there are actually two subjects in Lacan's work: the subject of the signifier and the subject of jouissance,[3] or at least two faces of the subject.

To briefly summarize a few points I made in chapter 4, the subject of the signifier might be termed the "Lévi-Straussian subject," in that this subject contains knowledge or acts on knowledge without having any idea that he is doing so. If he is asked why he built a hut in his village in such and such a place, his answer seems to have nothing to do with the fundamental oppositions that structure his world and effectively order his village's layout. In other words, the Lévi-Straussian subject lives and acts on the basis of a knowledge he does not know, of which he is unaware. It lives him, in a sense. An observer finds it in him without having to rely on what he is consciously aware of.

This is the same kind of knowledge discovered via hypnosis, and in the end it seems not to require a subject at all, in the usual sense of the term. It is what Lacan, in "Subversion of the Subject," terms the subject of the combinatory: There is a combinatory of oppositions provided by the person's language, family, and society, and that combinatory functions (E 806). In "Science and Truth," Lacan refers to this subject as the "subject of science" (E 862)—that is, the subject that can be studied by science—and claims paradoxically that "the subject upon which we operate in psychoanalysis can only be the subject of science" (E 858): the pure subject of the combinatory, the pure subject of language. (This is the strictly positional subject of game theory, the subject that falls under the "conjectural sciences.")

This claim is a bit disingenuous, for although it is true that psychoanalysis relies only on language to achieve the effects it seeks—language being its only medium—it nevertheless seeks to have an effect on affect, on the subject as affect, libido, or jouissance.[4] One of the difficulties one encounters in reading Lacan's work is that he rarely specifies which subject he is talking about at any one moment, preferring to slip surreptitiously from one meaning to the other. I would suggest that, in "Science and Truth," when Lacan talks about the "object," he is referring to the subject as affect, whereas when he talks about the "subject," he means the subject as structure, as the pure subject of the combinatory.

Note first that it is far easier to deal with the subject of the signifier than with the subject of the drives (or the subject as jouissance). The second *n'est pas commode,* is not easy to get a handle on. This difficulty led many post-Freudian analysts to look for other ways of dealing with what we might call the J-factor, the jouissance factor. (Wilhelm Reich, at a certain stage of his work, figured, "Why not just deal with it directly, by direct contact with the patient's body? Why bother to work it out via speech?")

Many contemporary cognitive-behavioral approaches to psychology can be understood as restricting their attention to the subject of the signifier as opposed to the subject as jouissance. Indeed, many cognitive-behavioral psychologists seem not to comprehend even intuitively that they are missing something: Everything is supposed to be rational, there being no need for, and certainly no room for, anything else in their system. They seek out and "correct" or destroy "irrational beliefs."

Linguistics—that newborn science that Lacan was so infatuated with in the 1950s, thinking it could serve at the outset as a model for the kind of scientificity proper to psychoanalysis, in other words, that psychoanalysis could become a science along the lines of a science like linguistics—restricts its attention to the subject of the signifier. The same is true of all structuralist discourses: The structuralist project, as Lacan himself shows in some of his work from the 1950s, is to draw knowledge out of the pure subject of the signifier, to elicit and map the knowledge inscribed therein.

Marking his subsequent rejection of linguistics as a model for psychoanalysis, in 1972 Lacan forges a new term for what he himself does with language, since what he does is not the same as linguistics: He calls it "linguistricks" (Seminar XX, 20/15). He does not simply draw out the knowledge contained in language, contained in grammar and idioms, for example; he uses language to have effects on something other than the pure subject of the signifier.

Speech

> Can we work with sexual jouissance directly? We cannot,
> and that is why there is speech.
> —*Lacan, Seminar XVIII, March 17, 1971*

It would seem that there must be some convergence or overlap between the subject of the signifier and the subject of jouissance if changes can be wrought in the second via the first. Lacan notices early on that the two come together in speech. Speech relies on the system of signifiers (or simply on "the signifier," as he is wont to say, implying thereby the entire signifying system of a language), borrowing its lexicon and grammar from it, and yet speech requires something else: enunciation. It has to be enunciated, and there is a bodily component that is thus introduced: breathing and all of the movements of the jaw, tongue, and so on required for the production of speech.[5]

Linguistics concerns itself with the subject of the enunciated or subject of the statement—for example, "I" in the sentence "I think so"—which it categorizes as the "shifter." And it takes into account the difference between the subject of the statement and the enunciating subject: If, repeating Freud, one says "Psychoanalysis is an impossible profession," the subject of the statement is "psychoanalysis," whereas the enunciating subject is the person who actually speaks those words. Linguistics is forced to take cognizance of the distinction between these two subjects.

But linguistics does not account for the enunciating subject per se. The enunciating subject is the one who may take pleasure in speaking, who may find it painful to speak, or who may make a slip while speaking. The enunciating subject is the one who may let slip something that is revealing of his or her feelings, desires, or pleasures.

Thus speech is one of the places these two subjects come into play simultaneously, and psychoanalysis, insofar as it works with speech, cannot ignore the one or the other.

Nor, I would suggest, can economics (to turn momentarily to the social sciences, which, as I asserted at the outset, have something in common with psychoanalysis). Economics should ideally take into account these same two subjects as they come into play on the "floor" of the stock market. I would argue that we can equate the subject of the signifier with the supposedly "rational" economic subject of the market, *Homo œconomicus*. Who then would the enunciating subject or subject as jouissance be? Is it not the subject who is taxed by U.S. Federal Reserve chairman Alan Greenspan with "irrational exuberance" for *acting* in such a way as to bid up stock prices "beyond all reason"? "Irrational exuberance," an expression that has been repeated thousands of times in the media since Greenspan first said it, is the very name of jouissance in the economic arena. "Irrational exuberance" is the potlatch of our times. Probably not the only potlatch, of course, but a significant one all the same.

If speech (as opposed to stock trading) is where the two subjects come into play in psychoanalysis, it is also because psychoanalysis constitutes itself as a speech situation, that is, a situation in which most other forms of human action are implicitly or explicitly excluded at the outset. It is not a group situation, in which the mass action of groups might have to be taken into account—mass hysteria, rioting, pillaging, and so on (unless waiting room behavior is, for some reason, considered to be part and parcel of the analytic situation itself). Sociology and political science would be ill-advised to ignore the subject of the latter actions, the subject as jouissance, believing that their fields can be exhaustively accounted for on the basis of the subject of the signifier alone.

Lacan's Early Work Revisited

In his very first model or graph of the analytic situation, the L schema—based on a model provided in Lévi-Strauss's *Structural Anthropology*[6]—

Lacan depicts the two subjects I have been discussing as being at logger-heads or working at cross-purposes (I have simplified the L schema in Figure 6.1).

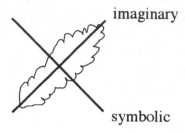

Figure 6.1. Simplified L schema II

The imaginary register, at this point in Lacan's work, corresponds to the subject as jealous rage, envy, and rivalry. It is tantamount to what Lacan later calls the subject's *jalouissance,* "jealouissance" (Seminar XX, 91/100), combining "jealousy" and "jouissance." The idea, at that stage, was that through speech, jealouissance could be dissipated, worked through, resolved—in a word, eliminated. In the clash between the subject of the signifier and the subject of jouissance, the latter had to be disposed of. The latter constituted an obstacle to the former and provided a kind of interference in the former.

As we saw in chapter 4, Lacan provides a complex Graph of Desire in which we find the advent of the subject in language in the lower half of the graph and the subject's intersection with jouissance at the top of the graph (I have simplified the graph in Figure 6.2).

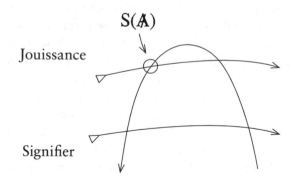

Figure 6.2. Simplified Graph of Desire

The subject follows a pathway starting from the bottom right-hand corner and intersects first the signifying chain (lower horizontal vector) and then jouissance (upper horizontal vector). The second intersection is fraught with trouble, for the first thing the subject encounters there is that there is no signifier that can account for or answer for his or her jouissance: S($\cancel{A}$). One's jouissance is without rhyme or reason, one might say. The subject's predicament between the signifier (lower level) and jouissance (upper level) is a thorny one, as it is depicted by Lacan: There is no easy alliance between them.

This discussion is not leading up to some way to reconcile these two subjects; Lacan does not introduce any particular formulation that shows how the two can be made to get along, so to speak. It is obvious that, in psychoanalysis, we deal with the subject of jouissance through the medium of speech, and that we attempt to use speech in ways that bring about change when it comes to the jouissance of the symptoms that the analysand complains of.

While psychoanalysts obviously have to grapple with the heterogeneity of the subject, it seems to me that *many* other fields in the humanities and social sciences have to come to terms with these *two* faces of the subject in theory building and praxis—no doubt in different ways than psychoanalysis due to the different aims that inform each field.[7] Having sketched out the two different subjects at stake in much of Lacan's work, let me turn now to knowledge insofar as it is associated with the first of these subjects.

Knowledge in a Prescientific Context

Over the course of at least twenty years, Lacan focuses on what might be called a prescientific type of knowledge and attempts to distinguish it from knowledge in a modern scientific context. That prescientific type of knowledge is associated by Lacan with Aristotelian science, a type of science that precedes the shifts often referred to as the Copernican revolution, although they were not made by Copernicus himself.

Why does Lacan focus on this and come back to it again and again in an almost obsessive manner? Is it not a moot point, of interest only to the history of science? Is Lacan a closet historian in his nonanalytic moments?

Lacan's claim here seems to be that psychoanalysis has had a difficult time detaching itself from both philosophy and psychology and keeps slipping into all kinds of prescientific constructs, all kinds of simplistic forms of pseudoscience and age-old philosophical notions. If psychoanalysis is to be something more credible than modern psychology—which leads to a proliferation of nosological categories as glorious as "imagined ugliness disorder" (known as Body Dismorphic Disorder in the DSM IV)[8]—then it has to examine what science is all about, not simply what people think it is about.

Modern science, for example, is ostensibly concerned with measurement and the production of "hard facts." Virtually the entire American psychological establishment has enlisted itself in the production of measures and statistics of all kinds.

But is that the kind of scientificity psychoanalysis can hope to achieve or should even wish to achieve? The *APA Monitor,* the monthly organ of the American Psychological Association, occasionally lists which aspects of Freud's theories have been borne out by empirical research. But when we consider the banal hypotheses psychologists have reduced Freud's theories to in order to test them and then examine the research design they have come up with to test such watered-down hypotheses, we may well wonder whether the supposed confirmations are of any more value than the alleged refutations!

According to Lacan, this is not at all the kind of scientificity at which psychoanalysis must aim: To his mind, psychoanalysis is not currently a science, and it is not by going in the direction of trying to produce measurable facts that it will become one. "It is not what is measured in science that is important, contrary to what people think" (Seminar XX, 116/128). We shall see what he thinks *is* important in science in a moment.

But first let us turn to Lacan's comments about antiquity's view of knowledge. Antiquity's view of the world is based on a fantasy, Lacan suggests, the fantasy of a preexisting harmony between mind *(nous)* and the world (Seminar XX, 116/128), between what man thinks and the world he thinks about, between the relations between the words with which he talks about the world and the relations existing in the world itself.

Modern science has rather decisively broken with this notion, presuming, if anything, the inadequacy of our preexisting language to characterize nature and the need for new concepts, new words, and new formulations. And yet, curiously enough, in the psychoanalytic journals, we find articles by the likes of Jules H. Massermann,[9] who discovers, according to Lacan, "with an unequaled naïveté, the verbatim correspondence of the grammatical categories of his childhood to relations found in reality" (E 274). In other words, in the middle of the twentieth century, we find an unquestioning approach to language and the categories and relations it provides in studies produced by analysts. This most prescientific of presumptions is still found in much of psychology today.[10]

The fantasy that characterized antiquity's view of the world goes quite far, according to Lacan: It is—and I do not think he was the first to say so—all about copulation (Seminar XX, 76/82), all an elaborate metaphor for relations between the sexes. Form penetrates or inseminates matter; form is active and matter passive; there *is* a relationship, a fundamental relationship, between form and matter, active and passive, the male principle and the female principle. All knowledge at that time participated, in

Lacan's words, "in the fantasy of an inscription of the sexual link" (76/82), in the fantasy that there is such a thing as a sexual relationship and that this link or relationship is verified all around us. The relation between knowledge and the world was consubstantial with a fantasy of copulation.

Surely no such fantasy could be at work in psychoanalysis today! But the fact of the matter is that, if there is one primordial fantasy at work in psychoanalysis today, it is that a harmonious relationship between the sexes *must be* possible. This view is based on what is thought to be a teleological perspective in Freud's work, a teleology that supposedly grows out of the "progression" of libidinal stages known as the oral, anal, and genital stages. Whereas in the oral and anal stages, the child relates to partial objects, not to another person as a whole, in the genital stage, post-Freudian analysts have often claimed, the child relates to another person as a whole person, not as a collection of partial objects.

A thick volume was devoted to such notions in France in the mid-1950s, *La psychanalyse d'aujourd'hui.*[11] In it, a whole generation of analysts put forward the idea that when one successfully reaches the genital stage, a perfectly harmonious state is reached in which one takes one's sexual partner as a subject, not an object, as a Kantian end-in-himself or -herself, not as a means to an end. And the crowning achievement of this stage is that one becomes what they call "oblative": truly altruistic, that is, capable of doing things for another person without any thought of the advantages it may bring to oneself.[12]

Had that generation of analysts ever seen anything of the sort? It would be hard to believe. Nevertheless, those analysts did not hesitate to postulate such a perfect state of harmony between the sexes and the total elimination of narcissism and selfishness and, in their work with their analysands, to promote genital relations as selfless and oral and anal relations as selfish. Even though no one had ever seen such a thing, *it had to exist.*

In other words, it was yet another fantasy, distorting psychoanalytic theory and practice.[13] Lacan's goal is to eliminate all such fantasies from psychoanalysis. That is, of course, more easily said than done, which is precisely why the study of the history of science takes on such great importance in any field that would like to become scientific at some point in the future, purging itself of unscientific elements: If one does not know the history of one's field, one is likely to repeat it.

The fantasy of harmony between the sexes has a long and distinguished lineage, insofar as we can trace it back to at least Plato's *Symposium,* where we see Aristophanes put forward the view that once we were all spherical beings lacking in nothing, but Zeus split us in two, and now we are all in search of our other half. We divided beings yearn to be grafted back together, failing which, we at least find relief in each other's arms (thanks to Zeus's having taken pity on us and turned our private parts around to the inside). As Aristophanes says, "Love thus seeks to refind our early estate, endeavoring to combine two into one and heal the human sore."[14] Love is what can make good the primordial split, and harmony can be achieved thereby.

A belief in a possible harmony, not only at some primordially lost moment in human history (in the Garden of Eden [phylogenesis]) or individual time (in the mother-child relation [ontogenesis]) but *now,* can be found in some forms of contemporary Jungian psychology in the West and in certain Chinese religions in the East (in the notion of yin and yang, for example).

Aristophanes' image of humans as originally spherical beings also points to the sphere as the shape that was considered most perfect, most harmonious, lacking in nothing. A great deal of ancient cosmology and astronomy up until Kepler's time was based on the fantasy of the perfection of the sphere, and much "scientific" work was devoted to *saving the truth (salva veritate)* by showing how the apparently noncircular motion of the planets could be explained on the basis of movement in accordance with that shape of shapes, the circle. Epicycles were employed even by Copernicus, and thus the Copernican revolution was not as Copernican as all that. All Copernicus said was that if the sun is considered as at the center of the world, the calculations can be simplified—which in that case meant something like reducing the number of epicycles from sixty to thirty.

As I mentioned in chapter 4, Lacan claims that it is not such a move, which keeps entirely intact the notions of center and periphery, that can constitute a revolution: Things keep revolving just as before. It is the introduction by Kepler of a not-so-perfect shape, the ellipse, that shakes things up a bit, problematizing the notion of the center (Seminar XX, 43/43). The still more important move after that, as Lacan sees it, is the idea that if a planet moves toward a point (a focus) that is empty, it is not so easy to describe that as turning or circling, as it had been called in the past: Perhaps it is something more like falling. This is where Newton comes in. Instead of saying what everyone else had been saying for millennia—"it turns"— Newton says, "it falls" (43/43).

Despite the Newtonian revolution, Lacan claims that for most of us, our "world view [. . .] remains perfectly spherical" (42/42). Despite the Freudian revolution that removes consciousness from the center of our view of ourselves, it ineluctably slips back to the center, or a center is ineluctably reestablished elsewhere. The "decentering" that psychoanalysis requires is difficult to sustain, Lacan says (42/42), and analysts keep slipping back into the old center/periphery way of thinking—hence the need for another "subversion," the Lacanian subversion.

One of the main points of "Subversion of the Subject" is that the subject is *not* someone who knows but, rather, someone who does not know. Despite Freud's emphasis on the unconscious, on a knowledge known unbeknown to the conscious, thinking subject—that is, the ego—despite Freud's emphasis on a knowledge that is inscribed, registered, or recorded somewhere, but that is not, strictly speaking, known by anyone, psychoanalysts have reverted to the idea of a conscious self: an ego endowed with synthetic functions, an ego that plays an active role in "integrating reality" and mediating between the tempestuous drives of the id and the severe moral strictures of the superego—in a word, an agent imbued with intentionality and efficacy (a notion of the ego found primarily in Freud's later works).

The radicality of Freud's initial move has been lost or covered over, and it is difficult to keep such fantasies from sneaking in the back door. Lacan suggests that the importance of the unknowing subject is found at virtually every step of the way in Freud's work. Of all the ancient myths in which a man kills his father and sleeps with his mother known at Freud's time—and there were apparently quite a number of them—why, Lacan asks, did Freud chose Oedipus? His answer: because *Oedipus did not know he had done those things* (Seminar VIII, 122). Oedipus was thus a perfect model for the unknowing subject, for a subject who acts without knowing why, in any conscious sense of the word "knowing." From the vantage point of psychoanalysis, "[t]here's no such thing as a knowing subject" (Seminar XX, 114/126).

Knowledge and the Whole

There seems to be something truly compelling about the visual realm and the images we encounter in that realm: The image of the circle (or at least of the egg shape) returns to haunt us even in Saussure's model of the sign (see Figure 6.3), to turn for a moment to other discourses.

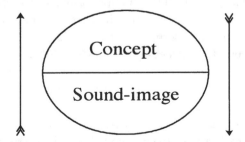

Figure 6.3. The Saussurian sign

As we saw in chapter 3, for Saussure the signifier and the signified, the sound-image and the concept, are indissolubly tied together. As Saussure says, "[T]he two elements [concept (signified) and sound-image (signifier)] are *intimately united*";[15] they seem, in the image he provides for the sign, to form a whole. This is an encapsulated sign, a sign in which the signifier and signified are not separate but correlative orders, forming a yin-yang-like configuration. Here I am leaving out the complexities that stem from the multiple relations among different signs, in order to focus on this way of conceptualizing, visualizing, or representing the sign itself.

We also saw in chapter 3 that Lacan begins his forays into linguistics by subverting the Saussurian sign: There is no harmonious, totalizing relationship between signifier and signified, he says. The signifier dominates the signified, and there is a genuine barrier between the two that abolishes the reciprocal arrows Saussure provides, suggesting a kind of mutuality or possibility that each order may have comparable effects on the other order. Lacan already subverts the sign in that way in "Instance of the Letter" (as we saw in chapter 3) and takes that subversion further still in the 1970s, repeatedly emphasizing the barrier or bar between the two realms and the fact that the signifier creates the signified, brings the signified into being (Seminar XX, 35/34). He strives to dissipate the hold Saussure's image of the sign has on us.

When Lacan takes up the theme of history, it is clear that he objects to Hegel's attempt to find some sort of totalizing meaning or teleology in history. Lacan is generally suspicious of the whole and is ever pointing to the hole in every whole, to the gap in every psychoanalytic theory that attempts to account for everything, whether to explain the whole of the patient's world or to reduce all of psychoanalytic experience to, say, a relationship between two bodies (in a "two-body psychology") or to a "communication situation."

Psychoanalysts seem to have a fatal attraction to such totalizing explanations, but they do not appear to be alone in that regard. Even in a field as abstract and seemingly free of the seduction of images and the imaginary as modern physics, there is an increasing interest, it seems, in "theories of everything," in a "unified field theory" that would account for all forces known and knowable. That strikes me as quite fanciful, as involving a view of scientific knowledge based on an image like that of the sphere—even if it is an *n*-dimensional sphere—as opposed to an image based on a Klein bottle, say, or a Möbius strip.

This is, in fact, at least one of the reasons Lacan introduces such images in his work in the early 1960s: to encourage his audience to stop thinking in terms of circles and spheres and to think instead in terms of surfaces that are less easily graspable in terms of categories like inside and outside, front-side and back-side, body and orifice (see especially Seminar IX). The notion of the world as constituting a whole, Lacan says, is based on "a view, a gaze, or an imaginary hold" (Seminar XX, 43/43), a view of a sphere from the outside, as it were—as if the world were over to one side, and we were looking at it from *some privileged outside point*.[16] But are we on the inside or the outside of a Klein bottle? It is more difficult to situate oneself in terms of some sort of exteriority when such surfaces are taken as models. Yet even those surfaces remain images and keep psychoanalysis rooted in the imaginary. Even the knots Lacan introduces in Seminar XX, some twelve years later, partake of the visual, though they are perhaps still harder to picture in the mind.

Lacan, in his attempt to get us to leave behind the visual, is led to the letter. If Kepler shook us out of our old Copernican ways of thinking by introducing the ellipse, Newton took us further still by introducing a kind of writing:

$$F = g\frac{mm'}{d^2}$$

This, according to Lacan, "is what rips us away from the imaginary function" (43/43).

Formalization without Mathematization

One way beyond fantasy is the reduction to letters. Indeed, in Seminar XX, Lacan says, "[N]othing seems to better constitute the horizon of analytic discourse than the use made of the letter by mathematics" (44/44); note that in mathematics, many of the letters do not have the kinds of meanings they have even in physics, where *m* stands for mass. Mathematicians like Bertrand Russell have been quoted as saying that the letters used in mathematics have no meaning, and to be devoid of meaning is to be devoid of the imaginary (as Lacan says, "[M]eaning is imaginary" [Seminar III, 65/54]).

Although Lacan ultimately concludes that "[t]he analytic thing will not be mathematical" (Seminar XX, 105/117), he nevertheless spends many years attempting to provide symbols—which he refers to as mathemes— with which to summarize and formalize psychoanalytic theory: $, *a*, *i(a)*, A, ($◊a$), ($◊D$), S($A̸$), Φ, and so on. His endeavor is in part an attempt to formulate certain structures in as rigorous a manner as analysis is currently able to. The symbols he introduces have nothing to do with measurement and thus cannot be replaced by numbers like those in Newton's formula for force and gravitation. And yet, when one is familiar with their multiple meanings, they seem to summarize a good deal of theorization in a very condensed form. Lacan's goal here seems to be to provide not a mathematization of psychoanalysis but, rather, a formalization. Formalization seems, at least at this stage of Lacan's work, to be a possible way of moving toward scientificity and is what Lacan finds most important about science—far more important than measurement.

In physics, formalization allowed theorists an independent field of speculation: One could play with the formulas themselves and work out all of their interrelations, without having the slightest idea what the new configurations meant or implied. One could make certain assumptions, not because they made any sort of intuitive sense, but simply because they simplified equations; those assumptions could then be tested through experimentation. But the formalization itself allowed for new breakthroughs; it gave physicists *a basis for a non-intuitive, non-image-based, non-imaginary approach to their field*. Indeed, modern physics became so far removed from any intuitive understanding of the phenomena supposedly under investigation that, rather than developing new theoretical advances to explain or account for the phenomena, physicists often had to think of what never-before-noticed phenomena might in fact validate the theories. No one had ever noticed, for example, that the sun bends the light that comes to us from Venus until modern physics posited the matter-like nature of photons and the sun's gravitational pull on them. To the best of my knowledge, there are still aspects of Albert Einstein's theories that have yet to be tested.

Obviously, there is no formalization of psychoanalysis in the offing that would allow for such an independent basis of theorization, but Lacan situates such a formalization at the horizon of a form of psychoanalysis that could claim to be scientific. How such a formalization could function independently if it did not simultaneously involve mathematization is hard to say, but he seems to think that set theory provides a model for *formalization without mathematization,* set theory being a kind of logic that can be used to generate many different areas of mathematics.

One of the paradoxes of the kind of field that psychoanalysis is, is that—unlike a field such as physics, in which physicists need never read the original texts written by Newton, James Maxwell, Hendrik Lorentz, or Einstein, learning all they need to know in order to "do" or "practice" physics by reading ordinary, current textbooks or by simply going to classes—in psychoanalysis, Freud's texts remain unsurpassed and are indispensable reading (at least they should be!). It is not as if later work in the field could somehow subsume all of Freud's contributions and pass them on in the form of a series of formulas that anyone could learn and use.

In Lacan's work, we see a two-pronged approach: We see Lacan attempt to reduce his own work and Freud's to mathemes—indeed, he ironically claims at one point to have reduced all of psychoanalysis to set theory[17]—and yet we see a kind of "fetishization" of the text, so to speak. We find in his work, on the one hand, a "structural" approach to reading Freud's texts and other texts (for example, Poe's "The Purloined Letter") that has spurred great interest in the humanities and in literary criticism in particular, and, on the other hand, an attention to writing that seeks to have effects on the reader that imply anything but the direct transmission of formulas and mathematically precise equations.

In his writing, we witness a veritable deluge of polysemia, double entendres, triple entendres, equivocations, evocations, enigmas, jokes, and so on. His texts and lectures seem designed to introduce us to the very kind of work analysis itself requires, sifting through layers of meaning, deciphering the text as if it were a long series of slips of the tongue. He says at one point that his writing style is deliberately designed to contribute to the training of analysts ("All of my rhetoric aims to contribute to the effect of training" [E 722]), but it no doubt goes further still. His writing affects us and, in certain cases, even upsets us.

If we think in terms of the distinction between the subject of the signifier—the subject of the pure combinatory or Lévi-Straussian subject—and the subject of jouissance, we might say, facetiously, that the mathemes are produced by Lacan as the subject of science, while the endless punning is produced by Lacan as the subject of jouissance, the enjoying subject. But then again, he seems to have at least as much fun with his mathemes as with his witticisms.[18]

Knowledge Begins with a Deficiency of Jouissance

In his discussion of Aristotle, Lacan says that knowledge finds its motor force in a deficiency of jouissance (Seminar XX, 52/54–55).[19] We find the pleasures available to us in life inadequate, and it is owing to that inadequacy that we expound systems of knowledge—perhaps, first and foremost, to explain why our pleasure is inadequate and then to propose how to change things so that it will not be. One cannot take the lack out of Lacan:[20] Knowledge is not motivated by some overflowing of life, some "natural exuberance." Monkeys may show signs of such exuberance at various moments, but they do not create logics, mathematical systems, philosophies, or psychologies. Articulated knowledge (that is, *savoir*), according to Lacan, is motivated by some failure of pleasure, some insufficiency of pleasure: in a word, dissatisfaction.

The French title of Seminar XX, *Encore*, reflects this; when we say *"encore,"* we mean give us more, that is not enough, do it again (it means other things as well, but they do not concern us as directly here). It means that what we experienced was not sufficient.

Is it true that we have less jouissance than other people or other animal species? Do we really see people around us who enjoy more than we do? Perhaps occasionally. The argument has often been made that racism, sexism, homophobia, and religious intolerance are based on the *belief* that some other group enjoys more than another group does, whatever that group may be. And yet that belief is usually based on next to nothing: Racists have rarely if ever seen any such thing in the peoples they discriminate against. But that does not stop them from believing it.

It seems that we do something animals could never do: We judge our jouissance against a standard of what we think *it should be,* against an absolute standard, norm, or benchmark. Standards and benchmarks do not exist in the animal kingdom; they are made possible only by language. In other words, language is what allows us to think that the jouissance we obtain is not what it should be.

Language is what allows us to *say* that there is the paltry satisfaction we get in various and sundry ways, and then another satisfaction, a better satisfaction, a satisfaction that would never fail us, never come up short, never disappoint us. Have we ever experienced such a reliable satisfaction? For most of us, the answer is probably no. But that does not stop us from believing there must be such a thing. There must be something better. Maybe we think we see some sign of it in some *other* group of people and envy and hate those people for it. Maybe we project it onto some group because we want to believe it exists somewhere. (I am obviously not trying to explain all aspects of racism, sexism, and so on here with this highly simplistic formulation.)

In any case, we think there must be something better; we say there must be something better; we *believe* there must be something better. By saying it over and over, whether to ourselves, to our friends, or to our analysts, we give a certain consistency to this other satisfaction, this Other jouissance. In the end, we wind up giving it so much consistency that the jouissance we do, in fact, obtain seems all the more inadequate. The little we had diminishes further still. It pales in comparison with the ideal we hold up for ourselves of a jouissance we could really count on, one that would never let us down.

Many things prop up the belief in this kind of jouissance. Hollywood certainly props it up, attempting to give it a kind of consistency few of us have probably ever known. In Hollywood's depiction of sexual relations— and sex is not the only realm in question when Lacan talks about jouissance, but it is certainly one of the more palpable ones—there is something inevitable and reliable about the satisfaction the actors ostensibly obtain from sex. I am not suggesting that no one ever has sexual experiences like the ones depicted on the silver screen; rather, I am suggesting that virtually no one has them with such regularity, that virtually no one has them so *infallibly.*[21]

What is the status of this unfailing jouissance that could never miss the mark? It does not exactly exist, according to Lacan, but it *insists* as an ideal, an idea, a possibility thought permits us to envision. In his vocabulary, it "ex-sists": It persists and makes its claims felt with a certain insistence from the outside, as it were—outside in the sense that it is not the wish "Let's do *that* again!" but, rather, "Isn't there something else you could do, something different you could try?"

When we think of the paltry jouissance we do have, we feel this Other jouissance is the one we should have, the one that should be. Since we can conceive of its possibility, it must be. This resonates with Medieval philosophy: Anselm of Canterbury says that "God is that than which nothing greater can be conceived." And since existence must be one of the properties of the most perfect thing going, God has to exist, otherwise He would not be the most perfect thing going. The ontological argument has been criticized for attempting to deduce existence from essence; perhaps it could be understood, from a Lacanian vantage point, as proving God's *ex-sistence.*[22]

The idea of an Other jouissance is closely related to the idea of God. There is a kind of fantasy at work here: the fantasy that we could attain such perfect, total, indeed, we might even say spherical, satisfaction. That fantasy takes on various forms in Buddhism, Zen, Catholicism, Tantrism, and Mysticism and goes by various names: Nirvana, Ecstasy, Enlightenment, Grace, and so on. (By calling it fantasy, I am not saying that it is necessarily unreal.)

The fantasy is so powerful that we feel this Other jouissance has to be, has to exist. Yet if it were not for this fantasy, we might be more content with the jouissance we do actually obtain. Thus, whereas Lacan says that, according to the fantasy, this Other jouissance should be (that is, should exist), from the point of view of the satisfactions we actually do obtain, it should not be because it merely makes matters worse. We might say that *it never fails to make matters worse.* This is the gist of the play on words Lacan makes over and over again in chapter 5 of Seminar XX, "c'est la jouissance qu'il ne faudrait pas" (a play on two different verbs, *falloir,* "it must be," and *faillir,* "to fail," that are written and pronounced identically in certain tenses; thus "it is the jouissance that must not be" and "it is the jouissance that cannot fail"): It is the idea of a jouissance that never fails and that never fails to diminish still further the little jouissance we already have.

These two jouissances (the paltry one and the Other) are not complementary, according to Lacan, otherwise "we would fall back into the whole" (Seminar XX, 68/73), the fantasy of complementarity, yin and yang, one for men, say, and one for women. Instead, they form a couple, if you will, akin to that constituted by the aporetic couple, being and nonbeing, over which certain Greek philosophers got rather "worked up" (Seminar XX, 25/22, 52/54, 56/61).

Sexuation

The discussion of these two jouissances brings us to the topic of what Lacan calls "sexuation." It should be recalled that sexuation is not biological sex: What Lacan calls masculine structure and feminine structure have to do not with one's biological organs but rather with the kind of jouissance one is able to obtain.[23] There is not, to the best of my knowledge, any easy overlap between sexuation and "gender," between sexuation and "sexual identity," or between sexuation and what is sometimes referred to as "sexual orientation." "Gender" is a recent term in English usage and was utterly unknown in France in the early 1970s in anything other than a grammatical sense. When I refer to men in the ensuing discussion, I mean those people who, regardless of their biological sex, fall under certain formulas—what Lacan calls "the formulas of sexuation"—the ones on the left in Figure 6.4 (Seminar XX, 73/78); and when I refer to women I mean those people who, regardless of their biological sex, fall under the formulas on the right.

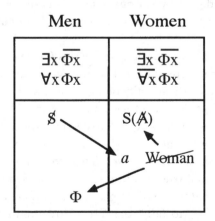

Figure 6.4. The formulas of sexuation

Lacan explicitly indicates here that he is attempting to define men and women in terms of a logic—hopefully not in terms of a fantasy (though a logic may well contain fantasy elements; Hegel's logic involves the fantasy of the whole, of totalizability), certainly not in terms of chromosomes, and not even in terms of the Oedipus complex.[24]

Lacan refers to the two jouissances that I have been referring to thus far as phallic jouissance and the Other jouissance (or jouissance of the Other). I have avoided saying "phallic jouissance" thus far, not wanting to put a name on it, especially such a loaded one. Why, after all, call it phallic?

There are many reasons, some of which I have elaborated on elsewhere; but here I would like to suggest that, reading *à la lettre,* we try to understand "phallic" as "fallible," we try to hear the "fallibility" in the "phallus." Phallic jouissance is the jouissance that fails us, that disappoints us. It is susceptible to failure and it fundamentally misses our partner. Why? Because it reduces our partner, as Other, to what Lacan refers to as object *a,* that partial object that serves as the cause of desire: our partner's voice or gaze that turns us on, or that body part we enjoy in our partner. It can be represented with Lacan's mathemes as $\$ \rightarrow a,$ which is, in fact, what we find under the formulas in the table Lacan provides (see Figure 6.4).[25]

To enjoy in this way, reducing one's partner to object *a,* is to enjoy like a man—that is, in the sense of someone characterized by masculine structure. Lacan even makes a pun here, saying that this kind of jouissance is "hommosexual," spelling it with two *m*s, *homme* being the term for "man" in French. Regardless of whether one is male or female (those are the biological terms) and regardless of whether one's partner is male or female, to enjoy in this way is to enjoy *like* a man.

As we saw in chapter 3, in Seminar XX (40/39), Lacan equates the phallus with the bar between the signifier and the signified ($\frac{S}{s}$). This should remind us of the high degree of abstraction Lacan brings to this often-contested Freudian concept; how we could understand the bar or barrier between the signifier and the signified as in any way related to the biological organ associated with the male of the species is truly difficult to see.[26] Why the barrier between the signifier and the signified? That barrier is such that there is a great deal of slippage between what I say I want in words or what I tell myself I want and the actual object I aim at. I tell my partner I want this, she gives it to me, and I say "That's not it! I want that." She gives me that, but that still is not it. Desire's object will not sit still; desire always sets off in search of something else. Since desire is articulated, made of the stuff of language—at least that is Lacan's contention, his certainly not being a naturalistic notion of desire—it has a very tough time designating any kind of exact signified or meaning, pinning something down. "I know that's what I said I wanted, but that's not exactly what I meant."

There is a barrier between my desire for something as formulated or articulated in signifiers (S) and what can satisfy me.[27] Thus, the satisfaction I take in realizing my desire is always disappointing. This satisfaction, subject to the bar between the signifier and the signified, *fails* to fulfill me—it always leaves something more to be desired. That is phallic jouissance. Just as one cannot take the lack out of Lacan, one cannot take the failure out of the phallus. Phallic jouissance lets one down, comes up short.[28]

The Other jouissance, on the other hand, may be infallible, but it is a bit trickier: Since Lacan often calls it *la jouissance de l'Autre,* it could be the jouissance the Other gets out of us—after all, Lacan says we are duped by jouissance, *joués* (Seminar XX, 66/70)—but then again, it could be our enjoyment of the Other or even our enjoyment as the Other (26/23–24). That ambiguity should be kept in mind as we turn to the formulas of sexuation themselves.

The Formulas of Sexuation

In the mid-1960s, Lacan borrows some of the language of functions from Gottlob Frege, the logician. In the formulas of sexuation put forward in the early 1970s, Φx is a function, even though Lacan puts a Φ in the place of the more usual f in $f(x)$. Φx is a function with a variable, and I think we can, at least at one level, read the variable "x" as "jouissance" (see Figure 6.4).[29] Reading x in this way,[30] the formulas can be understood as follows, assuming we keep in mind that Lacan does not use the universal and existential quantifiers in the same way that classical logic does:

$\forall x \Phi x$: All of a man's jouissance is phallic jouissance. Every single one of his satisfactions may come up short.

$\exists x \overline{\Phi x}$: Nevertheless, there is the belief in another jouissance, in a jouissance that could never come up short.

This way of formulating things may allow us to explain a number of comments Lacan makes about Søren Kierkegaard and about Taoism. Kierkegaard, Lacan seems to claim, thinks he can accede to love only by giving up his phallic jouissance. It is only if he stops reducing Woman, the Other (the Other sex, here, as Lacan says) to object *a*—it is only by renouncing the enjoyment he gets from object *a*—that he can attain something else, something Lacan describes as "a good at one remove" or "a good to the second power," "a good that is not caused by a little *a*" (Seminar XX, 71/77). Lacan refers to that as "castrating himself," since it involves giving up the jouissance of the organ; Kierkegaard attempts to castrate himself (figuratively, not physically) *in order to attain the dimension of existence.* (The formula in the upper left-hand corner is the only place existence comes in on the men's side of the table.) He seems to have to sacrifice (that is, castrate) one kind of love—love of object *a*—to achieve another kind of love, presumably a love that aims at something beyond object *a*.[31]

Turning from love to certain Taoist sexual practices, Lacan says that in Taoism, "one must withhold one's cum" in order to achieve a higher or greater pleasure (Seminar XX, 104/115). In certain Tantric practices, orgasm is deferred, often for hours, and the sexual partners supposedly become surrounded by a kind of blue halo, indicative of a higher or heightened state of pleasure. Note that Lacan associates phallic jouissance with organ pleasure, the pleasure of the genitalia (13/7); the idea here is that one must endlessly defer or altogether give up organ pleasure to obtain another kind of pleasure.

These examples point to a belief held by certain people that, through a certain kind of sacrifice, a man can attain an enjoyment beyond that of object *a,* an enjoyment that may be that of his partner as a divided subject or that of the Other, of the Other sex (enjoyment of someone—usually, but not necessarily, a female—as a representative of or stand-in for the Other). Here it seems that it is only by making such a sacrifice that he can truly love. Perhaps the courtly love tradition provides us with examples of this. Recall here what Lacan says in another context: "When one loves, it has nothing to do with sex" (27/25). If my interpretation of Lacan's comments here on Kierkegaard and Taoism are correct, the lower formula of sexuation for men ($\forall x \Phi x$) would then correspond to love of object *a*, and the upper formula ($\exists x \overline{\Phi x}$) would correspond to the *belief* in another kind of love: a love that we might term a "love beyond desire," since desire is caused by object *a*.[32]

Let us turn now to the formulas for women:

$\overline{\forall x} \Phi x$: Not all of a woman's jouissance is phallic jouissance.

$\overline{\exists x} \overline{\Phi x}$: There *is* not any that is not phallic jouissance, the emphasis going on the first "is." All the jouissances that do *exist* are phallic (in order to exist, according to Lacan, something must be articulable within our signifying system determined by the phallic signifier); but that does not mean there cannot be some jouissances that are not phallic. It is just that they do not exist; instead, they *ex-sist*. The Other jouissance can only ex-sist, it cannot exist, for to exist it would have to be spoken, articulated, symbolized.

Why is it that the Other jouissance cannot be spoken? If it were spoken, it would have to be articulated in signifiers, and if it were articulated in signifiers, it would be subject to the bar between signifier and signified. In other words, it would become fallible: capable of missing the mark. The bar brings on a disjunction between signifier and signified, the possibility—indeed, the inevitability—of slippage, noncorrespondence between signifier and signified. It brings on the whole signifying matrix where a loss of jouissance is unavoidable (object *a*), as we see in Lacan's formulation of the general structure of signification:

$$\frac{S_1}{\cancel{S}} \longrightarrow \frac{S_2}{a} \Leftarrow \text{loss or product}$$

This is why, Lacan seems to suggest, the Other jouissance must remain ineffable. A recurrent theme in the writings of the mystics is that what they experience in moments of rapture and ecstasy simply cannot be described: It is ineffable.[33] No words come at those moments. That is, presumably, why Lacan says women have not told the world more about this jouissance: It is inarticulable.

Is there anything that *can* be said about it? The most concrete thing Lacan says is that it corresponds to "making love," as opposed to sexual intercourse (which, at least for men, is related to object *a*), "making love" being akin to poetry (Seminar XX, 68/72). He even says at one point in the seminar that it is "the satisfaction of speech" (61/64).[34] How is such a satisfaction compatible with the notion that it is an *ineffable* experience where the bar between signifier and signified does not function? It seems to have something to do with a kind of speaking in which the signification of one's speech is perhaps eclipsed in importance by the act or fact of speaking itself. An example Lacan gives is speaking about love, for he says that "to speak of love is in itself a jouissance" (77/83). That is, after all, what the courtly love tradition was all about: conversing instead of engaging in "the act of love" (68/72), that is, in sexual intercourse.[35] This might be qualified as a kind of sublimation that provided its own pleasures ("'another satisfaction,' the satisfaction of speech" [61/64]).[36]

The ineffability of this Other jouissance may have something to do with the difficulty we have in saying anything terribly incisive or eloquent about the act of speaking itself. The jouissance involved in enunciating would seem to go beyond anything we can "state" or "formulate" about it. I cannot say why Lacan associates this Other jouissance specifically with women, apart from the oft-repeated point that many women seem to enjoy talking more than men do.[37]

In any case, the idea here seems to be that one *can* experience this Other jouissance, though one cannot say anything about it because it is ineffable. The fact that it does not *exist* (that is, is not articulable in speech) does not mean one cannot experience it: One's experience of it simply *ex-sists*. Lacan does not claim that everyone who has the ability to experience it actually experiences it; rather, "not all women" experience it. Nor does he suggest that a woman *has* to experience it to obtain psychic health or that women who do not are somehow "unhealthy" or "abnormal"—indeed, such terms are truly rare in Lacan's discourse, no matter what the context.

One crucial difference between men and women, structurally defined, then, seems to be that women do not have to renounce phallic jouissance to have Other jouissance: They can have the Other jouissance without giving up their phallic jouissance. They can have *both* this hommosexual jouissance—related to object *a,* and not to their partners as such—*and* the Other jouissance as well. For men, on the other hand, it seems to be an either/or. Does this reintroduce a fantasy dating back at least as far as Ovid, who has Tiresias say that women's enjoyment is greater than men's?

Whatever the case may be, this is what Lacan seems to mean by "sexuation": A man is someone who, regardless of chromosomes, can have one or the other (or at least thinks he can have the other by giving up the one) but not both; a woman is someone who, regardless of chromosomes, can potentially have both (see Figure 6.5).[38]

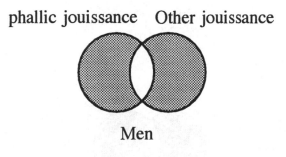

Men

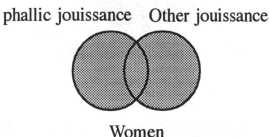

Women

Figure 6.5 Men's either/or, women's both/and

Note that, since "man" and "woman" in this discussion do not correspond to male and female, Lacan's discussions about relations between men and women can apply equally well to what are more conventionally referred to as "homosexual" relations, "homosexual" without the two *m*s. In female homosexuality, both partners could come under feminine structure, masculine structure, or one of each; the same goes for male homosexuality. There does not seem to me to be anything specific about homosexual object choice that immediately situates someone on one side or the other of Figure 6.4.

Subject and Other

As we saw in chapter 3, Lacan had been saying for many years that the psychoanalytic subject was everything the Cartesian subject was not: If the cogito was the intersection between being and thinking (Figure 6.6), the Lacanian subject was being in one place (imaginary or, perhaps, real), thinking in another (unconscious), with no overlap between them (Figure 6.7).

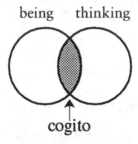

Figure 6.6. The Cartesian subject

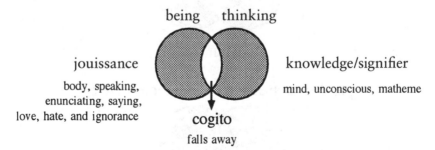

Figure 6.7. The Lacanian subject

We can modify that a bit here on the basis of Lacan's formulation: "The discordance between knowledge and being is our subject" (Seminar XX, 109/120). And since he asserts that "[t]here's no such thing as a knowing subject," I think we are justified in situating the cogito—the knowing subject par excellence—as what falls out between the two ("I am thinking, therefore [I *know* that] I am").

What, then, of the Lacanian Other? Lacan makes it sound here like a similar disjunction is involved (see Figure 6.8). There seem to be two faces of the Other: the locus of the signifier (which Lacan associates here with the father function) and "the God face [. . .] based on feminine jouissance" (71/77). Prior to the early 1970s, the Other is always very distinct from affect or jouissance in Lacan's work, the Other being the locus of the signifier, object *a* being associated with jouissance. But here the concept of the Other becomes a disjunction of these two radically opposed terms. Just as there are two faces of the subject, here there seem to be two faces of the Other. This may be where *lalangue,* whereby jouissance is "injected," so to speak, into the unconscious—that is, into the Other—comes in. Note that these two faces, Φ and S(Ⱥ), correspond to Woman's two partners in the table under the formulas of sexuation (Figure 6.4), suggesting that she finds one face of the Other under man and the Other face under woman.

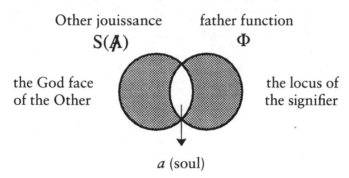

Other jouissance   father function
S(Ⱥ)   Φ

the God face   the locus of
of the Other   the signifier

a (soul)

Figure 6.8. The Lacanian Other

What drops out between the two? I would suggest that it is the soul, which seems to be associated here by Lacan with object *a* (what Lacan calls "soulove" is love, not of the Other, but of object *a*).[39]

Conclusion

It is often hard to say what exactly in analysands' discourse should be characterized as indicative of the Other jouissance. But we hear about the *idea* or *ideal* of an unfailing, infallible jouissance every day in analytic work. The gulf between the actually fallible jouissance and the ideally infallible jouissance is as palpable in clinical practice as in everyday discourse and the media (which, after all, are not unrelated). One need not endorse Lacan's account of masculine and feminine structure to agree with the idea that, in our discourse about sexuality, there are two quite different jouissances.[40]

Has Lacan introduced all kinds of fantasies of his own in this theorization of jouissance? The same old fantasies? Perhaps *disjunction* is the most important term here.

Whatever the case may be, the fantasy of the whole that Lacan strives to debunk in Seminar XX is alive and well in many disciplines today. To give but one example, E. O. Wilson, the renowned sociobiologist, recently published a book entitled *Consilience: The Unity of Knowledge,* in which he suggests that, using methods developed in the *natural* sciences, science will eventually be able to explain everything: psychology, literature, the arts, history, sociology, and even religion. The theory of the whole still has a considerable hold on many of us!

Notes

Preface

1. References to Lacan's *Écrits* are given as "E" followed by the page number in the French edition (Paris: Éditions du Seuil, 1966); the French pagination is included in the margins of the new English translation, *Écrits: A Selection* (New York and London: W. W. Norton and Company, 2002). References to Lacan's seminars that have been published in French (Paris: Éditions du Seuil, various) are given as "Seminar" followed by the volume number in Roman numerals and then the page number. Page references to seminars that have been published in English (New York and London: W. W. Norton and Company, various) include the French pagination followed by a slash and then the English pagination. Lacan's unpublished seminars are referred to by Roman numeral and the date of the lecture being cited (for example, Seminar X, March 13, 1963). Virtually all references to Freud's work are to *The Standard Edition of the Complete Psychological Works of Sigmund Freud* (London: Hogarth Press, 1953–74), abbreviated here as "SE", followed by volume and page numbers.

1. Lacanian Technique in "The Direction of the Treatment"

1. *Diagnostic and Statistical Manual of Mental Disorders,* 4th ed. (Washington, D.C.: American Psychiatric Association, 1994).

2. Lacan critiques the pregenital/genital distinction made in Sacha Nacht's "La thérapeutique psychanalytique," in *La psychanalyse d'aujourd'hui* (Paris: Presses Universitaires de France, 1956), which assumes, for example, that pregenital types (hysterics being oral, obsessives being anal) are never selflessly giving—or "oblative" in his terminology—whereas normal people are. He derides this distinction for many years, and suggests in Seminar XX that this notion of perfectly harmonious genital relations is one of the biggest myths ever fostered by psychoanalysis, associating it with the myth of the perfection of the sphere (reflected in the obsession with epicycles in ancient cosmology right up until Kepler, even after Copernicus) and with Aristophanes' claim that we were formerly spherical beings but were split by Zeus and can only hope to find satisfaction when we locate our other half (see chapter 6 below). Lacan does not believe in perfect unity of any kind, whether between man and woman, man and man, woman and woman, or analysand and analyst. His claim in the 1970s that "there's no such thing as a sexual relationship" (Seminar XX, 17/12) is a way of saying there is no perfectly harmonious genital relation, period.

3. In "Variations on the Standard Treatment," Lacan argues that the ego psychologists latched onto Freud's notion of the ego at the very point at which Freud revised that notion, starting around 1920. Stuck on the pre-1920s' notion of the ego, they could not understand anything about the functioning of the ego in Freud's subsequently developed second topography (E 334).

4. On this point, see chapter 10 of my *Clinical Introduction to Lacanian Psychoanalysis: Theory and Technique* (Cambridge, Mass.: Harvard University Press, 1997).

5. In *The Ego and the Id* (SE XIX), Freud provides at least four different glosses on the ego; see chapter 2 below for a discussion of them.

6. As Lacan indicates in "The Freudian Thing, or the Meaning of the Return to Freud in Psychoanalysis," while *each* of the two parties to the analytic situation can be characterized individually by the whole of the L schema (with its four positions), putting the two different parties together in the analytic game leads to a logical reduction. This reduction is akin to a *union* in set theory, for a and a' for the one collapse into a and a' for the other—the little other (or alter ego or "semblable" [see note 9 below]) for the one party being the other party's ego, and vice versa—and one subject becomes associated with S (the subject of the unconscious) and the other with A (the Other). As Lacan puts it there, "This is why I teach that there are not only two subjects present in the analytic situation, but two subjects each of whom is provided with two objects, the ego and the other, the latter beginning with a lowercase o. Now, due to the singularities of a dialectical mathematics with which we must familiarize ourselves, their union in the pair of subjects S and A includes only four terms in all, because the relation of exclusion that obtains between a and a' reduces the two couples thus indicated to a single couple in the juxtaposition of the subjects" (E 429–30). The complete L schema is found in the 1966 French edition of *Écrits* on page 53 (and in Seminar II, 284/243), and a simplified form appears on page 548. Note, however, that Lacan inverts the positions of a and a' in the two schemas; I have followed their positions in the complete schema. Cf. Freud's comment in SE XIX, 33, note 1: "I am accustoming myself to regarding every sexual act as an event between four individuals."

7. Lacan suggests that "the analyst strives to get the analysand to guess *[lui faire deviner]*" the fourth player's hand (E 589).

8. In 1951, Lacan had already said that we can interpret transference (or resistance) in a situation of stasis, where the analysis is not going anywhere, in order to set things in motion again, but we have to realize that it is essentially a lure to do so (E 225): It is a kind of measure of last resort. Interpreting the transference does not dissolve it, whether it be positive or negative; it does not make it go away. Such interpretation is situated within transference and may indeed give rise to still *more* transference. Interpretation of the transference as based on the belief that we can somehow step outside of the transference situation might be represented by adding a hypothetical point to Figure 1.1 in the extreme right-hand margin of the page, as if there were a possible metaposition or metadimension. It would imply that the analyst could speak (presumably such interpretation would still be made by speaking) without implicating herself in either the imaginary or symbolic registers. And

if we conceptualize the transference as involving all three Lacanian dimensions, imaginary, symbolic, and real, transference interpretation would have to postulate some fourth dimension or register from which to proceed that would somehow simultaneously extract the analyst from the other three dimensions.

9. Lacan's term *semblable* is sometimes translated as "fellow man" or "counterpart," but in Lacan's usage it refers specifically to the mirroring of two imaginary others (*a* and *a'*) who *resemble* each other (or at least see themselves in each other). "Fellow man" corresponds well to the French *prochain,* points to man (not woman), the adult (not the child), and suggests fellowship, whereas in Lacan's work *semblable* evokes rivalry and jealousy first and foremost. "Counterpart" suggests parallel hierarchical structures within which the two people take on similar symbolic roles, as in "The chief financial officer's counterpart in his company's foreign acquisition target was Mr. Juppé, the *directeur financier.*" Jacques-Alain Miller (in a personal communication) has suggested the translation "alter ego" for *semblable,* but since "alter ego" is also occasionally used independently by Lacan and since it has a number of inapposite connotations in English ("a trusted friend" and "the opposite side of one's personality"), I have preferred to revive the obsolete English "semblable" found, for example, in *Hamlet,* act 5, scene 2, line 124: "[H]is semblable is his mirror; and who else would trace him, his umbrage, nothing more."

10. A "fully realized subject" is someone who has completely come to be as a subject where it was, and since the ego, in Lacan's view, is a thing—an it—the ego must be progressively eliminated in the process of subjectification.

11. See also SE XXIII, 197.

12. Margaret Little, "Counter-Transference and the Patient's Response to It," *International Journal of Psycho-Analysis* 32 (1951): 32–40. Note that the article is not by Annie Reich, as the French version of Seminar I says, and that, ostensibly, the case is not Margaret Little's own case, as Lacan implies, but is, rather, that of a "very experienced" male analyst. Adding an interesting twist to the story, Little later revealed that the analyst was, in fact, Ella Sharpe and that Little herself was the patient in question. See Margaret Little, *Psychotic Anxieties and Containment: A Personal Record of an Analysis with Winnicott* (Northvale, N.J., and London: Jason Aronson, 1990), 36.

13. Lacan formulates the analyst's interpretation as follows: "You are in this state because you think I greatly begrudge you your success on the radio the other day, with this topic which, as you know, personally interests me in the highest degree" (Seminar I, 41/31).

14. Note that Lacan is certainly extrapolating here, for Little writes only that "[t]he interpretation was accepted, the distress cleared up quite quickly, and the analysis went on. Two years later (the analysis having ended in the meanwhile) [. . .] it came to him that what had troubled him at the time of his broadcast had been a very simple and obvious thing, sadness that his mother was not there to enjoy his success [. . .], and guilt that he had enjoyed it while she was dead had spoilt it for him" ("Counter-Transference," 32).

15. Note that Lacan finds the opposition often made between the "intellectual"

and the "affective" orders to be a false one (Seminar I, 69/57, 302–3/274). See chapter 2 below on this point.

16. Like so many things in the therapeutic universe, the emphasis on the body-to-body and person-to-person relationship between analyst and analysand has been returning in recent years in the form of what is sometimes referred to as "relational psychology." This is part of a larger trend in which analysts are encouraged to be "fully present" to the analysand and "authentic," that is, true to their own genuine feelings. In other words, analysts are encouraged to use their own personalities in the course of analytic work, to bring their own hurts, fears, and wants into therapy with their patients.

17. Or, as he puts it in Seminar IV, "transference occurs essentially at the level of symbolic articulation" (135).

18. This is what allows him to say that the analysis (or interpretation) of transference comes down to "the elimination of the subject supposed to know," for the latter is what props up the symbolic dimension of the transference; see Seminar XV (November 29, 1967). Lacan's comment in 1958 that "it is natural to analyze transference" seems to be ironic in the context in which it appears (E 636).

19. See Freud's various formulations in SE IV, 148–49.

20. For another example, see chapter 7 of *Group Psychology and the Analysis of the Ego* (SE XVIII).

21. After all, the Other's desire is not singular and monolithic but rather plural and protean.

22. In Seminar XIX, Lacan perhaps gives us a clue as to the origin of his reluctance to discuss his own cases when he mentions an incident that occurred at Sainte-Anne Hospital. He was giving a talk there and mentioned a phrase uttered by the mother of a male homosexual he was treating (a phrase found in his 1946 paper "Aggressiveness in Psychoanalysis" [E 104] with a slight variation): "And I thought he was impotent!" According to Lacan, ten people in the audience immediately realized who he was referring to, and that led to problems at the hospital. He quips, "That has inspired me since to be very prudent about discussing cases" (Seminar XIX, January 6, 1972).

23. Cf. "Science and Truth," where Lacan criticizes certain analysts for failing to see that Freud's reality principle, when understood properly (that is, in terms of linguistic structure), in no way excludes psychical reality in favor of "external reality," since the two are similarly structured by the signifier.

24. Lacan's discussion of resistance in Seminar I is motivated, at least in part, by a certain Dr. Z*'s comments (34–37/26–28). Dr. Z* admits quite openly there that he has the impression at times that his analysands are suddenly resisting him deliberately out of some ill will or perfidy; he has the sense that when his patients are on the verge of discovering something important, they stop short out of laziness. He admits that he gets infuriated by this and wants to force his patients to see the discovery that is close at hand and perhaps, too, to see that they are resisting seeing it. Dr. Z* even seems to want to make a virtue of this, suggesting that Freud was able to make so many breakthroughs precisely because he was especially bothered

by his patients' resistance to him. In other words, Dr. Z* seems to believe that it is a good thing for the analyst to be especially sensitive to and infuriated by such resistance on the patient's part.

One senses Lacan's slight embarrassment in responding to Dr. Z*'s confession in front of so many analysts and philosophers in the room: One of Lacan's sentences ends in an ellipsis, and a part of the discussion has been edited out of the published text. Dr. Z* considers the analyst's hypersensitivity to be a powerful aid in *defeating* the patient's resistance, whereas Lacan sees the whole process Dr. Z* describes as an abusive exercise of power, much like the abuse of power engaged in by Jean-Martin Charcot and other hypnotists who bypass the subject altogether. In a sense, we might say that it is Dr. Z*'s views and "misunderstanding" that provide the impetus to Lacan's discussion of resistance here and, in particular, to his discussion of Freud's conceptualization of resistance in "The Dynamics of Transference" (SE XII, 99–108). The title of the very next chapter of the seminar is "Resistance and the Defenses," and the subject of how to understand and deal with resistance and the defenses takes up the next couple of classes in Seminar I.

Lacan articulates his view of resistance here on the basis of his notions of full speech and empty speech, which are correlated with the symbolic and the imaginary dimensions.

Full Speech	Empty Speech
Revelation	Resistance
Symbolic	Imaginary

Full speech is the speech associated with revelation; it is the speech wherein the analysand talks about the past or the present and makes discoveries about her fantasies, her desires, her position in a nexus of family relationships, and so on. These discoveries are not necessarily new to the analyst, but they are to the analysand, and the analysand has the impression of breaking new ground and of "getting somewhere."

Analysts are painfully aware, however, that this kind of revelatory work cannot go on uninterruptedly forever; indeed, in certain analyses, it may be quite rare, long periods of stasis and stagnation being interrupted by all-too-brief, fleeting moments of revelation rather than the other way around. Lacan theorizes that the reason revelation cannot go on uninterruptedly for an indefinite period of time is that the reality (or "the real," as the French often call it) that the patient is trying to symbolize has never before been symbolized and that symbolization is an arduous process. Reality resists symbolization. Conceiving of the real as trauma, we note that events usually become traumatic precisely because no one ever helped the child who was affected by them speak those events, fit them into a fabric of meaning, and thus defuse their impact. When we try to bring the patient toward those events in analysis, there are no words there: Some kind of memory of the event persists despite an absence of historicization, story-fication, so to speak, or fictionalization—in a word, verbalization. Although language is imminent in affect, as we shall see in chapter 2, it does not seem to be always already there in the case of trauma: It has to be brought in ex post facto.

Lacan suggests that this is part of the very nature of trauma, of the "traumatic real," as he calls it: It resists being put into words. As in Freud's metaphor from the realm of physics, the closer the patient gets to the traumatic core, the stronger the repulsion, the stronger the force pushing him away. In a sense, then, Lacan wants us to consider the idea that it is not the patient who is in any way willfully resisting the therapeutic process; rather, it is the very nature of the job that the patient is faced with that is fraught with resistance. *The real resists symbolization.* The unframed real—the reality that, like the roots Roquentin encounters in Jean-Paul Sartre's *Nausea,* presents itself devoid of categories, not located in any symbolic context—resists such location or contextualization. The symbol is not imminent in the affect associated with traumatic experiences. An event is traumatic precisely insofar as the social context has not provided the symbolic or linguistic parameters in which the experience fits. This resistance to symbolization frustrates both parties to the therapy, patient and therapist alike. And each is inclined to take out his frustration on the only other person physically present in the room. Dr. Z* would like to grab his patient by the throat and throttle him or force him to speak the words that would finally free him, Dr. Z* apparently feeling as constrained by the real as his patient. The patient, too, is likely to take it out on the analyst: to sink his claws into the person who is presumably there to help him and yet is perceived as not helping.

The closer the patient gets to the pathogenic nucleus or core, Freud says in "The Dynamics of Transference," the more likely he is to veer away from it and latch onto something about the analyst. Lacan suggests that we understand that very broadly: "Resistance is the inflexion [or detour] discourse makes upon approaching this [pathogenic] nucleus" (Seminar I, 47/36), and it leads the patient to latch onto anything else that presents itself to his mind. This object could well be something in his visual or sensory field, such as the couch, the pictures on the wall, the smell in the room, the way the analyst shook his hand that day, or the sound of the analyst's breathing. Any of these things can be viewed as tied to the analyst, but the crucial point is that the real resists the analysand's attempts to get at it and creates a diversion, so to speak. That diversion generally involves something on the imaginary axis: something about how the analysand thinks he is being viewed or judged by the analyst, something related to comparisons between himself and his analyst, and so on.

If, for example, in the course of revelatory speech, the analyst echoes back something the analysand said, thereby stressing or emphasizing it, the analysand— succumbing to the resistance put up by the real he is approaching—may focus, not on the words echoed, but rather on the fact that the analyst picked out those words to stress: "I wonder why you chose to accentuate that, of all things?"

This might seem to put the analyst on the line: to question her ability to pick out the right things to highlight or, indeed, to question her ability to direct the treatment in general, to do anything of value for the patient. And, of course, it can be taken in that way: It can be taken by the analyst as an attack, as a jab, as an indirect attempt to offend her. In other words, it can, if we so choose, be taken up at the level of the imaginary axis: "My ability is being called into question, my credibility is at stake." It can, alternatively, be taken up at the level of the symbolic axis: The analyst can sidestep the perhaps somewhat intentional slight or blow and read it as a failure of symbolization, a failure to symbolize the real,

It is at such moments of failure that what Lacan calls the *presence* of the analyst is noticed, that the analyst as a person, as opposed to an abstract function or Other, comes to the fore. Even if the sessions are not held face-to-face (or in the same room or even in the same state, as, for example, when they are conducted over the phone), the analyst's silence or breathing or chair movements may be noticed, whereas they usually are not. While this is, perhaps, the time when the analyst feels most solicited as a person, as a flesh-and-blood human being with feelings of her own, she need not change roles: She need not respond as an ego (that is, on the basis of her own personality) instead of continuing to occupy the position of an abstract function or Other.

It is also at such moments of the failure of symbolization that the analyst may be taken to task for not helping the subject, for not interpreting or otherwise leading the patient to his own truth. Lacan says that it is when the avowal or confession of being does not come to term or to fruition that the patient sinks his claws into the analyst (it is rendered as "hooks on to" the analyst in the published translation; Seminar I, 59/48). He takes it out on the analyst, the only other person present in the room. The patient takes credit for the revelation and blames the analyst for the stasis and stagnation. There is no point in explaining to the patient that this is what is happening; there is no point in saying, "It is not really me that you are mad at, it is the symbolization process in general." It may make the analyst who feels attacked personally feel a little better to say something like that, but the analysand is likely to experience it with more immediacy: "No, I'm angry at you!"

25. This plan could be understood as the staging of a game between his own ego (identified here with "another man") and his mother's ego (identified here with his mistress), a scene he himself will *see* from an outside position, as it were.

26. By telling him her dream, she might be understood as putting him in the position of an analyst with respect to her, in the sense that she indicates thereby that it was dreamt for him.

27. This is not to suggest that the mistress's dream does not contain other desires as well, desires that may have less to do with her lover than the desire Lacan emphasizes here.

28. "All speech calls for a response" (E 247).

29. Phi and phi are discussed at greater length in chapter 5 below. Lacan's discussion in Seminar VIII could be understood as sketching out an explanation for the homosexual tendencies so often found in cases of obsession in men.

30. Perhaps the penis she presents in the dream is related in some way to the

extra penis the patient himself introduced into the situation with his request that she sleep with another man. In other words, perhaps she sensed that it was important to him at some level that another penis be involved.

31. If we can call that a fading of the subject, it is nevertheless not fading before object *a* but fading due to a lack of lack.

32. Colette Soler, "The Relation to Being: The Analyst's Place of Action," trans. Mario Beira, *Analysis* 10 (2001). Originally published in Spanish in *El Analiticon* 2 (1987): 40–58. On "lack of being," cf. Seminar II, 261/223.

2. Lacan's Critique of the Ego Psychology Troika

1. Cf. Lacan's discussion of the "rigorous logic" governing analysts' "intellectual productions" (E 316).

2. Wilhelm Reich's "character analysis" also gets occasional billing, as in "Variations on the Standard Treatment" (E 337–43).

3. See, for example, Freud's use of the term "ego-psychology" (or "psychology of the ego") in SE XXII, 58.

4. Anna Freud, *The Ego and the Mechanisms of Defense* (New York: International Universities Press, [1936] 1966).

5. Heinz Hartmann, "Ich-Psychologie und Anpassungsproblem," *Internationale Zeitschrift für Psychoanalyse und Imago* 24 (1939). In English, *Ego Psychology and the Problem of Adaptation* (New York: International Universities Press, 1958). This is where the term "nonconflictual zone" (or "conflict-free sphere") was first introduced.

6. Heinz Hartmann, Ernst Kris, and Rudolf Loewenstein, "Comments on the Formation of Psychic Structure," in *The Psychoanalytic Study of the Child,* vol. 2 (New York: International Universities Press, 1946), 26.

7. Heinz Hartmann and Ernst Kris, "The Genetic Approach in Psychoanalysis," in *The Psychoanalytic Study of the Child,* vol. 1 (New York: International Universities Press, 1945). See Lacan's comments on this supposed "nonconflictual sphere" in Seminar XIV (May 10, 1967).

8. Heinz Hartmann, Ernst Kris, and Rudolf Loewenstein, "Notes on the Theory of Aggression," in *The Psychoanalytic Study of the Child,* vol. 3/4 (New York: International Universities Press, 1949), 10. See also their comment that "thinking, perception, and action [are] three of the foremost functions of the ego" ("Comments on the Formation of Psychic Structure," 14). Cf. the *Outline of Psychoanalysis,* where Freud says that "the waking ego governs motility" (SE XXIII, 166).

9. Their concern with the "synchronization" of Freud's work is also mentioned in this 1946 paper on page 12.

10. See D. Rapaport, *The Structure of Psychoanalytic Theory: A Systematizing Attempt* (New York: International Universities Press, [1958] 1960); and J. A. Arlow and C. Brenner, *Psychoanalytic Concepts and the Structural Theory* (New York: International Universities Press, 1964).

11. Lacan refers to the child's ego as a "little other" because it is modeled on the "little others"—the young brothers, sisters, cousins, and neighbors—around

the child. The phenomenon of transitivism—seen, for example, in the fact that on certain occasions one child falls down and another child watching cries—suggests that there is little sharp distinction at this level between one child's ego and another child's ego. The Other with a capital O can be understood here as the unconscious insofar as it is the locus of one's mother tongue and all the ideals, values, desires, contradictory notions, and ambiguous phraseology that this tongue has been used to convey by one's parents and other people around one in the course of one's lifetime.

12. As Lacan indicates in Seminar XIV (December 21, 1966), Freud penned his by-now famous assertion *Wo Es war, soll Ich werden* (SE XXII, 80) *after* formulating his second topography in the 1920s, suggesting that his use of *Ich* alone and of *das Ich* cannot simply be equated.

13. Note, for example, that although Lacan criticizes Anna Freud's *chosisme* in 1953 (Seminar I) and criticizes in numerous texts the way ego psychologists encourage the patient to view himself as an object, by 1956 he seems to have decided to outdo them in objectification, conceptualizing the ego as a thing, pure and simple, reserving that which is not objectified for the subject, an altogether different "agency."

14. Arthur Rimbaud, *Oeuvres complètes* (Paris: Gallimard, 1954), 268.

15. Regarding the faculty of consciousness, which the ego psychologists also attribute to the ego, Lacan points out that such a view was common in preanalytic thinking and that although Freud initially used that preanalytic terminology, he later rejected it when he introduced the notion of unconscious thought. Lacan even introduces a model in Seminar II to show just how "nonsubjective" consciousness can be: He asks us to imagine the earth without any more human beings—after a nuclear holocaust, for example—and a lake near some mountains. He then raises the question: Do the mountains reflect in the lake? Is there an image in the lake of them? Of course there is, he replies, and we know it because, before the holocaust, we can install a camera that will automatically take and develop pictures that will prove the existence of the reflection. He asks us to consider this to be a "phenomenon of consciousness that has been perceived by no ego, that has been reflected in no ego-like experience, there being no ego or consciousness of an ego at that time" (Seminar II, 62/47).

This is simply part of his argument that consciousness is not some sort of holy grail but, rather, that consciousness-like phenomena can be mimicked and need not be considered the ego's pride and joy. In "The Freudian Thing" he provides a similar example, that of a lectern placed between two mirrors, its mirror image reflecting ad infinitum. There he says that "[t]he ego's privileged status compared to things must be sought elsewhere than in this false recurrence to infinity of the reflection which constitutes the mirage of consciousness" (E 424).

16. See Douglas Kirsner's recent book, *Unfree Associations: Inside Psychoanalytic Institutes* (London: Process Press, 2000).

17. In Ernest Jones, *Papers on Psycho-Analysis* (Boston: Beacon Press, 1961).

18. I have changed the term "dual" to "dyadic" in all my quotations from the

seminar, since Lacan does not use the term *relation duelle* to talk about dual relations as contemporary clinicians do, where the therapist has two distinct relationships with the patient (teacher and therapist, for example), but rather to talk about a dyad involving only two elements: ego *(a)* and alter ego *(a')*.

19. Anna Freud makes it clear right from the outset that, to her way of thinking, "a transference reaction in the true sense of the term" is a reaction to the analyst as ego (identified here with the mother's ego, as we shall see), that is, a reaction in the imaginary register. The symbolic (the girl's relation to her father, as we shall also see) is excluded de jure as "not connected with the analytic situation at all"!

20. Ernst Kris, "Ego Psychology and Interpretation in Psychoanalytic Therapy," *Psycho-Analytic Quarterly* 20 (1951): 15–30. Lacan even returns to the case briefly in Seminar XIV (March 8, 1967).

21. Note the similarity here to a solution Freud suggests is adopted by certain homosexual women: a "retiring" from the oedipal rivalry with their mothers by leaving men to their mothers (SE XVIII, 158–60).

22. Jacques Lacan, "Response to Jean Hyppolite's Commentary on Freud's 'Verneinung,'" *La psychanalyse* 1 (1956): 41–58.

23. This is what makes it clear that this text, first published in 1956, was completed after Lacan's discussion of the case in Seminar III (January 11, 1956).

24. Cf. Freud's comments: "However much the analyst may be tempted to become a teacher, model and ideal for other people and to create men in his own image, he should not forget that that is not his task in the analytic relationship" (SE XXIII, 175).

25. Nevertheless, Klein is sometimes taken to task for overemphasizing the reality of the here and now, and object relations, for overemphasizing an imaginary "two-body psychology" (Seminar I, 18/11).

3. Reading "The Instance of the Letter in the Unconscious"

1. Indications of an attempt at control are found in numerous seminars, where Lacan suggests that he is at great pains to introduce material in such a way as to forestall as many misunderstandings as possible, having obviously been disheartened by the echoes he received from his students of what they had understood in what he tried to convey (see, for example, Seminar XV, November 22 and 29, 1967).

2. Lacan often indicates just how important he considers such difficulty to be; consider, for example, his remarks in Seminar XVIII about his *Écrits*: "As many people told me right away, 'We can't understand anything in it.' Note that that is a lot: Something you don't understand anything about allows for hope; it is the sign that you are affected by it. So it's a good thing you didn't understand anything because you can never understand anything other than what you of course already have in your head" (March 17, 1971).

3. Lacan seems to want his readers to adopt the attitude displayed by Chrysippus, the Stoic philosopher, when he said to his preceptor, "Give me the doctrines and I will find arguments to support them." Consider what he says in his postface to Seminar XI (not included in the English translation): "You don't understand dis

writing *[stécriture]*. So much the better—it'll give you a reason to explain it" (253). *Stécriture* is a neologism based on a slang pronunciation of the word *cette* (this), *ste,* and *écriture* (writing), and can also be seen to condense *sténographie* (stenography) and *écriture.*

4. Actually, one can find the notion that anxiety arises when the object is about to be lost *(la cession de l'objet),* but one has to sift through hundreds of pages to find it! See Seminar X, July 3, 1963.

5. In Seminar XIX, for example, he mentions that at a talk he had recently given in Milan, he tried to ensure that his Italian audience would not "believe they could situate me *[me repérer]*" (*repérer* also means "to map," "locate," or "pin down") on the basis of the *"poubellication"* known as *Écrits* (June 14, 1972). The talk in Milan was published as "Discours de Jacques Lacan à l'Université de Milan le 12 mai 1972," in *Lacan in Italia, 1953–1978: En Italie Lacan* (Milan: La Salamandra, 1978), 32–55.

6. This, of course, does not stop people from trying to create such systems; see, for example, John Rawls, *A Theory of Justice* (Cambridge, Mass.: Belknap, 1971). Lacan suggests that his own work cannot be taken as a system due to his very theory of the subject: "What I enunciate about the subject as himself an effect of discourse absolutely rules out the possibility that my discourse could constitute a system" (Seminar XVI, November 27, 1968).

7. Lacan's lack of attention to detail, leaving so many errors in all of the extant editions of *Écrits,* also suggests a non-anal concern with taking things further and little interest in bequeathing us a lovely jewel of a finished product.

8. See Jean-Luc Nancy and Philippe Lacoue-Labarthe, *Le titre de la lettre* (Paris: Galilée, 1973). In English, *The Title of the Letter,* trans. F. Raffoul and D. Pettigrew (Albany: State University of New York Press, 1992).

9. Lacan even goes so far as to claim that the unconscious *is* those very "twists and turns" (E 620).

10. Freud's endlessly revised editions of his texts and occasional summaries of psychoanalysis as a whole perhaps also fostered such readings. Note that the revisions, however, often amounted to simply adding footnotes that contradict or substantially modify the thesis put forward in the "main body of the text," without suppressing any of the latter, hence effectively allowing the different perspectives to stand side by side, as it were.

11. He never characterizes his oral seminars as *poubellication*—a term condensing "publication" and *poubelle,* "garbage can," which he uses to characterize his *Écrits* (Seminar XX, 29/26)—or suggests that he has to forget himself *(s'oublier)* or forget everything *(tout-blier)* to give them (Seminar XX, 57/61). He even went so far as to say, on one occasion, that in rereading his seminars he was struck by the fact that there are no screwups or big errors in them, whereas there are in his *Écrits.* His excuse is that he writes fast: "What I write, I rework ten times. But it's true that the tenth time I write very fast, and that's why there remain foul-ups *[bavures]* in it—because it's a text. A text, as the name indicates, can only be woven by forming knots. When you make knots there is something that remains and that hangs down" (Seminar XIX, May 10, 1972). The somewhat tongue-in-cheek or

ironic character of this comment is underscored by the fact that the French term for knots, *noeuds,* also means "balls." Note that these comments from the 1970s seem to contradict the points he makes about writing in "Instance of the Letter."

12. Indeed, in Freudian terms we might say that it is a "compromise formation" between the two.

13. There are other, not-so-generous things we could say about the unfinished nature of his analysis. For example, we could point to his allusion in a note here (E 506, note 1) to his former analyst, Loewenstein, without naming him, giving only the title of his work and demonstrating a rivalrous relationship with him: He asserts that referring to Roman Jakobson's published works "renders superfluous the 'personal communications' that I could tout as much as anyone else," Loewenstein being the one who indicates having personal communications with Jakobson in his paper. Lacan goes on, in the same note, to associate Loewenstein with Rosencrantz and Guildenstern. The highbrow nature of the reference should not mislead us as to its derisory intent! Lacan even takes a furtive jab at Loewenstein in the main body of the text when he claims to have had to "pay homage somewhere here to a noble victim of the error of seeking in the letter" (E 509), "the letter" no doubt referring, in this instance, to a personal communication with Jakobson.

14. In "Function and Field of Speech and Language," he mentions that he is deliberately breaking "with the traditional style—that places a 'paper' somewhere between a compilation and a synthesis—in order to adopt an ironic style suitable to a radical questioning of the foundations of our discipline" (E 238). He seems to go further still in breaking with tradition in "Instance of the Letter," going well beyond irony alone.

15. As he says in Seminar XIX, "I strive to ensure that access to the meaning [of what I say] not be too easy, such that you must contribute some elbow grease of your own (or work hard at it) *[mettre du vôtre]*" (January 6, 1972).

16. Note that Lacan may have only reluctantly agreed to publish his papers in the collection known since as *Écrits* after Paul Ricoeur published his thick volume *De l'interprétation* (Paris: Seuil, 1965), translated as *Freud and Philosophy: An Essay on Interpretation,* trans. D. Savage (New Haven: Yale University Press, 1970). Lacan certainly did not want Ricoeur to take credit for the return to Freud that Lacan himself had been championing. Lacan claims that the texts in his *Écrits* had to be pried away from him (see, for example, Seminar XVIII, March 10, 1971).

17. In a more speculative vein, note that Noam Chomsky's *Syntactic Structures* (The Hague: Mouton, 1957), taking linguistics in a non-Saussurian direction, came out in 1957 (the same year as "Instance of the Letter"), although I do not know how early in the year it appeared. Lacan may nevertheless have been familiar with Chomsky's article "On Accent and Juncture in English," included in *For Roman Jakobson,* ed. M. Halle, H. Lunt, and H. MacLean (The Hague: Mouton, 1956), 65–80.

18. Charles Rycroft, "The Nature and Function of the Analyst's Communication to the Patient," *International Journal of Psycho-Analysis* 37, no. 6 (1956): 469–72.

19. Consider, for example, his comment in "The Mirror Stage as Formative of the *I* Function, as Revealed in Psychoanalytic Experience": "It is this moment that decisively tips the whole of human knowledge into being mediated by the other's desire [and] constitutes its objects in an abstract equivalence due to competition from other people" (E 98).

Lacan clears a path that might be understood to lie midway between a kind of Hegelian totalizing system building and a deconstructionist approach in which one never proposes any positive thesis whatsoever. The latter is a rather safe, negative task which leaves the philosopher unexposed to criticism; its usefulness to clinicians is often, however, rather limited.

20. Ferdinand de Saussure, *Cours de linguistique générale,* ed. T. de Mauro (Paris: Payot, [1916] 1972), 98–99; in English, *Course in General Linguistics,* trans. W. Baskin (New York: McGraw-Hill, 1959) and, more recently, trans. R. Harris (Chicago: Open Court, 1983). Page references here to Saussure are to the critical French edition, whose pagination is included in Harris's translation.

21. Lacan draws a far clearer distinction between the letter and the signifier in his later work, especially in the 1970s. He begins to do so when he rereads his own text "The Seminar on 'The Purloined Letter'" in Seminar XVIII, indicating there that we must not confuse the two, the letter being "in the real" and the signifier "in the symbolic" (May 12, 1971). He continues to elaborate on the letter in the remainder of Seminar XVIII and in later seminars as well. He refers to the signifier as material again in Seminar XVI (December 11, 1968).

22. Note that Saussure's language is sometimes even suggestive of a sexual relationship between the signifier and the signified: "[T]hey are intimately united" (*Cours,* 99); he refers to a "coupling of thought [the signified] with phonic matter [the signifier]" (*Cours,* 156); and he says that "Phonic substance [the signifier] is [. . .] not a mold whose forms thought [the signified] must necessarily marry" (*Cours,* 155). Compare my discussion in chapter 6 regarding knowledge as participating "in the fantasy of an inscription of the sexual link" (Seminar XX, 76/82).

23. Consider the following from "Discours de Jacques Lacan à l'Université de Milan le 12 mai 1972," in the bilingual edition *Lacan in Italia:* "[T]o tell oneself that language is there so that signification can come into being is a notion that is, to say the least, hasty." In Seminar III, Lacan asserts that "the definition of the signifier is not to signify anything" (214/190), which he explicitly returns to and reformulates in Seminar XIX by saying that the signifier "has no signification" (June 21, 1972).

24. James Joyce, *Finnegans Wake* (London: Faber and Faber, 1975), 11.

25. Perhaps suggesting that indignation is for the Ladies and scorn for the Gentlemen.

26. The term "signifying chain" seems to have originated with Louis Hjelmslev.

27. This is an important reason why word-for-word translations are often so useless.

28. Consider Lacan's comments on analytic interpretation in Seminar XI: "It is false to say that interpretation is open to any and every meaning because

interpretation is merely a question of the connection between one signifier and another, and thus of a crazy *[folle]* connection. Interpretation is not open to any and every meaning" (225–26/249–50; see also 189/209). As for the phrase I often hear bandied about, "the sliding of the signifier," it is nowhere to be found in *Écrits*. In "Subversion of the Subject" one finds "the sliding of signification" (E 805), which is virtually synonymous with "the sliding of the signified." And in "The Seminar on 'The Purloined Letter'" we find "the displacement *[Entstellung]* of the signifier" (E 11, 30), which concerns the "path" of the letter purloined by the minister in Edgar Allan Poe's short story. If Lacan does, in fact, ever employ the expression "the sliding of the signifier," it is probably to imply the movement or unfolding of the signifying chain as one speaks.

29. Something similar to this *is* found in Saussure's figure on page 146.

30. Note a possible kind of *sens* or directionality of the letter here.

31. Situated on the Graph of Desire (E 817 and Figure 4.15 below), the sliding of the signified runs left to right between $s(A)$ and A until a retrograde movement of signification ties down the signified, anchoring one or more meanings. Meaning begins to slide again as soon as the next sentence begins, but is once again closed or "buckled down" as the sentence ends. This does not mean, of course, that the buckled-down meaning(s) cannot be modified or called into question thereafter.

32. Roman Jakobson, "Slavic Epic Verse" (1952), in *Roman Jakobson: Selected Writings,* vol. 4 (Paris and The Hague: Mouton, 1966), 414–63.

33. Consider the beginning of the song "Jamaica Farewell" by Jimmy Buffett.

34. Note that many of the things formerly associated (metonymically) with Booz—his qualities and clothing, for example—become associated with the sheaf. "Booz," the occulted signifier, remains "present by virtue of its (metonymic) connection to the rest of the chain" (E 507).

35. Of course, in many cases analysts themselves introduce the several staves by evoking the other possible meanings of the words and expressions that are used by the analysand to convey his "intended meaning."

36. In English, see "Position of the Unconscious," trans. B. Fink, in *Reading Seminar XI: Lacan's Four Fundamental Concepts of Psychoanalysis,* ed. R. Feldstein, B. Fink, and M. Jaanus (Albany: State University of New York Press, 1995).

37. This account intersects the obsessive's fantasy as laid out in chapter 2.

38. The cross here might also evoke the "passion of the signified" (see Seminar XX). Cf. Tennyson's poem "Crossing the Bar."

39. Figure 3.10 can even serve us as another way of visualizing the bar between the signifier and the signified, implying, as it does, that there is no overlap between the two, no zone of mutuality or reciprocity.

4. Reading "The Subversion of the Subject"

1. Seminar V contains several pages of commentary on the graph at the back, as well as detailed commentary in the body of the seminar. It is always important, in working out the details of one of Lacan's schemas, to consider the problems he was grappling with and how different parts of the schema relate to those problems.

2. See my *Lacanian Subject: Between Language and Jouissance* (Princeton: Princeton University Press, 1995), appendix I.

3. Alienation is related to what Lacan calls a "forced choice," like that a mugger gives you: "Your money or your life!" If you try to keep your money, you lose both your money and your life, and if, instead, you part with your money, the life (or being) you retain is diminished because you can now afford less of the good things in life (Seminar XI, 192–93/211–12). Similarly, in order to retain your life in some form, retain some being (as a social animal), you have to submit to meaning making (express yourself in a language others speak) and thereby lose some life, some being (animal being).

4. Note that A stands for *Autre,* "Other."

5. See my *Clinical Introduction to Lacanian Psychoanalysis: Theory and Technique* (Cambridge, Mass.: Harvard University Press, 1997), chapter 7.

6. See my detailed discussion of Lacan on Hamlet in "Reading *Hamlet* with Lacan," in *Lacan, Politics, Aesthetics,* ed. R. Feldstein and W. Apollon (Albany: State University of New York Press, 1996), 181–98.

7. This portion of Seminar VI was published in *Ornicar?* 25 (1982): 13–36; quotation at 23.

8. The question of enjoying what one knows is discussed at length in Seminar XX, especially 88–90/96–98.

9. Lacan explicitly dissociates the phallus from the Name-of-the-Father in Seminar XVIII (June 16, 1971).

10. This is one of the reasons why $-\varphi$ gets substituted for s in the following equation, which (as I argue in chapter 5) is implicitly found in "Subversion of the Subject" (E 823):

$$\frac{S}{s} = \frac{\Phi}{(-\varphi)}$$

11. Demand no longer figures in the top of the graph, except as part of the drive, but Lacan mentions that demand (whether it is the subject's demand addressed to the Other or the Other's demand addressed to the subject) disappears from the drive. Thus, what is going on at that point in the graph is not *addressed to* the Other. (The subject here has to answer for his own jouissance; there is no answer in the Other that explains why he enjoys.)

12. One final reconstruction of a facet of the graph, which may be helpful in reading chapter 5, involves replacing S(Ⱥ) in the complete graph by –1 (minus one, as what is unthinkable about the subject).

13. Malcolm Bowie, *Lacan* (Cambridge, Mass.: Harvard University Press, 1991), 196, for example.

5. The Lacanian Phallus and the Square Root of Negative One

1. Alan Sokal and Jean Bricmont, *Fashionable Nonsense: Postmodern Intellectuals' Abuse of Science* (New York: Picador, 1998).

2. "For the function of language in speech is not to inform but to evoke" (E 299).

3. Recall his comment at the beginning of "Instance of the Letter": "Writing [. . .] allows for the kind of tightening up that must, to my taste, leave the reader no other way out than the way in, which I prefer to be difficult" (E 493).

4. See his comments in Seminar XI (223–25/247–49) on their paper "L'inconscient: Une étude psychanalytique," in *VIe Colloque de Bonneval: L'Inconscient* (Paris: Desclée de Brouwer, 1966), 95–130. In English, "The Unconscious: A Psychoanalytic Study," trans. Patrick Coleman, *Yale French Studies* 48 (1972): 118–75. He mentions there that $\frac{S}{s}$ could theoretically be understood as a fraction, in some sense, but he himself rarely uses it in that way.

5. This does not mean it will not evoke fond or not-so-fond memories in some people of time spent there, but the name itself does not have multiple meanings in the English language.

6. Saul Kripke, *Naming and Necessity* (Cambridge, Mass.: Harvard University Press, 1972).

7. For a counterexample, see Seminar XIX, where, eleven years later, Lacan says, "There is a big difference between the signifier/signified relationship and signification. Signification constitutes *[fait]* a sign, and a sign has nothing to do with a signifier" (December 2, 1971).

8. This aspect of the mirror stage is discussed in Seminar VIII and in "Remarque sur le rapport de Daniel Lagache" ("Remarks on Daniel Lagache's Presentation") (E 647–84).

9. Note that Lacan does not situate it as either purely real (a biological organ) or purely imaginary (an image of the penis); rather, it denotes imaginary castration or "the imaginary function of castration" (E 825).

10. This is not to imply that Lacan always uses the words "phallus" and "phallic" in this sense; there are many places in his work where these terms seem to refer to nothing more than the penis as a biological organ (especially in his work prior to 1958).

11. Note that object *a* has not yet been formulated by Lacan as the real cause of desire at this stage in his work; that only occurs in a fully developed way in Seminar VIII.

12. Lacan's grammar in the French is rarely any more difficult than it is here: "[L'organe érectile] est égalable au $\sqrt{-1}$ de la signification plus haut produite, de la jouissance qu'il restitue par le coefficient de son énoncé à la fonction de manque de signifiant: (–1)" (E 822). The word *de* is particularly open to interpretation here, and the passage could alternatively be translated as follows: "[T]he erectile organ can be set equal to $\sqrt{-1}$ times *[de]* the signification produced above, times *[de]* the jouissance it restores—by the coefficient of its statement—to the function of lack of a signifier: (–1)." The coefficient of the statement $(-\varphi)$ here would seem to be –1.

13. Lacan refers to the phallus as the signifier of jouissance again in Seminar XVI (May 21, 1969), but he does not always do so. In Seminar XIX, for example, he says that "the signifier is jouissance and the phallus is merely the signified" (December 8, 1971).

14. In this sense, all meaning making is related to the phallus—all signification is phallic, so to speak—simply because the phallus is the very name of the relation between the signifier and the signified. See Lacan's later comments on whether the title of the article should be understood as involving a subjective genitive or an objective genitive (Seminar XIX, January 19, 1972; February 3, 1972). He indicates, in the same seminar, that after rereading the article, he found "there's no need to change anything in it, even though at that time no one truly understood a word of it."

15. Note that Lacan refers to the phallus as a "symbol," a "name," and a "signifier," all of which are at times conceptualized differently in his work; while perhaps suggesting a certain lack of rigor in his use of terminology, the use of all three nevertheless suggests the exceptional status, in his view, of the phallus among all other signifiers.

6. Hors Texte—Knowledge and Jouissance

1. Lacan indicates that he himself did not take up the Freudian concept of the superego for many years but that when he finally did, it was not in the form of "moral conscience" but, rather, in the form of the imperative, "Enjoy!" (Seminar XVIII, June 16, 1971).

2. Lacan might say that affect takes refuge in the body as a representational site of the unconscious.

3. The latter often goes by the name of object *a*. Miller's seminar was given weekly in Paris under the auspices of the University of Paris VIII (Saint-Denis).

4. In chapter 4, I qualified Lacan's claim here as polemical, for it is designed to dissuade psychoanalysts from reading the patient's gestures and body language as if they were somehow more real than his speech.

5. What are we to make, then, of machines that read aloud written texts or computer files? The absence of selective stress (other than programmed) on different words or clauses in such reading would seem to point, at the very least, to the absence of the subject of enunciation (or the enunciating subject)—that is, to the subject of jouissance.

6. Claude Lévi-Strauss, *Structural Anthropology,* trans. C. Jacobson and B. G. Schoepf (New York: Basic Books, 1963), 125.

7. In literary theory, for example, one must take into account not only the structures of the text but also what Roland Barthes calls the "pleasure of the text" (and their interrelations). In other words, one must consider the pleasure of the reader and the writer, as well as the performative aspects of the text. We should, of course, do the same in psychoanalysis, considering that the field is defined not only by a practice that is passed on, but also by a series of texts that are read and reread.

8. *Diagnostic and Statistical Manual of Mental Disorders,* 4th ed. (Washington, D.C.: American Psychiatric Association, 1994).

9. Jules H. Massermann, "Language, Behaviour, and Dynamic Psychiatry," *International Journal of Psycho-Analysis* 25, nos. 1–2 (1944): 1–8.

10. According to Lacan, it is also found in Jean Piaget's work on children; see his comments on Piaget in "Science and Truth" (E 859–60).

11. *La psychanalyse d'aujourd'hui* (Paris: Presses Universitaires de France, 1956). This volume was discussed in another context in chapter 1.

12. In Seminar XIX, Lacan refers to the notion of "oblativity" as an "obsessive's sensational invention" (January 6, 1972).

13. I doubt anyone needs to be reminded that a similar fantasy is at work in contemporary psychology, at least in its most popular form: the by-now absolute-best-selling pop-psychology book of all time, John Gray's *Men Are from Mars, Women Are from Venus* (New York: HarperCollins, 1993). The title itself seems promising, suggesting that *nothing predestines men and women for complementary relations.* But everything in the book after the first two chapters is designed to help the reader overcome difference and establish *the One that has to be,* the One that the age-old fantasy requires.

14. Plato, *Lysis, Symposium, Gorgias,* trans. W. R. M. Lamb, Loeb Classical Library (Cambridge, Mass.: Harvard University Press, [1925] 1967), 141.

15. Ferdinand de Saussure, *Cours de linguistique générale,* ed. T. de Mauro (Paris: Payot, [1916], 1972), 99; in English, *Course in General Linguistics,* trans. W. Baskin (New York: McGraw-Hill, 1959), 66–67. Note that Saussure's language is sometimes suggestive of a sexual relationship between the signifier and the signified: "[T]hey are intimately united" (*Cours,* 99); he refers to a "coupling of thought [the signified] with phonic matter [the signifier]" (*Cours,* 156); and he says that "[p]honic substance [the signifier] is [. . .] not a mold whose forms thought [the signified] must necessarily marry" (*Cours,* 155).

16. Such a privileged point would amount to a metaposition akin to that implicit in psychoanalytic theories that encourage interpretation of transference as a supposed way to step outside of the transference; see, on this point, chapter 1.

17. See, for example, Lacan, "Transfert à Saint-Denis," *Ornicar?* 17–18 (1979): 278.

18. The very rigidity of the distinction I have drawn between these two subjects may seem problematic and susceptible of deconstruction. Do these two concepts not themselves form a unified, unitary, binary structure, not so dissimilar from Saussure's conception of the sign? And does Lacan not further polarize the binary nature of the structure with his notion of the One and the Other, the Other as always and inescapably Other, in the 1970s?

This rigid binary opposition may, perhaps, be understood to be thrown into question by another concept Lacan introduces in the early 1970s—*lalangue,* or llanguage—for it seems to inject jouissance into the unconscious, that is, into the Other. It may also be called into question by the concept of writing, for "what is written are the conditions of jouissance and what is counted are the remainders" of jouissance (Seminar XX, 118/131). But as I have not introduced these concepts here, I will not attempt to resolve the opposition, confining myself to pointing out the possibility. The notion of the subject as a disjunction—the subject as a disjunction between signifier and affect—to which I turn later in this chapter, may help here as well.

19. He says the same for the Stoics regarding material implication, that is, the deduction of the true from the false (Seminar XX, 56/60).

20. As Shelly Silver used to say.

21. Perhaps the stereotypical cigarette smoked after sex in movies nevertheless points to a recognized lack in that jouissance, there being something more to be desired: an oral, respiratory pleasure that has gone unsatisfied.

22. Lacan suggests in Seminar XVI that people have failed to grasp the true import of Anselm's argument (February 12, 1969, for example).

23. See, for example, my *Lacanian Subject* (Princeton: Princeton University Press, 1995), chapter 8.

24. Whether there is any point in defining men and women at all is, of course, an open question.

25. Elsewhere in this seminar Lacan says, "[T]he object is a *raté*," a missing, a failure: "The essence of the object is failure" (Seminar XX, 55/58).

26. Here it would seem that the bar, rather than serving as the copula or means of copulation, as we might see it in Saussure's model of the "coupling" of the signifier and signified, serves instead as a barrier.

27. This is true of my partner as well; in my relation to my partner, "I ask [her]," as Lacan says, "to refuse what I offer [her] because that's not it" (Seminar XX, 101/111).

28. Lacan gives phallic jouissance a number of other names in later seminars: He calls it "symbolic jouissance" and even "semiotic jouissance" (Seminar XXI, June 11, 1974).

29. In "Science and Truth" (E 863) Lacan borrows the term "nonsaturated," which Frege apparently uses to talk about a function that does not have a variable, that is, f instead of $f(x)$. In that text, it seems that the subject without an object is the pure, unsaturated subject of the signifier, we might say, whereas the subject with an object is the "saturated" subject of jouissance.

30. This reading is rather different from the one I provided in *The Lacanian Subject*, chapter 8, but it is in fact offered by Lacan at one point in Seminar XVIII (June 16, 1971), when he first begins to elaborate the formulas of sexuation.

31. We could, perhaps, also read the upper left-hand formula as asserting that there exists something in him that wishes to make that sacrifice, give up phallic jouissance, in the hope of finding "true love."

32. Kierkegaard feels, it seems, that this kind of love beyond desire "has to exist"; in that sense it appears to insist, for him, like the belief in God. We might then be led to conclude that it *ex-sists* for him.

33. See, for example, Saint John of the Cross's poem "I Entered I Know Not Where."

34. Recall what he says in 1964: "For the time being, I am not fucking, I am talking to you. Well I can have exactly the same satisfaction as if I were fucking. That's what [sublimation] means" (Seminar XI, 151/165–66).

35. There is, of course, some debate as to the degree to which sex was altogether excluded from courtly love relations.

36. In Seminar XIX, Lacan refers to "the jouissance of speaking" (May 4, 1972).

37. We need not assume there is some sort of complete consistency to Lacan's work in this regard, for he adds to and changes things as he goes along in the

seminar. He says, for example, in chapter 1 that "Jouissance, qua sexual, is phallic" (Seminar XX, 14/9), but he later qualifies object *a*, the "star" of phallic jouissance, as *a*-sexual (Seminar XX, 115/127). Is *"a*-sexual" to be understood as "asexual"? If so, is phallic jouissance asexual or sexual? Is the Other jouissance sexual or asexual? It would seem to be sexual because it reaches the Other sex as such, not just object *a*, and yet, he says, "When one loves, it has nothing to do with sex" (Seminar XX, 27/25). Or is the term *"a*-sexual" not to be understood in the same way as "asexual," implying instead a form of sexuality that is dependent on object *a*? Similarly, Lacan never really tells us if a man (like Kierkegaard) is actually able to accede to a love beyond that of object *a* or merely believes that he can do so by giving up phallic jouissance. If he accedes to a love beyond desire, is it the same as the Other jouissance? Lacan's characterization of phallic jouissance and the Other jouissance seems to remain something of a work in progress.

38. If we think of phallic jouissance as the satisfaction that corresponds to desire—and the terms S and *a* that form fantasy, which Lacan says props up desire, are there (in the table under the formulas of sexuation, Seminar XX, 73/78)—then a man can desire his partner, or love his partner, but not both at the same time, whereas a woman can do both. Is this a fair account of what Lacan is saying? If it is, it would seem to point to a love beyond desire—equivalent to what Lacan jokingly refers to here as a jouissance beyond the phallus. This form of love might correspond to love of the Other or to what Lacan qualifies in the last chapter of the seminar as a "subject-to-subject relationship" (Seminar XX, 131–32/144), in which the object seems to drop out; we might schematize this latter relationship as follows:

$$(S \Diamond a \Diamond S) \quad \rightarrow \quad (S \Diamond S)$$
[hommosexual desire]   [love]

But that might be going too far. It would, perhaps, be safer to say that a man is able to attain one kind of love *or* the other (love for the object or love for the Other sex) with one and the same partner, whereas a woman is able to attain both kinds of love with the same partner (or phallic jouissance with a man or male instance and the Other jouissance with a woman or feminine instance?). I am obviously extrapolating here, since Lacan never says "with one and the same partner."

39. In Seminar XIX, Lacan proposes that the relation to object *a* is what Socrates, in the *Symposium,* calls the soul (May 10, 1972).

40. Colette Soler and Geneviève Morel provide a number of examples of the ways in which the Other jouissance is evoked in work with analysands, and suggest that the experience of the Other jouissance is not, ultimately, something we work with directly in psychoanalysis. This is because the Other jouissance is not inscribed in the unconscious (our main concern in psychoanalysis), which is structured like a language and thus determined by the phallus as a bar between signifier and signified. See Soler's "What Does the Unconscious Know about Women?" and Morel's "Feminine Conditions of Jouissance," both in *Reading Seminar XX: Lacan's Major Work on Love, Knowledge, and Feminine Sexuality,* ed. S. Barnard and B. Fink (Albany: State University of New York Press, 2002).

Index

Bruce Fink is a practicing Lacanian psychoanalyst, analytic supervisor, and professor of psychology at Duquesne University in Pittsburgh, Pennsylvania. He is the author of two other books on Lacan, *The Lacanian Subject: Between Language and Jouissance* and *A Clinical Introduction to Lacanian Psychoanalysis: Theory and Technique*. He has also translated Lacan's work into English, most recently in *Écrits: A Selection*.